YOUR 15-MONTH CANDID,
COMPLETE AND INDIVIDUAL FORECAST

CANCER
1987
SUPER HOROSCOPE
JUNE 21—JULY 20

ARROW BOOKS LIMITED
62-65 Chandos Place
London WC2N 4NW

CONTENTS

THE PUBLISHERS REGRET THAT THEY CANNOT ANSWER INDIVIDUAL LETTERS REQUESTING PERSONAL HOROSCOPE INFORMATION.

FIRST PUBLISHED IN GREAT BRITAIN BY ARROW BOOKS 1986
© GROSSET & DUNLAP, INC., 1974, 1978, 1979, 1980, 1981, 1982
© CHARTER COMMUNICATIONS, INC., 1983, 1984, 1985
COPYRIGHT © 1986 BY THE BERKLEY PUBLISHING GROUP

PRINTED IN GREAT BRITAIN BY
GUERNSEY PRESS CO. LTD
GUERNSEY C.I.
ISBN 0 09 948700 4

NOTE TO THE CUSP-BORN

First find the year of your birth, and then find the sign under which you were born according to your day of birth. Thus, you can determine if you are a true Cancer (or Gemini or Leo), according to the variations of the dates of the Zodiac. (See also page 7.)

Are you *really* a Cancer? If your birthday falls during the fourth week of June, at the beginning of Cancer, will you still retain the traits of Gemini, the sign of the Zodiac before Cancer? And what if you were born late in July—are you more Leo than Cancer? Many people born at the edge, or cusp, of a sign have difficulty determining exactly what sign they are. If you are one of these people, here's how you can figure it out, once and for all.

Consult the following table. It will tell you the precise days on which the Sun entered and left your sign for the year of your birth. If you were born at the beginning or end of Cancer, yours is a lifetime reflecting a process of subtle transformation. Your life on Earth will symbolize a significant change in consciousness, for you are either about to enter a whole new way of living or are leaving one behind.

If you were born during the fourth week of June, you may want to read the Gemini book as well as Cancer. Because Gemini holds the keys to the more hidden sides of your personality; many of your dilemmas and uncertainties about the world and people around you, your secret wishes, and your potential for cosmic unfoldment.

Although you feel you have a lot to say, you will often withdraw and remain silent. Sometimes, the more you say the more confused a situation can get. Talking can drain you, and you are vulnerable to gossip. You feel secure surrounded by initimates you can trust, but sometimes the neighbors—even your own relatives—seem to be talking behind your back and you sense a vague plot in the air.

You symbolize the birth of feeling, the silent but rich condition of a fertilized seed growing full with life. The family is always an issue. At best you are a "feeling" type whose power of sensing things remains a force behind everything you think and do.

If you were born the fourth week of July, you may want to read the horoscope book for Leo as well as Cancer, for Leo could be your greatest asset. You need a warm embrace, the comfort and safety of being cared for, protected, fed. You need strong ties to the past, to the family. Attachments are natural for you. You want to be your own person, yet you often find ties and attachments prohibiting you from the rebirth you are anticipating. You may find it hard to separate yourself from dependencies without being drawn backward again and again.

You symbolize the fullness of growth, the condition of being *nearly* ripe, the new life about to emerge from the shadows into the sunshine.

DATES SUN ENTERS CANCER
(LEAVES GEMINI)

June 21 every year from 1900 to 2000, except for the following:

June 22:				June 20:
1902	1914	1923	1939	1988
03	15	26	43	92
06	18	27	47	96
07	19	31	51	
10	22	35	55	
11				

DATES SUN LEAVES CANCER
(ENTERS LEO)

July 23 every year from 1900 to 2000, except for the following:

July 22:				
1928	1953	1968	1981	1992
32	56	69	84	93
36	57	72	85	94
40	60	73	86	96
44	61	76	88	97
48	64	77	89	98
52	65	80	90	

HISTORY AND USES
OF ASTROLOGY

Does astrology have a place in the fast-moving, ultra-scientific world we live in today? Can it be justified in a sophisticated society whose outriders are already preparing to step off the moon into the deep space of the planets themselves? Or is it just a hangover of ancient superstition, a psychological dummy for neurotics and dreamers of every historical age?

These are the kind of questions that any inquiring person can be expected to ask when they approach a subject like astrology which goes beyond, but never excludes, the materialistic side of life.

The simple, single answer is that astrology works. It works for tens of millions of people in the western world alone. In the United States there are 10 million followers and in Europe, an estimated 25 million. America has more than 4000 practicing astrologers, Europe nearly three times as many. Even down-under Australia has its hundreds of thousands of adherents. The importance of such vast numbers of people from diverse backgrounds and cultures is recognized by the world's biggest newspapers and magazines who probably devote more of their space to this subject in a year than to any other. In the eastern countries, astrology has enormous followings, again, because it has been proved to work. In countries like India, brides and grooms for centuries have been chosen on the basis of astrological compatibility. The low divorce rate there, despite today's heavy westernizing influence, is attributed largely to this practice.

In the western world, astrology today is more vital than ever before; more practicable because it needs a sophisticated society like ours to understand and develop its contribution to the full; more valid because science itself is confirming the precepts of astrological knowledge with every new exciting step. The ordinary person who daily applies astrology intelligently does not have to wonder whether it is true nor believe in it blindly. He can see it working for himself. And, if he can use it—and this book is designed to help the reader to do just that—he can make living a far richer experience, and become a more developed personality and a better person.

Astrology is the science of relationships. It is not just a study of planetary influences on man and his environment. It is the study of man himself.

We are at the center of our personal universe, of all our relationships. And our happiness or sadness depends on how we act, how we relate to the people and things that surround us. The emotions that we generate have a distinct affect—for better or worse—on the world around us. Our friends and our enemies will confirm this. Just look in the mirror the next time you are angry. In other words, each of us is a kind of sun or planet or star and our influence on our personal universe, whether loving, helpful or destructive, varies with our changing moods, expressed through our individual character.

And to an extent that includes the entire galaxy, this is true of the planetary bodies. Their radiations affect each other, including the earth and all the things on it. And in comparatively recent years, giant constellations called "quasars" have been discovered. These exist far beyond the night stars that we can observe, and science says these quasars are emitting radiating influences more powerful and different than ever recorded on earth. Their effect on man from an astrological point of view is under deep study. Compared with these inter-stellar forces, our personal "radiations" are negligible on the planetary scale. But ours are just as potent in the way they affect our moods, and our ability to control them. To this extent they determine much of the happiness and satisfaction in our lives. For instance, if we were bound and gagged and had to hold some strong emotion within us without being able to move, we would soon start to feel very uncomfortable. We are obviously pretty powerful radiators inside, in our own way. But usually, we are able to throw off our emotion in some sort of action—we have a good cry, walk it off, or tell someone our troubles—before it can build up too far and make us physically ill. Astrology helps us to understand the universal forces working on us, and through this understanding, we can become more properly adjusted to our surroundings and find ourselves coping where others may flounder.

Closely related to our emotions is the "other side" of our personal universe, our physical welfare. Our body, of course, is largely influenced by things around us over which we have very little control. The phone rings, we hear it. The train runs late. We snag our stocking or cut our face shaving. Our body is under a constant bombardment of events that influence our lives to varying degrees.

The question that arises from all this is, what makes each of us act so that we have to involve other people and keep the ball of activity and evolution rolling? This is the question that both science and astrology are involved with. The scientists have attacked it from different angles: anthropology, the study of human evolution as body, mind and response to environment; anatomy, the study of bodily structure; psychology, the science of the human mind; and so on. These studies have produced very impressive classifications and valuable information, but because the approach to the problem is fragmented, so is the result. They remain "branches" of science. Science generally studies effects. It keeps turning up wonderful answers but no lasting solutions. Astrology, on the other hand approaches the question from the broader viewpoint. Astrology began its inquiry with the totality of human experience and saw it as an effect. It then looked to find the cause, or at least the prime movers, and during thousands of years of observation of man and his *universal* environment, came up with the extraordinary principle of planetary influence—or astrology, which, from the Greek, means the science of the stars.

Modern science, as we shall see, has confirmed much of astrology's foundations—most of it unintentionally, some of it reluctantly, but still, indisputably.

It is not difficult to imagine that there must be a connection between outer space and the earth. Even today, scientists are not too sure how our earth was created, but it is generally agreed that it is only a tiny part of the universe. And as a part of the universe, people on earth see and feel the influence of heavenly bodies in almost every aspect of our existence. There is no doubt that the sun has the greatest influence on life on this planet. Without it there would be no life, for without it there would be no warmth, no division into day and night, no cycles of time or season at all. This is clear and easy to see. The influence of the moon, on the other hand, is more subtle, though no less definite.

There are many ways in which the influence of the moon manifests itself here on earth, both on human and animal life. It is a well-known fact, for instance, that the large movements of water on our planet—that is the ebb and flow of the tides—are caused by the moon's gravitational pull. Since this is so, it follows that these water movements do not occur only in the oceans, but that all bodies of water are affected, even down to the tiniest puddle.

The human body, too, which consists of about 70 percent water, falls within the scope of this lunar influence. For example the menstrual cycle of most women corresponds to the lunar month; the period of pregnancy in humans is 273 days, or equal to nine lunar months. Similarly, many illnesses reach a crisis at the change of the moon, and statistics in many countries have shown that the crime rate is highest at the time of the full moon. Even human sexual desire has been associated with the phases of the moon. But, it is in the movement of the tides that we get the clearest demonstration of planetary influence, and the irresistible correspondence between the so-called metaphysical and the physical.

Tide tables are prepared years in advance by calculating the future positions of the moon. Science has known for a long time that the moon is the main cause of tidal action. But only in the last few years has it begun to realize the possible extent of this influence on mankind. To begin with, the ocean tides do not rise and fall as we might imagine from our personal observations of them. The moon as it orbits around the earth, sets up a circular wave of attraction which pulls the oceans of the world after it, broadly in an east to west direction. This influence is like a phantom wave crest, a loop of power stretching from pole to pole which passes over and around the earth like an invisible shadow. It travels with equal effect across the land masses and, as scientists were recently amazed to observe, caused oysters placed in the dark in the middle of the United States where there is no sea, to open their shells to receive the non-existent tide. If the land-locked oysters react to this invisible signal, what effect does it have on us who not so long ago in evolutionary time, came out of the sea and still have its salt in our blood and sweat?

Less well known is the fact that the moon is also the primary force behind the circulation of blood in human beings and animals, and the movement of sap in trees and plants. Agriculturists have established that the moon has a distinct influence on crops, which explains why for centuries people have planted according to moon cycles. The habits of many animals, too, are directed by the movement of the moon. Migratory birds, for instance, depart only at or near the time of the full moon. Just as certain fish, eels in particular, move only in accordance with certain phases of the moon.

Know Thyself—Why?

In today's fast-changing world, everyone still longs to know what the future holds. It is the one thing that everyone has in common: rich and poor, famous and infamous, all are deeply concerned about tomorrow.

But the key to the future, as every historian knows, lies in the past. This is as true of individual people as it is of nations. You cannot understand your future without first understanding your past, which is simply another way of saying that you must first of all know yourself.

The motto "know thyself" seems obvious enough nowadays, but it was originally put forward as the foundation of wisdom by the ancient Greek philosophers. It was then adopted by the "mystery religions" of the ancient Middle East, Greece and Rome, and is still used in all genuine schools of mind training or mystical discipline, both in those of the East, based on yoga, and those of the West. So it is universally accepted now, and has been through the ages.

But how do you go about discovering what sort of person you are? The first step is usually classification into some sort of system of types. Astrology did this long before the birth of Christ. Psychology has also done it. So has modern medicine, in its way.

One system classifies men according to the source of the impulses they respond to most readily: the muscles, leading to direct bodily action; the digestive organs, resulting in emotion, or the brain and nerves. Another such system says that character is determined by the endocrine glands, and gives us labels like "pituitary," "thyroid" and "hyperthyroid" types. These different systems are neither contradictory nor mutually exclusive. In fact, they are very often different ways of saying the same thing.

Very popular and useful classifications were devised by Dr. C. G. Jung, the eminent disciple of Freud. Jung observed among the different faculties of the mind, four which have a predominant influence on character. These four faculties exist in all of us without exception, but not in perfect balance. So when we say, for instance, that a man is a "thinking type," it means that in any situation he tries to be rational. It follows that emotion, which some say is the opposite of thinking, will be his weakest function. This type can be sensible and reasonable, or calculating and unsympathetic. The emotional type, on the other hand, can often be recognized by exaggerated language—everything is either marvelous or terrible—and in extreme cases they even invent dramas and quarrels out of nothing just to make life more interesting.

The other two faculties are intuition and physical sensation. The sensation type does not only care for food and drink, nice clothes and furniture; he is also interested in all forms of physical experience. Many scientists are sensation types as are athletes and nature-lovers. Like sensation, intuition is a form of perception and we all possess it. But it works through that part of the mind which is not under conscious control—consequently it sees meanings and connections which are not obvious to thought or emotion. Inventors and original thinkers are always intuitive, but so, too, are superstitious people who see meanings where none exist.

Thus, sensation tells us what is going on in the world, feeling (that is, emotion) tells us how important it is to ourselves, thinking enables us to interpret it and work out what we should do about it, and intuition tells us what it means to ourselves and others. All four faculties are essential, and all are present in every one of us. But some people are guided chiefly by one, others by another.

Besides these four types, Jung observed a division into extrovert and introvert, which cuts across them. By and large, the introvert is one who finds truth inside himself rather than outside. He is not, therefore, ideally suited to a religion or a political party which tells him what to believe. Original thinkers are almost necessarily introverts. The extrovert, on the other hand, finds truth coming to him from outside. He believes in experts and authorities, and wants to think that nature and the laws of nature really exists, that they are what they appear to be and not just generalities made by men.

A disadvantage of all these systems of classification, is that one cannot tell very easily where to place oneself. Some people are reluctant to admit that they act to please their emotions. So they deceive themselves for years by trying to belong to whichever type they think is the "best." Of course, there is no best; each has its faults and each has its good points.

The advantage of the signs of the Zodiac is that they simplify classification. Not only that, but your date of birth is personal—it is unarguably yours. What better way to know yourself than by going back as far as possible to the very moment of your birth? And this is precisely what your horoscope is all about.

What Is a Horoscope?

If you had been able to take a picture of the heavens at the moment of your birth, that photograph would be your horoscope. Lacking such a snapshot, it is still possible to recreate the picture—and this is at the basis of the astrologer's art. In other words, your horoscope is a representation of the skies with the planets in the exact positions they occupied at the time you were born.

This information, of course, is not enough for the astrologer. He has to have a background of significance to put the photograph on. You will get the idea if you imagine two balls—one inside the other. The inner one is transparent. In the center of both is the astrologer, able to look up, down and around in all directions. The outer sphere is the Zodiac which is divided into twelve approximately equal segments, like the segments of an orange. The inner ball is our photograph. It is transparent except for the images of the planets. Looking out from the center, the astrologer sees the planets in various segments of the Zodiac. These twelve segments are known as the signs or houses.

The position of the planets when each of us is born is always different. So the photograph is always different. But the Zodiac and its signs are fixed.

Now, where in all this are you, the subject of the horoscope?

You, or your character, is largely determined by the sign the sun is in. So that is where the astrologer looks first in your horoscope.

There are twelve signs in the Zodiac and the sun spends approximately one month in each. As the sun's motion is almost perfectly regular, the astrologers have been able to fix the dates governing each sign. There are not many people who do not know which sign of the Zodiac they were born under or who have not been amazed at some time or other at the accuracy of the description of their own character. Here are the twelve signs, the ancient zodiacal symbol, and their dates for the year 1987.*

ARIES	Ram	March 20–April 20
TAURUS	Bull	April 20–May 21
GEMINI	Twins	May 21–June 21
CANCER	Crab	June 21–July 23
LEO	Lion	July 23–August 23
VIRGO	Virgin	August 23–September 23
LIBRA	Scales	September 23–October 23
SCORPIO	Scorpion	October 23–November 22
SAGITTARIUS	Archer	November 22–December 22
CAPRICORN	Sea-Goat	December 22–January 20
AQUARIUS	Water-Bearer	January 20–February 18
PISCES	Fish	February 18–March 20

The time of birth—apart from the date—is important in advanced astrology because the planets travel at such great speed that the patterns they form change from minute to minute. For this reason, each person's horoscope is his and his alone. Further on we will see that the practicing astrologer has ways of determining and reading these minute time changes which dictate the finger character differences in us all.

However, it is still possible to draw significant conclusions and make meaningful predictions based simply on the sign of the Zodiac a person is born under. In a horoscope, the signs do not necessarily correspond with the divisions of the houses. It could be that a house begins half way across a sign. It is the interpretation of such combinations of different influences that distinguishes the professional astrologer from the student and the follower.

However, to gain a workable understanding of astrology, it is not necessary to go into great detail. In fact, the beginner is likely to find himself confused if he attempts to absorb too much too quickly. It should be remembered that this is a science and to become proficient at it, and especially to grasp the tremendous scope of possibilities in man and his affairs and direct them into a worthwhile reading, takes a great deal of study and experience.

*These dates are fluid and change with the motion of the Earth from year to year.

If you do intend to pursue it seriously you will have to learn to figure the exact moment of birth against the degrees of longitude and latitude of the planets at that precise time. This involves adapting local time to Greenwich Mean Time (G.M.T.), reference to tables of houses to establish the Ascendant, as well as making calculations from Ephemeris—the tables of the planets' positions.

After reading this introduction, try drawing up a rough horoscope to get the "feel" of reading some elementary characteristics and natal influences.

Draw a circle with twelve equal segments. Write in counterclockwise the names of the signs—Aries, Taurus, Gemini etc.— one for each segment. Look up an ephemeris for the year of the person's birth and note down the sign each planet was in on the birthday. Do not worry about the number of degrees (although if a planet is on the edge of a sign its position obviously should be considered). Write the name of the planet in the segment/sign on your chart. Write the number 1 in the sign where the sun is. This is the first house. Number the rest of the houses, counterclockwise till you finish at 12. Now you can investigate the probable basic expectation of experience of the person concerned. This is done first of all by seeing what planet or planets is/are in what sign and house. (See also page 72.)

The 12 houses control these functions:

1st.	Individuality, body appearance, general outlook on life	(Personality house)
2nd.	Finance, business	(Money house)
3rd.	Relatives, education, correspondence	(Relatives house)
4th.	Family, neighbors	(Home house)
5th.	Pleasure, children, attempts, entertainment	(Pleasure house)
6th.	Health, employees	(Health house)
7th.	Marriage, partnerships	(Marriage house)
8th.	Death, secret deals, difficulties	(Death house)
9th.	Travel, intellectual affairs	(Travel house)
10th.	Ambition, social standing	(Business and Honor house)
11th.	Friendship, social life, luck	(Friends house)
12th.	Troubles, illness, loss	(Trouble house)

The characteristics of the planets modify the influence of the Sun according to their natures and strengths.

Sun: Source of life. Basic temperament according to sun sign. The will.
Moon: Superficial nature. Moods. Changeable. Adaptive. Mother.
Mercury: Communication. Intellect. Reasoning power. Curiosity. Short travels.
Venus: Love. Delight. Art. Beautiful possessions.
Mars: Energy. Initiative. War. Anger. Destruction. Impulse.
Jupiter: Good. Generous. Expansive. Opportunities. Protection.
Saturn: Jupiter's opposite. Contraction. Servant. Delay. Hardwork. Cold. Privation. Research. Lasting rewards after long struggle.
Uranus: Fashion. Electricity. Revolution. Sudden changes. Modern science.
Neptune: Sensationalism. Mass emotion. Devastation. Delusion.
Pluto: Creates and destroys. Lust for power. Strong obsessions.

Superimpose the characteristics of the planets on the functions of the house in which they appear. Express the result through the character of the birth (sun) sign, and you will get the basic idea of how astrology works.

Of course, many other considerations have been taken into account in producing the carefully worked out predictions in this book: The aspects of the planets to each other; their strength according to position and sign; whether they are in a house of exaltation or decline; whether they are natural enemies or not; whether a planet occupies his own sign; the position of a planet in relation to its own house or sign; whether the planet is male, female or neuter; whether the sign is a fire, earth, water or air sign. These are only a few of the colors on the astrologer's pallet which he must mix with the inspiration of the artist and the accuracy of the mathematician.

The Problem of Love

Love, of course, is never a problem. The problem lies in recognizing the difference between infatuation, emotion, sex and, sometimes, the downright deceit of the other person. Mankind, with its record of broken marriages, despair and disillusionment, is obviously not very good at making these distinctions.

Can astrology help?

Yes. In the same way that advance knowledge can usually help in any human situation. And there is probably no situation as human, as poignant, as pathetic and universal, as the failure of man's love.

Love, of course, is not just between man and woman. It involves love of children, parents, home and so on. But the big problems usually involve the choice of partner.

Astrology has established degrees of compatibility that exist between people born under the various signs of the Zodiac. Because people are individuals, there are numerous variations and modifications and the astrologer, when approached on mate and marriage matters makes allowances for them. But the fact remains that some groups of people are suited for each other and some are not and astrology has expressed this in terms of characteristics which all can study and use as a personal guide.

No matter how much enjoyment and pleasure we find in the different aspects of each other's character, if it is not an overall compatibility, the chances of our finding fulfillment or enduring happiness in each other are pretty hopeless. And astrology can help us to find someone compatible.

History of Astrology

The origins of astrology have been lost far back in history, but we do know that reference is made to it as far back as the first written records of the human race. It is not hard to see why. Even in primitive times, people must have looked for an explanation for the various happenings in their lives. They must have wanted to know why people were different from one to another. And in their search they turned to the regular movements of the sun, moon and stars to see if they could provide an answer.

It is interesting to note that as soon as man learned to use his tools in any type of design, or his mind in any kind of calculation, he turned his attention to the heavens. Ancient cave dwellings reveal dim crescents and circles representative of the sun and moon, rulers of day and night. Mesopotamia and the civilization of Chaldea, in itself the foundation of those of Babylonia and Assyria, show a complete picture of astronomical observation and well-developed astrological interpretation.

Humanity has a natural instinct for order. The study of anthropology reveals that primitive people—even as far back as prehistoric times—were striving to achieve a certain order in their lives. They tried to organize the apparent chaos of the universe. They had the desire to attach meaning to things. This demand for order has persisted throughout the history of man. So that observing the regularity of the heavenly bodies made it logical that primitive peoples should turn heavenwards in their search for an understanding of the world in which they found themselves so random and alone.

And they did find a significance in the movements of the stars. Shepherds tending their flocks, for instance, observed that when the cluster of stars now known as the constellation Aries was in sight, it was the time of fertility and they associated it with the Ram. And they noticed that the growth of plants and plant life corresponded with different phases of the moon, so that certain times were favorable for the planting of crops, and other times were not. In this way, there grew up a tradition of seasons and causes connected with the passage of the sun through the twelve signs of the Zodiac.

Astrology was valued so highly that the king was kept informed of the daily and monthly changes in the heavenly bodies, and the results of astrological studies regarding events of the future. Head astrologers were clearly men of great rank and position, and the office was said to be a hereditary one.

Omens were taken, not only from eclipses and conjunctions of the moon or sun with one of the planets, but also from storms and earthquakes. In the eastern civilizations, particularly, the reverence inspired by astrology appears to have remained unbroken since the very earliest days. In ancient China, astrology, astronomy and religion went hand in hand. The astrologer, who was also an astronomer, was part of the official government service and had his own corner in the Imperial Palace. The duties of the Imperial astrologer, whose office was one of the most important in the land, were clearly defined, as this extract from early records shows:

"This exalted gentleman must concern himself with the stars in the heavens, keeping a record of the changes and movements of the Planets, the Sun and the Moon, in order to examine the movements of the terrestial world with the object of prognosticating good and bad fortune. He divides the territories of the nine regions of the empire in accordance with their dependence on particular celestial bodies. All the fiefs and principalities are connected with the stars and from this their prosperity or misfortune should be ascertained. He makes prognostications according to the twelve years of the Jupiter cycle of good and evil of the terrestial world. From the colors of the five kinds of clouds, he determines the coming of floods or droughts, abundance or famine. From the twelve winds, he draws conclusions about the state of harmony of heaven and earth, and takes note of good and bad signs that result from their accord or disaccord. In general, he concerns himself with five kinds of phenomena so as to warn the Emperor to come to the aid of the government and to allow for variations in the ceremonies according to their circumstances."

The Chinese were also keen observers of the fixed stars, giving them such unusual names as Ghost Vehicle, Sun of Imperial Concubine, Imperial Prince, Pivot of Heaven, Twinkling Brilliance or Weaving Girl. But, great astrologers though they may have been, the Chinese lacked one aspect of mathematics that the Greeks applied to astrology—deductive geometry. Deductive geometry was the basis of much classical astrology in and after the time of the Greeks, and this explains the different methods of prognostication used in the East and West.

Down through the ages the astrologer's art has depended, not so much on the uncovering of new facts, though this is important, as on the interpretation of the facts already known. This is the essence of his skill. Obviously one cannot always tell how people will react (and this underlines the very important difference between astrology and predestination which will be discussed later on) but one can be prepared, be forewarned, to know what to expect.

But why should the signs of the zodiac have any effect at all on the formation of human character? It is easy to see why people thought they did, and even now we constantly use astrological expressions in our everyday speech. The thoughts of "lucky star," "ill-fated," "star-crossed," "mooning around," are interwoven into the very structure of our language.

In the same way that the earth has been created by influences from outside, there remains an indisputable togetherness in the working of the universe. The world, after all, is a coherent structure, for if it were not, it would be quite without order and we would never know what to expect. A dog could turn into an apple, or an elephant sprout wings and fly at any moment without so much as a by your leave. But nature, as we know, functions according to laws, not whims, and the laws of nature are certainly not subject to capricious exceptions.

This means that no part of the universe is ever arbitrarily cut off from any other part. Everything is therefore to some extent linked with everything else. The moon draws an imperceptible tide on every puddle; tiny and trivial events can be effected by outside forces (such as the fall of a feather by the faintest puff of wind). And so it is fair to think that the local events at any moment reflect to a very small extent the evolution of the world as a whole.

From this principle follows the possibility of divination, and also knowledge of events at a distance, provided one's mind were always as perfectly undisturbed, as ideally smooth, as a mirror or unruffled lake. Provided, in other words, that one did not confuse the picture with hopes, guesses, and expectations. When people try to foretell the future by cards or crystal ball gazing they find it much easier to confuse the picture with expectations than to reflect it clearly.

But the present does contain a good deal of the future to which it leads—not all, but a good deal. The diver halfway between bridge and water is going to make a splash; the train whizzing towards the station will pass through it unless interfered with; the burglar breaking a pane of glass has exposed himself to the possibility of a prison sentence. Yet this is not a doctrine of determinism, as was emphasized earlier. Clearly, there are forces already at work in the present, and any one of them could alter the situation in some way. Equally, a change of decision could alter the whole situation as well. So the future depends, not on an irresistible force, but on a small act of free will.

An individual's age, physique, and position on the earth's surface are remote consequences of his birth. Birth counts as the original cause for all that happens subsequently. The horoscope, in this case, means "this person represents the further evolution of the state of the universe pictured in this chart." Such a chart can apply equally to man or woman, dog, ship or even limited company.

If the evolution of an idea, or of a person, is to be understood as a totality, it must continue to evolve from its own beginnings, which is to say, in the terms in which it began. The brown-eyed person will be faithful to brown eyes all his life; the traitor is being faithful to some complex of ideas which has long been evolving in him; and the person born at sunset will always express, as he evolves, the psychological implications or analogies of the moment when the sun sinks out of sight.

This is the doctrine that an idea must continue to evolve in terms of its origin. It is a completely non-materialist doctrine, though it never fails to apply to material objects. And it implies, too, that the individual will continue to evolve in terms of his moment of origin, and therefore possibly of the sign of the Zodiac rising on the eastern horizon at his birth. It also implies that the signs of the Zodiac themselves will evolve in the collective mind of the human race in the same terms that they were first devised and not in the terms in which modern astrologers consciously think they ought to work.

For the human race, like every other kind of animal, has a collective mind, as Professor Jung discovered in his investigation of dreams. If no such collective mind existed, no infant could ever learn anything, for communication would be impossible. Furthermore, it is absurd to suggest that the conscious mind could be older than the "unconscious," for an infant's nervous system functions correctly before it has discovered the difference between "myself" and "something else" or discovered what eyes and hands are for. Indeed, the involuntary muscles function correctly even before birth, and will never be under conscious control. They are part of what we call the "unconscious" which is not really "unconscious" at all. To the contrary, it is totally aware of itself and everything else; it is merely that part of the mind that cannot be controlled by conscious effort.

And human experience, though it varies in detail with every individual, is basically the same for each one of us, consisting of sky and earth, day and night, waking and sleeping, man and woman, birth and death. So there is bound to be in the mind of the human race a very large number of inescapable ideas, which are called our natural archetypes.

There are also, however, artificial or cultural archetypes which are not universal or applicable to everyone, but are nevertheless inescapable within the limits of a given culture. Examples of these are the cross in Christianity, and the notion of "escape from the wheel of rebirth" in India. There was a time when these ideas did not exist. And there was a time, too, when the scheme of the Zodiac did not exist. One would not expect the Zodiac to have any influence on remote and primitive peoples, for example, who have never heard of it. If the Zodiac is only an archetype, their horoscopes probably would not work and it would not matter which sign they were born under.

But where the Zodiac is known, and the idea of it has become worked into the collective mind, then there it could well appear to have an influence, even if it has no physical existence. For ideas do not have a physical existence, anyway. No physical basis has yet been discovered for the telepathy that controls an anthill; young swallows migrate before, not after, their parents; and the weaver-bird builds its intricate nest without being taught. Materialists suppose, but cannot prove, that "instinct" (as it is called, for no one knows how it works) is controlled by nucleic acid in the chromosomes. This is not a genuine explanation, though, for it only pushes the mystery one stage further back.

Does this mean, then, that the human race, in whose civilization the idea of the twelve signs of the Zodiac has long been embedded, is divided into only twelve types? Can we honestly believe that it is really as simple as that? If so, there must be pretty wide ranges of variation within each type. And if, to explain the variation, we call in heredity and environment, experiences in early childhood, the thyroid and other glands, and also the four functions of the mind mentioned at the beginning of this introduction, and extroversion and introversion, then one begins to wonder if the original classification was worth making at all. No sensible person believes that his favorite system explains everything. But even so, he will not find it much use at all if it does not even save him the trouble of bothering with the others.

Under the Jungian system, everyone has not only a dominant or principal function, but also a secondary or subsidiary one, so that the four can be arranged in order of potency. In the intuitive type, sensation is always the most inefficient function, but the second most inefficient function can be either thinking (which tends to make original thinkers such as Jung himself) or else feeling (which tends to make artistic people). Therefore, allowing for introversion and extroversion, there are at least four kinds of intuitive types, and sixteen types in all. Furthermore, one can see how the sixteen types merge into each other, so that there are no unrealistic or unconvincingly rigid divisions.

In the same way, if we were to put every person under only one sign of the Zodiac, the system becomes too rigid and unlike life. Besides, it was never intended to be used like that. It may be convenient to have only twelve types, but we know that in practice there is every possible gradation between aggressiveness and timidity, or between conscientiousness and laziness. How, then, do we account for this?

The Tyrant and the Saint

Just as the thinking type of man is also influenced to some extent by sensation and intuition, but not very much by emotion, so a person born under Leo can be influenced to some extent by one or two (but not more) of the other signs. For instance, famous persons born under the sign of Gemini include Henry VIII, whom nothing and no-one could have induced to abdicate, and Edward VIII, who did just that. Obviously, then, the sign Gemini does not fully explain the complete character of either of them.

Again, under the opposite sign, Sagittarius, were both Stalin, who was totally consumed with the notion of power, and Charles V, who freely gave up an empire because he preferred to go into a monastery. And we find under Scorpio, many uncompromising characters such as Luther, de Gaulle, Indira Gandhi and Montgomery, but also Petain, a successful commander whose name later became synonymous with collaboration.

A single sign is therefore obviously inadequate to explain the differences between people; it can only explain resemblances, such as the combativeness of the Scorpio group, or the far-reaching devotion of Charles V and Stalin to their respective ideals—the Christian heaven and the Communist utopia.

But very few people are born under one sign only. As well as the month of birth, as was mentioned earlier, the day matters, and, even more, the hour, which ought, if possible, to be noted to the nearest minute. Without this, it is impossible to have an actual horoscope, for the word horoscope means literally, "a consideration of the hour."

The month of birth tells you only which sign of the Zodiac was occupied by the sun. The day and hour tell you what sign was occupied by the moon. And the minute tells you which sign was rising on the eastern horizon. This is called the Ascendant, and it is supposed to be the most important thing in the whole horoscope.

If you were born at midnight, the sun is then in an important position, although invisible. But at one o'clock in the morning the sun is not important, so the moment of birth will not matter much. The important thing then will be the Ascendant, and possibly one or two of the planets. At a given day and hour, say, dawn on January 1st, or 9:00 p.m. on the longest day, the Ascendant will always be the same at any given place. But the moon and planets alter from day to day, at different speeds and have to be looked up in an astronomical table.

The sun is said to signify one's heart, that is to say, one's deepest desires and inmost nature. This is quite different from the moon, which, as we have seen, signifies one's superficial way of behaving. When the ancient Romans referred to the Emperor Augustus as a Capricornian, they meant that he had the moon in Capricorn; they did not pay much attention to the sun, although he was born at sunrise. Or, to take another example, a modern astrologer would call Disraeli a Scorpion because he had Scorpio rising, but most people would call him Sagittarian because he had the sun there. The Romans would have called him Leo because his moon was in Leo.

The sun, as has already been pointed out, is important if one is born near sunrise, sunset, noon or midnight, but is otherwise not reckoned as the principal influence. So if one does not seem to fit one's birth month, it is always worthwhile reading the other signs, for one may have been born at a time when any of them were rising or occupied by the moon. It also seems to be the case that the influence of the sun develops as life goes on, so that the month of birth is easier to guess in people over the age of forty. The young are supposed to be influenced mainly by their Ascendant which characterizes the body and physical personality as a whole.

It should be clearly understood that it is nonsense to assume that all people born at a certain time will exhibit the same characteristics, or that they will even behave in the same manner. It is quite obvious that, from the very moment of its birth, a child is subject to the effects of its environment, and that this in turn will influence its character and heritage to a decisive extent. Also to be taken into account are education and economic conditions, which play a very important part in the formation of one's character as well.

However, it is clearly established that people born under one sign of the Zodiac do have certain basic traits in their character which are different from those born under other signs. It is obvious to every thinking person that certain events produce different reactions in various people. For instance, if a man slips on a banana skin and falls heavily on the pavement, one passer-by may laugh and find this extremely amusing, while another may just walk on, thinking: "What a fool falling down like that. He should look where he is going." A third might also walk away saying to himself: "It's none of my business—I'm glad it wasn't me." A fourth might walk past and think: "I'm sorry for that man, but I haven't the time to be bothered with helping him." And a fifth might stop to help the fallen man to his feet, comfort him and take him home. Here is just one event which could produce entirely different reactions in different people. And, obviously, there are many more. One that comes to mind immediately is the violently opposed views to events such as wars, industrial strikes, and so on. The fact that people have different attitudes to the same event is simply another way of saying that they have different characters. And this is not something that can be put down to background, for people of the same race, religion, or class, very often express quite different reactions to happenings or events. Similarly, it is often the case that members of the same family, where there is clearly uniform background of economic and social standing, education, race and religion, often argue bitterly among themselves over political and social issues.

People have, in general, certain character traits and qualities which, according to their environment, develop in either a positive or a negative manner. Therefore, selfishness (inherent selfishness, that is) might emerge as unselfishness; kindness and consideration as cruelty and lack of consideration towards others. In the same way, a naturally constructive person, may, through frustration, become destructive, and so on. The latent characteristics with which people are born can, therefore, through environment and good or bad training, become something that would appear to be its opposite, and so give the lie to the astrologer's description of their character. But this is not the case. The true character is still there, but it is buried deep beneath these external superficialities.

Careful study of the character traits of different signs can be immeasurable help, and can render beneficial service to the intelligent person. Undoubtedly, the reader will already have discovered that, while he is able to get on very well with some people, he just "cannot stand" others. The causes sometimes seem inexplicable. At times there is intense dislike, at other times immediate sympathy. And there is, too, the phenomenon of love at first sight, which is also apparently inexplicable. People appear to be either sympathetic or unsympathetic towards each other for no apparent reason.

Now if we look at this in the light of the Zodiac, we find that people born under different signs are either compatible or incompatible with each other. In other words, there are good and bad interrelating factors among the various signs. This does not, of course, mean that humanity can be divided into groups of hostile camps. It would be quite wrong to be hostile or indifferent toward people who happen to be born under an incompatible sign. There is no reason why everybody should not, or cannot, learn to control and adjust their feelings and actions, especially after they are aware of the positive qualities of other people by studying their character analyses, among other things.

Every person born under a certain sign has both positive and negative qualities, which are developed more or less according to his free will. Nobody is entirely good or entirely bad, and it is up to each one of us to learn to control himself on the one hand, and at the same time to endeavor to learn about himself and others.

It cannot be repeated often enough that, though the intrinsic nature of man and his basic character traits are born in him, nevertheless it is his own free will that determines whether he will make really good use of his talents and abilities—whether, in other words, he will overcome his vices or allow them to rule him. Most of us are born with at least a streak of laziness, irritability, or some other fault in our nature, and it is up to each one of us to see that we exert sufficient willpower to control our failings so that they do not harm ourselves or others.

Astrology can reveal our inclinations and tendencies. Our weaknesses should not be viewed as shortcomings that are impossible to change. The horoscope of a man may show him to have criminal leanings, for instance, but this does not mean he will definitely become a criminal.

The ordinary man usually finds it difficult to know himself. He is often bewildered. Astrology can frequently tell him more about himself than the different schools of psychology are able to do. Knowing his failings and shortcomings, he will do his best to overcome them, and make himself a better and more useful member of society and a helpmate to his family and friends. It can also save him a great deal of unhappiness and remorse.

And yet it may seem absurd that an ancient philosophy, something that is known as a "pseudo-science," could be a prop to the men and women of the twentieth century. But below the materialistic surface of modern life, there are hidden streams of feeling and thought. Symbology is reappearing as a study worthy of the scholar; the psychosomatic factor in illness has passed from the writings of the crank to those of the specialist; spiritual healing in all its forms is no longer a pious hope but an accepted phenomenon. And it is into this context that we consider astrology, in the sense that it is an analysis of human types.

Astrology and medicine had a long journey together, and only parted company a couple of centuries ago. There still remain in medical language such astrological terms as "saturnine," "choleric," and "mercurial," used in the diagnosis of physical tendencies. The herbalist, for long the handyman of the medical profession, has been dominated by astrology since the days of the Greeks. Certain herbs traditionally respond to certain planetary influences, and diseases must therefore be treated to ensure harmony between the medicine and the disease.

No one expects the most eccentric of modern doctors to go back to the practices of his predecessors. We have come a long way since the time when phases of the moon were studied in illness. Those days were a medical nightmare, with epidemics that were beyond control, and an explanation of the Black Death sought in conjunction with the planets. Nowadays, astrological diagnosis of disease has literally no parallel in modern life. And yet, age-old symbols of types and of the vulnerability of, say, the Saturnian to chronic diseases or the choleric to apoplexy and blood pressure and so on, are still applicable.

But the stars are expected to foretell and not only to diagnose. The astrological forecaster has a counterpart on a highly conventional level in the shape of the weather prophet, racing tipster and stock market forecaster, to name just three examples. All in their own way are aiming at the same result. They attempt to look a little further into the pattern of life and also try to determine future patterns accurately.

Astrological forecasting has been remarkably accurate, but often it is wide of the mark. The brave man who cares to predict world events takes dangerous chances. Individual forecasting is less clear cut; it can be a help or a disillusionment. Then welcome to the nagging question: if it is possible to foreknow, is it right to foretell? A complex point of ethics on which it is hard to pronounce judgment. The doctor faces the same dilemma if he finds that symptoms of a mortal disease are present in his patient and that he can only prognosticate a steady decline. How much to tell an individual in a crisis is a problem that has perplexed many distinguished scholars. Honest and conscientious astrologers in this modern world, where so many people are seeking guidance, face the same problem.

The ancient cults, the symbols of old religions, are eclipsed for the moment. They may return with their old force within a decade or two. But at present the outlook is dark. Human beings badly need assurance, as they did in the past, that all is not chaos. Somewhere, somehow, there is a pattern that must be worked out. As to the why and wherefore, the astrologer is not expected to give judgment. He is just someone who, by dint of talent and training, can gaze into the future.

Five hundred years ago it was customary to call in a learned man who was an astrologer who was probably also a doctor and a philosopher. By his knowledge of astrology, his study of planetary influences, he felt himself qualified to guide those in distress. The world has moved forward at a fantastic rate since then, and in this twentieth century speed has been the keyword everywhere. Tensions have increased, the spur of ambition has been applied indiscriminately. People are uncertain of themselves. At first sight it seems fantastic in the light of modern thinking that they turn to the most ancient of all studies, and get someone to calculate a horoscope for them. But is it *really* so fantastic if you take a second look? For astrology is concerned with tomorrow, with survival. And in a world such as ours, those two things are the keywords of the time in which we live.

HOW TO USE
THESE PREDICTIONS

A person reading the predictions in this book should understand that they are produced from the daily position of the planets for a group of people and are not, of course, individually specialized. To get the full benefit of them he should relate the predictions to his own character and circumstances, co-ordinate them, and draw his own conclusions from them.

If he is a serious observer of his own life he should find a definite pattern emerge that will be a helpful and reliable guide.

The point is that we always retain our free will. The stars indicate certain directional tendencies but we are not compelled to follow. We can do or not do, and wisdom must make the choice.

We all have our good and bad days. Sometimes they extend into cycles of weeks. It is therefore advisable to study daily predictions in a span ranging from the day before to several days ahead; also to re-read the monthly predictions for similar cycles.

Daily predictions should be taken very generally. The word "difficult" does not necessarily indicate a whole day of obstruction or inconvenience. It is a warning to you to be cautious. Your caution will often see you around the difficulty before you are involved. This is the correct use of astrology.

In another section, detailed information is given about the influence of the moon as it passes through the various signs of the Zodiac. It includes instructions on how to use the Moon Tables. This information should be used in conjunction with the daily forecasts to give a fuller picture of the astrological trends.

THE MOON

Moon is the nearest planet to the earth. It exerts more observable influence on us from day to day than any other planet. The effect is very personal, very intimate, and if we are not aware of how it works it can make us quite unstable in our ideas. And the annoying thing is that at these times we often see our own instability but can do nothing about it. A knowledge of what can be expected may help considerably. We can then be prepared to stand strong against the moon's negative influences and use its positive ones to help us to get ahead. Who has not heard of going with the tide?

Moon reflects, has no light of its own. It reflects the sun—the life giver—in the form of vital movement. Moon controls the tides, the blood rhythm, the movement of sap in trees and plants. Its nature is inconstancy and change so it signifies our moods, our superficial behavior—walking, talking and especially thinking. Being a true reflector of other forces, moon is cold, watery like the surface of a still lake, brilliant and scintillating at times, but easily ruffled and disturbed by the winds of change.

The moon takes 28½ days to circle the earth and the Zodiac. It spends just over 2¼ days in each sign. During that time it reflects the qualities, energies and characteristics of the sign and, to a degree, the planet which rules the sign. While the moon in its transit occupies a sign incompatible with our own birth sign, we can expect to feel a vague uneasiness, perhaps a touch of irritableness. We should not be discouraged nor let the feeling get us down, or, worse still, allow ourselves to take the discomfort out on others. Try to remember that the moon has to change signs within 55 hours and, provided you are not physically ill, your mood will probably change with it. It is amazing how frequently depression lifts with the shift in the moon's position. And, of course, when the moon is transiting a sign compatible or sympathetic to yours you will probably feel some sort of stimulation or just plain happy to be alive.

In the horoscope, the moon is such a powerful indicator that competent astrologers often use the sign it occupied at birth as the birth sign of the person. This is done particularly when the sun is on the cusp, or edge, of two signs. Most experienced astrologers, however, coordinate both sun and moon signs by reading and confirming from one to the other and secure a far more accurate and personalized analysis.

For these reasons, the moon tables which follow this section (see pages 28–35) are of great importance to the individual. They show the days and the exact times the moon will enter each sign of the Zodiac for the year. Remember, you have to adjust the indicated times to local time. The corrections, already calculated for most of the main cities, are at the beginning of the tables. What follows now is a guide to the influences that will be reflected to the earth by the moon while it transits each of the twelve signs. The influence is at its peak about 26 hours after the moon enters a sign.

MOON IN ARIES

This is a time for action, for reaching out beyond the usual self-imposed limitations and faint-hearted cautions. If you have plans in your head or on your desk, put them into practice. New ventures, applications, new jobs, new starts of any kind—all have a good chance of success. This is the period when original and dynamic impulses are being reflected onto the earth. The energies are extremely vital and favor the pursuit of pleasure and adventure in practically every form. Sick people should feel an improvement. Those who are well will probably find themselves exuding confidence and optimism. People fond of physical exercise should find their bodies growing with tone and well-being. Boldness, strength, determination should characterize most of your activities with a readiness to face up to old challenges. Yesterday's problems may seem petty and exaggerated—so deal with them. Strike out alone. Self-reliance will attract others to you. This is a good time for making friends. Business and marriage partners are more likely to be impressed with the man and woman of action. Opposition will be overcome or thrown aside with much less effort than usual. CAUTION: Be dominant but not domineering.

MOON IN TAURUS

The spontaneous, action-packed person of yesterday gives way to the cautious, diligent, hardworking "thinker." In this period ideas will probably be concentrated on ways of improving finances. A great deal of time may be spent figuring out and going over schemes and plans. It is the right time to be careful with detail. People will find themselves working longer than usual at their desks. Or devoting more time to serious thought about the future. A strong desire to put order into business and financial arrangements may cause extra work. Loved ones may complain of being neglected and may fail to appreciate that your efforts are for their ultimate benefit. Your desire for system may extend to criticism of arrangements in the home and lead to minor upsets. Health may be affected through overwork. Try to secure a reasonable amount of rest and relaxation, although the tendency will be to "keep going" despite good advice. Work done conscientiously in this period should result in a solid contribution to your future security. CAUTION: Try not to be as serious with people as the work you are engaged in.

MOON IN GEMINI

The humdrum of routine and too much work should suddenly end. You are likely to find yourself in an expansive, quicksilver world of change and self-expression. Urges to write, to paint, to experience the freedom of some sort of artistic outpouring, may be very strong. Take full advantage of them. You may find yourself finishing something you began and put aside long ago. Or embarking on something new which could easily be prompted by a chance meeting, a new acquaintance, or even an advertisement. There may be a yearning for a change of scenery, the feeling to visit another country (not too far away), or at least to get away for a few days. This may result in short, quick journeys. Or, if you are planning a single visit, there may be some unexpected changes or detours on the way. Familiar activities will seem to give little satisfaction unless they contain a fresh element of excitement or expectation. The inclination will be towards untried pursuits, particularly those that allow you to express your inner nature. The accent is on new faces, new places. CAUTION: Do not be too quick to commit yourself emotionally.

MOON IN CANCER

Feelings of uncertainty and vague insecurity are likely to cause problems while the moon is in Cancer. Thoughts may turn frequently to the warmth of the home and the comfort of loved ones. Nostalgic impulses could cause you to bring out old photographs and letters and reflect on the days when your life seemed to be much more rewarding and less demanding. The love and understanding of parents and family may be important, and, if it is not forthcoming you may have to fight against a bit of self-pity. The cordiality of friends and the thought of good times with them that are sure to be repeated will help to restore you to a happier frame of mind. The feeling to be alone may follow minor setbacks or rebuffs at this time, but solitude is unlikely to help. Better to get on the telephone or visit someone. This period often causes peculiar dreams and upsurges of imaginative thinking which can be very helpful to authors of occult and mystical works. Preoccupation with the more personal world of simple human needs should overshadow any material strivings. CAUTION: Do not spend too much time thinking—seek the company of loved ones or close friends.

MOON IN LEO

New horizons of exciting and rather extravagant activity open up. This is the time for exhilarating entertainment, glamorous and lavish parties, and expensive shopping sprees. Any merrymaking that relies upon your generosity as a host has every chance of being a spectacular success. You should find yourself right in the center of the fun, either as the life of the party or simply as a person whom happy people like to be with. Romance thrives in this heady atmosphere and friendships are likely to explode unexpectedly into serious attachments. Children and younger people should be attracted to you and you may find yourself organizing a picnic or a visit to a fun-fair, the cinema or the seaside. The sunny company and vitality of youthful companions should help you to find some unsuspected energy. In career, you could find an opening for promotion or advancement. This should be the time to make a direct approach. The period favors those engaged in original research. CAUTION: Bask in popularity but not in flattery.

MOON IN VIRGO

Off comes the party cap and out steps the busy, practical worker. He wants to get his personal affairs straight, to rearrange them, if necessary, for more efficiency, so he will have more time for more work. He clears up his correspondence, pays outstanding bills, makes numerous phone calls. He is likely to make inquiries, or sign up for some new insurance and put money into gilt-edged investment. Thoughts probably revolve around the need for future security—to tie up loose ends and clear the decks. There may be a tendency to be "finicky," to interfere in the routine of others, particularly friends and family members. The motive may be a genuine desire to help with suggestions for updating or streamlining their affairs, but these will probably not be welcomed. Sympathy may be felt for less fortunate sections of the community and a flurry of some sort of voluntary service is likely. This may be accompanied by strong feelings of responsibility on several fronts and health may suffer from extra efforts made. CAUTION: Everyone may not want your help or advice.

MOON IN LIBRA

These are days of harmony and agreement and you should find yourself at peace with most others. Relationships tend to be smooth and sweet-flowing. Friends may become closer and bonds deepen in mutual understanding. Hopes will be shared. Progress by cooperation could be the secret of success in every sphere. In business, established partnerships may flourish and new ones get off to a good start. Acquaintances could discover similar interests that lead to congenial discussions and rewarding exchanges of some sort. Love, as a unifying force, reaches its optimum. Marriage partners should find accord. Those who wed at this time face the prospect of a happy union. Cooperation and tolerance are felt to be stronger than dissension and impatience. The argumentative are not quite so loud in their bellowings, nor as inflexible in their attitudes. In the home, there should be a greater recognition of the other point of view and a readiness to put the wishes of the group before selfish insistence. This is a favorable time to join an art group. CAUTION: Do not be too independent—let others help you if they want to.

MOON IN SCORPIO

Driving impulses to make money and to economize are likely to cause upsets all round. No area of expenditure is likely to be spared the axe, including the household budget. This is a time when the desire to cut down on extravagance can become near fanatical. Care must be exercised to try to keep the aim in reasonable perspective. Others may not feel the same urgent need to save and may retaliate. There is a danger that possessions of sentimental value will be sold to realize cash for investment. Buying and selling of stock for quick profit is also likely. The attention may turn to having a good clean up round the home and at the office. Neglected jobs could suddenly be done with great bursts of energy. The desire for solitude may intervene. Self-searching thoughts could disturb. The sense of invisible and mysterious energies at work could cause some excitability. The reassurance of loves ones may help. CAUTION: Be kind to the people you love.

MOON IN SAGITTARIUS

These are days when you are likely to be stirred and elevated by discussions and reflections of a religious and philosophical nature. Ideas of far-away places may cause unusual response and excitement. A decision may be made to visit someone overseas, perhaps a person whose influence was important to your earlier character development. There could be a strong resolution to get away from present intellectual patterns, to learn new subjects and to meet more interesting people. The superficial may be rejected in all its forms. An impatience with old ideas and unimaginative contacts could lead to a change of companions and interests. There may be an upsurge of religious feeling and metaphysical inquiry. Even a new insight into the significance of astrology and other occult studies is likely under the curious stimulus of the moon in Sagittarius. Physically, you may express this need for fundamental change by spending more time outdoors: sports, gardening or going for long walks. CAUTION: Try to channel any restlessness into worthwhile study.

MOON IN CAPRICORN

Life in these hours may seem to pivot around the importance of gaining prestige and honor in the career, as well as maintaining a spotless reputation. Ambitious urges may be excessive and could be accompanied by quite acquisitive drives for money. Effort should be directed along strictly ethical lines where there is no possibility of reproach or scandal. All endeavors are likely to be characterized by great earnestness, and an air of authority and purpose which should impress those who are looking for leadership or reliability. The desire to conform to accepted standards may extend to sharp criticism of family members. Frivolity and unconventional actions are unlikely to amuse while the moon is in Capricorn. Moderation and seriousness are the orders of the day. Achievement and recognition in this period could come through community work or organizing for the benefit of some amateur group. CAUTION: Dignity and esteem are not always self-awarded.

MOON IN AQUARIUS

Moon in Aquarius is in the second last sign of the Zodiac where ideas can become disturbingly fine and subtle. The result is often a mental "no-man's land" where imagination cannot be trusted with the same certitude as other times. The dangers for the individual are the extremes of optimism and pessimism. Unless the imgination is held in check, situations are likely to be misread, and rosy conclusions drawn where they do not exist. Consequences for the unwary can be costly in career and business. Best to think twice and not speak or act until you think again. Pessimism can be a cruel self-inflicted penalty for delusion at this time. Between the two extremes are strange areas of self-deception which, for example, can make the selfish person think he is actually being generous. Eerie dreams which resemble the reality and even seem to continue into the waking state are also possible. CAUTION: Look for the fact and not just for the image in your mind.

MOON IN PISCES

Everything seems to come to the surface now. Memory may be crystal clear, throwing up long-forgotten information which could be valuable in the career or business. Flashes of clairvoyance and intuition are possible along with sudden realizations of one's own nature, which may be used for self-improvement. A talent, never before suspected, may be discovered. Qualities not evident before in friends and marriage partners are likely to be noticed. As this is a period in which the truth seems to emerge, the discovery of false characteristics is likely to lead to disenchantment or a shift in attachments. However, where qualities are realized it should lead to happiness and deeper feeling. Surprise solutions could bob up for old problems. There may be a public announcement of the solving of a crime or mystery. People with secrets may find someone has "guessed" correctly. The secrets of the soul or the inner self also tend to reveal themselves. Religious and philosophical groups may make some interesting discoveries. CAUTION: Not a time for activities that depend on secrecy.

MOON TABLES

TIME CORRECTIONS FOR
GREENWICH MOON TABLES

London, Glasgow, Dublin, Dakar..Same time

Vienna, Prague, Rome, Kinshasa, Frankfurt,
Stockholm, Brussels, Amsterdam, Warsaw,
Zurich..Add 1 hour

Bucharest, Istanbul, Beirut, Cairo, Johannesburg,
Athens, Cape Town, Helsinki, Tel Aviv.............................Add 2 hours

Dhahran, Baghdad, Moscow, Leningrad, Nairobi,
Addis Ababa, Zanzibar...Add 3 hours

Delhi, Calcutta, Bombay, Colombo...................................Add 5 ½ hours

Rangoon...Add 6 ½ hours

Saigon, Bangkok, Chungking...Add 7 hours

Canton, Manila, Hong Kong, Shanghai, Peking....................Add 8 hours

Tokyo, Pusan, Seoul, Vladivostok, Yokohama.......................Add 9 hours

Sydney, Melbourne, Guam, Port Moresby............................Add 10 hours

Azores, Reykjavik...Deduct 1 hour

Rio de Janeiro, Montevideo, Buenos Aires,
Sao Paulo, Recife..Deduct 3 hours

LaPaz, San Juan, Santiago, Bermuda, Caracas,
Halifax..Deduct 4 hours

New York, Washington, Boston, Detroit, Lima,
Havana, Miami, Bogota...Deduct 5 hours

Mexico, Chicago, New Orleans, Houston........................Deduct 6 hours

San Francisco, Seattle, Los Angeles, Hollywood,
Ketchikan, Juneau...Deduct 8 hours

Honolulu, Fairbanks, Anchorage, Papeete.....................Deduct 10 hours

1987 MOON TABLES—GREENWICH TIME

JANUARY		FEBRUARY		MARCH	
Day Moon Enters		**Day Moon Enters**		**Day Moon Enters**	
1. Aquar.	0:29 pm	1. Pisces		1. Aries	0:42 pm
2. Aquar.		2. Aries	2:31 am	2. Aries	
3. Pisces	1:22 pm	3. Aries		3. Taurus	6:16 pm
4. Pisces		4. Taurus	9:00 am	4. Taurus	
5. Aries	5:17 pm	5. Taurus		5. Taurus	
6. Aries		6. Gemini	7:33 pm	6. Gemini	3:17 am
7. Aries		7. Gemini		7. Gemini	
8. Taurus	1:31 am	8. Gemini		8. Cancer	3:29 pm
9. Taurus		9. Cancer	8:20 am	9. Cancer	
10. Gemini	0:49 pm	10. Cancer		10. Cancer	
11. Gemini		11. Leo	8:48 pm	11. Leo	4:20 am
12. Gemini		12. Leo		12. Leo	
13. Cancer	1:30 am	13. Leo		13. Virgo	3:15 pm
14. Cancer		14. Virgo	7:55 am	14. Virgo	
15. Leo	2:10 pm	15. Virgo		15. Libra	11:48 pm
16. Leo		16. Libra	5:01 pm	16. Libra	
17. Leo		17. Libra		17. Libra	
18. Virgo	1:35 am	18. Libra		18. Scorpio	5:58 am
19. Virgo		19. Scorpio	0:05 am	19. Scorpio	
20. Libra	11:15 am	20. Scorpio		20. Sagitt.	10:46 am
21. Libra		21. Sagitt.	5:03 am	21. Sagitt.	
22. Scorpio	6:23 pm	22. Sagitt.		22. Capric.	1:52 pm
23. Scorpio		23. Capric.	6:42 am	23. Capric.	
24. Sagitt.	10:07 pm	24. Capric.		24. Aquar.	4:40 pm
25. Sagitt.		25. Aquar.	9:08 am	25. Aquar.	
26. Capric.	11:22 pm	26. Aquar.		26. Pisces	6:59 pm
27. Capric.		27. Pisces	10:13 am	27. Pisces	
28. Aquar.	11:26 pm	28. Pisces		28. Aries	10:26 pm
29. Aquar.				29. Aries	
30. Pisces	11:40 pm			30. Aries	
31. Pisces				31. Taurus	3:38 am

1987 MOON TABLES—GREENWICH TIME

APRIL		MAY		JUNE	
Day Moon Enters		**Day Moon Enters**		**Day Moon Enters**	
1. Taurus		1. Gemini		1. Leo	3:20 am
2. Gemini	Noon	2. Cancer	7:25 am	2. Leo	
3. Gemini		3. Cancer		3. Virgo	4:11 pm
4. Cancer	11:30 pm	4. Leo	8:09 pm	4. Virgo	
5. Cancer		5. Leo		5. Virgo	
6. Cancer		6. Leo		6. Libra	2:21 am
7. Leo	0:36 pm	7. Virgo	8:14 am	7. Libra	
8. Leo		8. Virgo		8. Scorpio	8:50 am
9. Virgo	11:41 pm	9. Libra	5:19 pm	9. Scorpio	
10. Virgo		10. Libra		10. Sagitt.	11:41 am
11. Virgo		11. Scorpio	10:48 pm	11. Sagitt.	
12. Libra	8:11 am	12. Scorpio		12. Capric.	0:10 pm
13. Libra		13. Scorpio		13. Capric.	
14. Scorpio	1:24 pm	14. Sagitt.	1:14 am	14. Aquar.	11:50 am
15. Scorpio		15. Sagitt.		15. Aquar.	
16. Sagitt.	4:56 pm	16. Capric.	2:41 am	16. Pisces	1:31 pm
17. Sagitt.		17. Capric.		17. Pisces	
18. Capric.	7:36 pm	18. Aquar.	3:54 am	18. Aries	5:15 pm
19. Capric.		19. Aquar.		19. Aries	
20. Aquar.	10:25 pm	20. Pisces	6:51 am	20. Aries	
21. Aquar.		21. Pisces		21. Taurus	0:22 am
22. Aquar.		22. Aries	11:49 am	22. Taurus	
23. Pisces	1:33 am	23. Aries		23. Gemini	10:14 am
24. Pisces		24. Taurus	6:56 pm	24. Gemini	
25. Aries	6:18 am	25. Taurus		25. Cancer	9:29 pm
26. Aries		26. Taurus		26. Cancer	
27. Taurus	0:11 pm	27. Gemini	3:53 am	27. Cancer	
28. Taurus		28. Gemini		28. Leo	10:00 am
29. Gemini	8:42 pm	29. Cancer	3:01 pm	29. Leo	
30. Gemini		30. Cancer		30. Virgo	10:43 pm
		31. Cancer			

1987 MOON TABLES—GREENWICH TIME

JULY	AUGUST	SEPTEMBER
Day Moon Enters	**Day Moon Enters**	**Day Moon Enters**
1. Virgo	1. Libra	1. Sagitt.
2. Virgo	2. Scorpio 0:49 am	2. Capric. 5:03 pm
3. Libra 10:02 am	3. Scorpio	3. Capric.
4. Libra	4. Sagitt. 6:35 am	4. Aquar. 6:39 pm
5. Scorpio 5:50 pm	5. Sagitt.	5. Aquar.
6. Scorpio	6. Capric. 8:41 am	6. Pisces 6:59 pm
7. Sagitt. 9:46 pm	7. Capric.	7. Pisces
8. Sagitt.	8. Aquar. 8:53 am	8. Aries 8:04 pm
9. Capric. 10:36 pm	9. Aquar.	9. Aries
10. Capric.	10. Pisces 8:32 am	10. Taurus 11:11 pm
11. Aquar. 10:15 pm	11. Pisces	11. Taurus
12. Aquar.	12. Aries 9:34 am	12. Taurus
13. Pisces 10:03 pm	13. Aries	13. Gemini 5:49 am
14. Pisces	14. Taurus 1:39 pm	14. Gemini
15. Pisces	15. Taurus	15. Cancer 4:37 pm
16. Aries 0:21 am	16. Gemini 9:52 pm	16. Cancer
17. Aries	17. Gemini	17. Cancer
18. Taurus 6:09 am	18. Gemini	18. Leo 5:18 am
19. Taurus	19. Cancer 9:25 am	19. Leo
20. Gemini 3:35 pm	20. Cancer	20. Virgo 5:40 pm
21. Gemini	21. Leo 10:24 pm	21. Virgo
22. Gemini	22. Leo	22. Virgo
23. Cancer 3:29 am	23. Leo	23. Libra 3:56 am
24. Cancer	24. Virgo 10:37 am	24. Libra
25. Leo 4:13 pm	25. Virgo .	25. Scorpio 0:22 pm
26. Leo	26. Libra 9:22 pm	26. Scorpio
27. Leo	27. Libra	27. Sagitt. 6:28 pm
28. Virgo 4:32 am	28. Libra	28. Sagitt.
29. Virgo	29. Scorpio 6:34 am	29. Capric. 10:57 pm
30. Libra 3:55 pm	30. Scorpio	30. Capric.
31. Libra	31. Sagitt. 1:04 pm	

1987 MOON TABLES—GREENWICH TIME

OCTOBER		NOVEMBER		DECEMBER	
Day Moon Enters		Day Moon Enters		Day Moon Enters	
1. Capric.		1. Pisces		1. Aries	
2. Aquar.	2:00 am	2. Aries	1:45 pm	2. Taurus	0:58 am
3. Aquar.		3. Aries		3. Taurus	
4. Pisces	4:04 am	4. Taurus	6:02 pm	4. Gemini	8:08 am
5. Pisces		5. Taurus		5. Gemini	
6. Aries	5:48 am	6. Taurus		6. Cancer	5:07 pm
7. Aries		7. Gemini	0:10 am	7. Cancer	
8. Taurus	9:04 am	8. Gemini		8. Cancer	
9. Taurus		9. Cancer	9:17 am	9. Leo	4:37 am
10. Gemini	3:01 pm	10. Cancer		10. Leo	
11. Gemini		11. Leo	8:52 pm	11. Virgo	5:27 pm
12. Gemini		12. Leo		12. Virgo	
13. Cancer	0:35 am	13. Leo		13. Virgo	
14. Cancer		14. Virgo	9:48 am	14. Libra	5:19 am
15. Leo	1:00 pm	15. Virgo		15. Libra	
16. Leo		16. Libra	9:09 pm	16. Scorpio	2:34 pm
17. Leo		17. Libra		17. Scorpio	
18. Virgo	1:30 am	18. Libra		18. Sagitt.	7:16 pm
19. Virgo		19. Scorpio	4:44 am	19. Sagitt.	
20. Libra	0:11 pm	20. Scorpio		20. Capric.	9:18 pm
21. Libra		21. Sagitt.	9:14 am	21. Capric.	
22. Scorpio	7:31 pm	22. Sagitt.		22. Aquar.	9:45 pm
23. Scorpio		23. Capric.	11:50 am	23. Aquar.	
24. Scorpio		24. Capric.		24. Pisces	10:48 pm
25. Sagitt.	0:47 am	25. Aquar.	1:31 pm	25. Pisces	
26. Sagitt.		26. Aquar.		26. Pisces	
27. Capric.	4:34 am	27. Pisces	3:51 pm	27. Aries	1:17 am
28. Capric.		28. Pisces		28. Aries	
29. Aquar.	7:35 am	29. Aries	7:37 pm	29. Taurus	6:38 am
30. Aquar.		30. Aries		30. Taurus	
31. Pisces	10:19 am			31. Gemini	2:29 pm

1987 PHASES OF THE MOON—GREENWICH TIME

New Moon	First Quarter	Full Moon	Last Quarter
(1986)	Jan. 6	Jan. 15	Jan. 22
Jan. 29	Feb. 5	Feb. 13	Feb. 21
Feb. 28	March 7	March 15	March 22
March 29	April 6	April 14	April 20
April 28	May 6	May 13	May 20
May 27	June 4	June 11	June 18
June 26	July 4	July 11	July 17
July 25	Aug. 2	Aug. 9	Aug. 16
Aug. 24	Sept. 1	Sept. 7	Sept. 14
Sept. 23	Sept. 30	Oct. 7	Oct. 14
Oct. 22	Oct. 29	Nov. 5	Nov. 13
Nov. 20	Nov. 28	Dec. 5	Dec. 13
Dec. 20	Dec. 27	(1988)	(1988)

Summer time to be considered where applicable.

1987 PLANTING GUIDE

	Aboveground Crops	Root Crops	Pruning	Weeds-Pests
January	4-8-9-13-14-31	21-22-23-24-27-28	23-24	16-17-18-19-25-26
February	1-4-5-9-10-28	17-18-19-20-23-24	19-20	14-15-21-22-25-26
March	4-5-9-10-31	16-17-18-19-23-27-28	18-19-27-28	21-25
April	1-5-6-12-13-28	14-15-19-20-23-24	15-23-24	17-21-22-25-26
May	2-3-10-11-12-30-31	16-17-20-21-25-26	20-21	14-15-18-19-23
June	6-7-8-9-26-27	13-17-21-22	17	15-19-20-24
July	4-5-6-10-31	11-14-15-18-19-23-24	14-15-23-24	12-13-16-17-21-22
August	1-2-3-6-7-27-28-29-30	10-11-15-19-20-21	10-11-19-20-21	12-13-17-18-22-23
September	3-23-24-25-26-30	11-12-16-17	16-17	9-10-13-14-18-19-20-21-22
October	1-4-5-23-24-27-28	8-9-13-14-21	13-14	7-11-12-16-17-18-19
November	1-24-28	6-9-10-17-18-19	9-10-19	7-8-12-13-14-15
December	2-3-21-25-26-29-30	7-8-14-15-16-17	7-8-17	5-9-10-11-12-13-19

1987 FISHING GUIDE

	Good	Best
January	6-12-15-16-17-18-29	13-14-22
February	11-12-13-14-15-16-21	5-10-28
March	7-12-13-14-15-22-29	16-17-18
April	11-16-17	6-12-13-14-15-20-28
May	6-14-15-27	10-11-12-13-16-20
June	4-10-11-12-14-18	8-9-13-26
July	8-9-12-13-17-25	4-10-11-14
August	8-9-12-16-24	2-6-7-10-11
September	1-4-5-6-8-9-10-14	7-23-30
October	6-7-10-29	4-5-8-9-14-22
November	2-3-4-7-8-13	5-6-20-28
December	4-5-6-13-20-27	2-3-7-8

MOON'S INFLUENCE OVER DAILY AFFAIRS

The Moon makes a complete transit of the Zodiac every 27 days 7 hours and 43 minutes. In making this transit the Moon forms different aspects with the planets and consequently has favorable or unfavorable bearings on affairs and events for persons according to the sign of the Zodiac under which they were born.

Whereas the Sun exclusively represents fire, the Moon rules water. The action of the Moon may be described as fluctuating, variable, absorbent and receptive. It is well known that the attraction to the Moon in combination with the movement of the Earth is responsible for the tides. The Moon has a similar effect on men. A clever navigator will make use of the tides to bring his ship to the intended destination. You also can reach your "destination" better by making use of your tides.

When the Moon is in conjunction with the Sun it is called a New Moon; when the Moon and Sun are in opposition it is called a Full Moon. From New Moon to Full Moon, first and second quarter—which takes about two weeks—the Moon is increasing or waxing. From Full Moon to New Moon, third and fourth quarter, the Moon is said to be decreasing or waning. The Moon Table indicates the New Moon and Full Moon and the quarters.

ACTIVITY	*MOON IN*
Business	
buying and selling	Sagittarius, Aries, Gemini, Virgo
new, requiring public support	1st and 2nd quarter
meant to be kept quiet	3rd and 4th quarter
Investigation	3rd and 4th quarter
Signing documents	1st & 2nd quarter, Cancer, Scorpio, Pisces
Advertising	2nd quarter, Sagittarius
Journeys and trips	1st & 2nd quarter, Gemini, Virgo
Renting offices, etc.	Taurus, Leo, Scorpio, Aquarius
Painting of house/apartment	3rd & 4th quarter, Taurus, Scorpio, Aquarius
Decorating	Gemini, Libra, Aquarius
Buying clothes and accessories	Taurus, Virgo
Beauty salon or barber shop visit	1st & 2nd quarter, Taurus, Leo, Libra, Scorpio, Aquarius
Weddings	1st & 2nd quarter

MOON'S INFLUENCE OVER YOUR HEALTH

ARIES	Head, brain, face, upper jaw
TAURUS	Throat, neck, lower jaw
GEMINI	Hands, arms, lungs, shoulders, nervous system
CANCER	Esophagus, stomach, breasts, womb, liver
LEO	Heart, spine
VIRGO	Intestines, liver
LIBRA	Kidneys, lower back
SCORPIO	Sex and eliminative organs
SAGITTARIUS	Hips, thighs, liver
CAPRICORN	Skin, bones, beeth, knees
AQUARIUS	Circulatory system, lower legs
PISCES	Feet, tone of being

Try to avoid work being done on that part of the body when the Moon is in the sign governing that part.

MOON'S INFLUENCE OVER PLANTS

Centuries ago it was established that seeds planted when the Moon is in certain signs and phases called "fruitful" will produce more than seeds planted when the Moon is in a Barren sign.

FRUITFUL SIGNS	*BARREN SIGNS*	*DRY SIGNS*
Taurus	Aries	Aries
Cancer	Gemini	Gemini
Libra	Leo	Sagittarius
Scorpio	Virgo	Aquarius
Capricorn	Sagittarius	
Pisces	Aquarius	

ACTIVITY	MOON IN
Mow lawn, trim plans	Fruitful sign, 1st & 2nd quarter
Plant flowers	Fruitful sign, 2nd quarter; best in Cancer and Libra
Prune	Fruitful sign, 3rd & 4th quarter
Destroy pests; spray	Barren sign, 4th quarter
Harvest potatoes, root crops	Dry sign, 3rd & 4th quarter; Taurus, Leo, and Aquarius

THE SIGNS: DOMINANT CHARACTERISTICS

March 21–April 20

The Positive Side of Aries

The Arien has many positive points to his character. People born under this first sign of the Zodiac are often quite strong and enthusiastic. On the whole, they are forward-looking people who are not easily discouraged by temporary setbacks. They know what they want out of life and they go out after it. Their personalities are strong. Others are usually quite impressed by the Arien's way of doing things. Quite often they are sources of inspiration for others traveling the same route. Aries men and women have a special zest for life that is often contagious; for others, they are often the example of how life should be lived.

The Aries person usually has a quick and active mind. He is imaginative and inventive. He enjoys keeping busy and active. He generally gets along well with all kinds of people. He is interested in mankind, as a whole. He likes to be challenged. Some would say he thrives on opposition, for it is when he is set against that he often does his best. Getting over or around obstacles is a challenge he generally enjoys. All in all, the Arien is quite positive and young-thinking. He likes to keep abreast of new things that are happening in the world. Ariens are often fond of speed. They like things to be done quickly and this sometimes aggravates their slower colleagues and associates.

The Aries man or woman always seems to remain young. Their whole approach to life is youthful and optimistic. They never say die, no matter what the odds. They may have an occasional setback, but it is not long before they are back on their feet again.

The Negative Side of Aries

Everybody has his less positive qualities—and Aries is no exception. Sometimes the Aries man or woman is not very tactful in communicating with others; in his hurry to get things done he is apt to

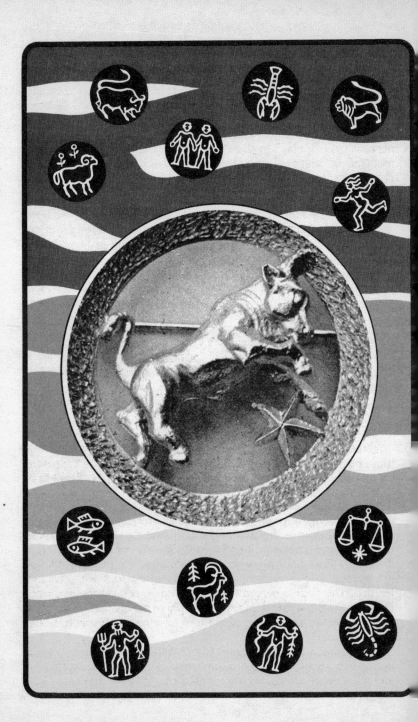

be a little callous or inconsiderate. Sensitive people are likely to find him somewhat sharp-tongued in some situations. Often in his eagerness to achieve his aims, he misses the mark altogether. At times the Arien is too impulsive. He can occasionally be stubborn and refuse to listen to reason. If things do not move quickly enough to suit the Aries man or woman, he or she is apt to become rather nervous or irritable. The uncultivated Arien is not unfamiliar with moments of doubt and fear. He is capable of being destructive if he does not get his way. He can overcome some of his emotional problems by steadily trying to express himself as he really is, but this requires effort.

April 21–May 20

The Positive Side of Taurus

The Taurus person is known for his ability to concentrate and for his tenacity. These are perhaps his strongest qualities. The Taurus man or woman generally has very little trouble in getting along with others; it's his nature to be helpful toward people in need. He can always be depended on by his friends, especially those in trouble.

The Taurean generally achieves what he wants through his ability to persevere. He never leaves anything unfinished but works on something until it has been completed. People can usually take him at his word; he is honest and forthright in most of his dealings. The Taurus person has a good chance to make a success of his life because of his many positive qualities. The Taurean who aims high seldom falls short of his mark. He learns well by experience. He is thorough and does not believe in short-cuts of any kind. The Taurean's thoroughness pays off in the end, for through his deliberateness he learns how to rely on himself and what he has learned. The Taurus person tries to get along with others, as a rule. He is not overly critical and likes people to be themselves. He is a tolerant person and enjoys peace and harmony—especially in his home life.

The Taurean is usually cautious in all that he does. He is not a person who believes in taking unnecessary risks. Before adopting any one line of action, he will weigh all of the pros and cons. The

Taurus person is steadfast. Once his mind is made up it seldom changes. The person born under this sign usually is a good family person—reliable and loving.

The Negative Side of Taurus

Sometimes the Taurus man or woman is a bit too stubborn. He won't listen to other points of view if his mind is set on something. To others, this can be quite annoying. The Taurean also does not like to be told what to do. He becomes rather angry if others think him not too bright. He does not like to be told he is wrong, even when he is. He dislikes being contradicted.

Some people who are born under this sign are very suspicious of others—even of those persons close to them. They find it difficult to trust people fully. They are often afraid of being deceived or taken advantage of. The Taurean often finds it difficult to forget or forgive. His love of material things sometimes makes him rather avaricious and petty.

May 21–June 20

The Positive Side of Gemini

The person born under this sign of the Heavenly Twins is usually quite bright and quick-witted. Some of them are capable of doing many different things. The Gemini person very often has many different interests. He keeps an open mind and is always anxious to learn new things.

The Geminian is often an analytical person. He is a person who enjoys making use of his intellect. He is governed more by his mind than by his emotions. He is a person who is not confined to one view; he can often understand both sides to a problem or question. He knows how to reason; how to make rapid decisions if need be.

He is an adaptable person and can make himself at home almost anywhere. There are all kinds of situations he can adapt to. He is a person who seldom doubts himself; he is sure of his talents and his

ability to think and reason. The Geminian is generally most satisfied when he is in a situation where he can make use of his intellect. Never short of imagination, he often has strong talents for invention. He is rather a modern person when it comes to life; the Geminian almost always moves along with the times—perhaps that is why he remains so youthful throughout most of his life.

Literature and art appeal to the person born under this sign. Creativity in almost any form will interest and intrigue the Gemini man or woman.

The Geminian is often quite charming. A good talker, he often is the center of attraction at any gathering. People find it easy to like a person born under this sign because he can appear easygoing and usually has a good sense of humor.

The Negative Side of Gemini

Sometimes the Gemini person tries to do too many things at one time—and as a result, winds up finishing nothing. Some Geminians are easily distracted and find it rather difficult to concentrate on one thing for too long a time. Sometimes they give in to trifling fancies and find it rather boring to become too serious about any one thing. Some of them are never dependable, no matter what they promise.

Although the Gemini man or woman often appears to be well-versed on many subjects, this is sometimes just a veneer. His knowledge may be only superficial, but because he speaks so well he gives people the impression of erudition. Some Geminians are sharp-tongued and inconsiderate; they think only of themselves and their own pleasure.

June 21–July 20

The Positive Side of Cancer

The Cancerians's most positive point is his understanding nature. On the whole, he is a loving and sympathetic person. He would never go out of his way to hurt anyone. The Cancer man or woman

is often very kind and tender; they give what they can to others. They hate to see others suffering and will do what they can to help someone in less fortunate circumstances than themselves. They are often very concerned about the world. Their interest in people generally goes beyond that of just their own families and close friends; they have a deep sense of brotherhood and respect humanitarian values. The Cancerian means what he says, as a rule; he is honest about his feelings.

The Cancer man or woman is a person who knows the art of patience. When something seems difficult, he is willing to wait until the situation becomes manageable again. He is a person who knows how to bide his time. The Cancerian knows how to concentrate on one thing at a time. When he has made his mind up he generally sticks with what he does, seeing it through to the end.

The Cancerian is a person who loves his home. He enjoys being surrounded by familiar things and the people he loves. Of all the signs, Cancer is the most maternal. Even the men born under this sign often have a motherly or protective quality about them. They like to take care of people in their family—to see that they are well loved and well provided for. They are usually loyal and faithful. Family ties mean a lot to the Cancer man or woman. Parents and in-laws are respected and loved. The Cancerian has a strong sense of tradition. He is very sensitive to the moods of others.

The Negative Side of Cancer

Sometimes the Cancerian finds it rather hard to face life. It becomes too much for him. He can be a little timid and retiring, when things don't go too well. When unfortunate things happen, he is apt to just shrug and say, "Whatever will be will be." He can be fatalistic to a fault. The uncultivated Cancerian is a bit lazy. He doesn't have very much ambition. Anything that seems a bit difficult he'll gladly leave to others. He may be lacking in initiative. Too sensitive, when he feels he's been injured, he'll crawl back into his shell and nurse his imaginary wounds. The Cancer woman often is given to crying when the smallest thing goes wrong.

Some Cancerians find it difficult to enjoy themselves in environments outside their homes. They make heavy demands on others, and need to be constantly reassured that they are loved.

July 21–August 21

The Positive Side of Leo

Often Leos make good leaders. They seem to be good organizers and administrators. Usually they are quite popular with others. Whatever group it is that he belongs to, the Leo man is almost sure to be or become the leader.

The Leo person is generous most of the time. It is his best characteristic. He or she likes to give gifts and presents. In making others happy, the Leo person becomes happy himself. He likes to splurge when spending money on others. In some instances it may seem that the Leo's generosity knows no boundaries. A hospitable person, the Leo man or woman is very fond of welcoming people to his house and entertaining them. He is never short of company.

The Leo person has plenty of energy and drive. He enjoys working toward some specific goal. When he applies himself correctly, he gets what he wants most often. The Leo person is almost never unsure of himself. He has plenty of confidence and aplomb. He is a person who is direct in almost everything he does. He has a quick mind and can make a decision in a very short time.

He usually sets a good example for others because of his ambitious manner and positive ways. He knows how to stick to something once he's started. Although the Leo person may be good at making a joke, he is not superficial or glib. He is a loving person, kind and thoughtful.

There is generally nothing small or petty about the Leo man or woman. He does what he can for those who are deserving. He is a person others can rely upon at all times. He means what he says. An honest person, generally speaking, he is a friend that others value.

The Negative Side of Leo

Leo, however, does have his faults. At times, he can be just a bit too arrogant. He thinks that no one deserves a leadership position except him. Only he is capable of doing things well. His opinion of himself is often much too high. Because of his conceit, he is sometimes rather unpopular with a good many people. Some Leos are too materialistic; they can only think in terms of money and profit.

Some Leos enjoy lording it over others—at home or at their place of business. What is more, they feel they have the right to. Egocentric to an impossible degree, this sort of Leo cares little about how others think or feel. He can be rude and cutting.

August 22–September 22

The Positive Side of Virgo

The person born under the sign of Virgo is generally a busy person. He knows how to arrange and organize things. He is a good planner. Above all, he is practical and is not afraid of hard work.

The person born under this sign, Virgo, knows how to attain what he desires. He sticks with something until it is finished. He never shirks his duties, and can always be depended upon. The Virgo person can be thoroughly trusted at all times.

The man or woman born under this sign tries to do everything to perfection. He doesn't believe in doing anything half-way. He always aims for the top. He is the sort of a person who is constantly striving to better himself—not because he wants more money or glory, but because it gives him a feeling of accomplishment.

The Virgo man or woman is a very observant person. He is sensitive to how others feel, and can see things below the surface of a situation. He usually puts this talent to constructive use.

It is not difficult for the Virgoan to be open and earnest. He believes in putting his cards on the table. He is never secretive or under-handed. He's as good as his word. The Virgo person is generally plain-spoken and down-to-earth. He has no trouble in expressing himself.

The Virgo person likes to keep up to date on new developments in his particular field. Well-informed, generally, he sometimes has a keen interest in the arts or literature. What he knows, he knows well. His ability to use his critical faculties is well-developed and sometimes startles others because of its accuracy.

The Virgoan adheres to a moderate way of life; he avoids excesses. He is a responsible person and enjoys being of service.

The Negative Side of Virgo

Sometimes a Virgo person is too critical. He thinks that only he can do something the way it should be done. Whatever anyone else does is inferior. He can be rather annoying in the way he quibbles over insignificant details. In telling others how things should be done, he can be rather tactless and mean.

Some Virgos seem rather emotionless and cool. They feel emo-

tional involvement is beneath them. They are sometimes too tidy, too neat. With money they can be rather miserly. Some try to force their opinions and ideas on others.

September 23–October 22

The Positive Side of Libra

Librans love harmony. It is one of their most outstanding character traits. They are interested in achieving balance; they admire beauty and grace in things as well as in people. Generally speaking, they are kind and considerate people. Librans are usually very sympathetic. They go out of their way not to hurt another person's feelings. They are outgoing and do what they can to help those in need.

People born under the sign of Libra almost always make good friends. They are loyal and amiable. They enjoy the company of others. Many of them are rather moderate in their views; they believe in keeping an open mind, however, and weighing both sides of an issue fairly before making a decision.

Alert and often intelligent, the Libran, always fair-minded, tries to put himself in the position of the other person. They are against injustice; quite often they take up for the underdog. In most of their social dealings, they try to be tactful and kind. They dislike discord and bickering, and most Libras strive for peace and harmony in all their relationships.

The Libra man or woman has a keen sense of beauty. They appreciate handsome furnishings and clothes. Many of them are artistically inclined. Their taste is usually impeccable. They know how to use color. Their homes are almost always attractively arranged and inviting. They enjoy entertaining people and see to it that their guests always feel at home and welcome.

The Libran gets along with almost everyone. He is well-liked and socially much in demand.

The Negative Side of Libra

Some people born under this sign tend to be rather insincere. So eager are they to achieve harmony in all relationships that they will even go so far as to lie. Many of them are escapists. They find facing

the truth an ordeal and prefer living in a world of make-believe.

In a serious argument, some Librans give in rather easily even when they know they are right. Arguing, even about something they believe in, is too unsettling for some of them.

Librans sometimes care too much for material things. They enjoy possessions and luxuries. Some are vain and tend to be jealous.

October 23–November 22

The Positive Side of Scorpio

The Scorpio man or woman generally knows what he or she wants out of life. He is a determined person. He sees something through to the end. The Scorpion is quite sincere, and seldom says anything he doesn't mean. When he sets a goal for himself he tries to go about achieving it in a very direct way.

The Scorpion is brave and courageous. They are not afraid of hard work. Obstacles do not frighten them. They forge ahead until they achieve what they set out for. The Scorpio man or woman has a strong will.

Although the Scorpion may seem rather fixed and determined, inside he is often quite tender and loving. He can care very much for others. He believes in sincerity in all relationships. His feelings about someone tend to last; they are profound and not superficial.

The Scorpio person is someone who adheres to his principles no matter what happens. He will not be deterred from a path he believes to be right.

Because of his many positive strengths, the Scorpion can often achieve happiness for himself and for those that he loves.

He is a constructive person by nature. He often has a deep understanding of people and of life, in general. He is perceptive and unafraid. Obstacles often seem to spur him on. He is a positive person who enjoys winning. He has many strengths and resources; challenge of any sort often brings out the best in him.

The Negative Side of Scorpio

The Scorpio person is sometimes hypersensitive. Often he imagines injury when there is none. He feels that others do not bother to

recognize him for his true worth. Sometimes he is given to excessive boasting in order to compensate for what he feels is neglect

The Scorpio person can be rather proud and arrogant. They can be rather sly when they put their minds to it and they enjoy outwitting persons or institutions noted for their cleverness.

Their tactics for getting what they want are sometimes devious and ruthless. They don't care too much about what others may think. If they feel others have done them an injustice, they will do their best to seek revenge. The Scorpion often has a sudden, violent temper; and this person's interest in sex is sometimes quite unbalanced or excessive.

November 23–December 20

The Positive Side of Sagittarius

People born under this sign are often honest and forthright. Their approach to life is earnest and open. The Sagittarian is often quite adult in his way of seeing things. They are broadminded and tolerant people. When dealing with others the person born under the sign of Sagittarius is almost always open and forthright. He doesn't believe in deceit or pretension. His standards are high. People who associate with the Sagittarian, generally admire and respect him.

The Sagittarian trusts others easily and expects them to trust him. He is never suspicious or envious and almost always thinks well of others. People always enjoy his company because he is so friendly and easy-going. The Sagittarius man or woman is often good-humored. He can always be depended upon by his friends, family, and co-workers.

The person born under this sign of the Zodiac likes a good joke every now and then; he is keen on fun and this makes him very popular with others.

A lively person, he enjoys sports and outdoor life. The Sagittarian is fond of animals. Intelligent and interesting, he can begin an animated conversation with ease. He likes exchanging ideas and discussing various views.

He is not selfish or proud. If someone proposes an idea or plan that is better than his, he will immediately adopt it. Imaginative yet practical, he knows how to put ideas into practice.

He enjoys sport and game, and it doesn't matter if he wins or loses. He is a forgiving person, and never sulks over something that has not worked out in his favor.

He is seldom critical, and is almost always generous.

The Negative Side of Sagittarius

Some Sagittarians are restless. They take foolish risks and seldom learn from the mistakes they make. They don't have heads for money and are often mismanaging their finances. Some of them devote much of their time to gambling.

Some are too outspoken and tactless, always putting their feet in their mouths. They hurt others carelessly by being honest at the wrong time. Sometimes they make promises which they don't keep. They don't stick close enough to their plans and go from one failure to another. They are undisciplined and waste a lot of energy.

December 21–January 19

The Positive Side of Capricorn

The person born under the sign of Capricorn is usually very stable and patient. He sticks to whatever tasks he has and sees them through. He can always be relied upon and he is not averse to work.

An honest person, the Capricornian is generally serious about whatever he does. He does not take his duties lightly. He is a practical person and believes in keeping his feet on the ground.

Quite often the person born under this sign is ambitious and knows how to get what he wants out of life. He forges ahead and never gives up his goal. When he is determined about something, he almost always wins. He is a good worker—a hard worker. Although things may not come easy to him, he will not complain, but continue working until his chores are finished.

He is usually good at business matters and knows the value of money. He is not a spendthrift and knows how to put something away for a rainy day; he dislikes waste and unnecessary loss.

The Capricornian knows how to make use of his self-control. He

can apply himself to almost anything once he puts his mind to it. His ability to concentrate sometimes astounds others. He is diligent and does well when involved in detail work.

The Capricorn man or woman is charitable, generally speaking, and will do what is possible to help others less fortunate. As a friend, he is loyal and trustworthy. He never shirks his duties or responsibilities. He is self-reliant and never expects too much of the other fellow. He does what he can on his own. If someone does him a good turn, then he will do his best to return the favor.

The Negative Side of Capricorn

Like everyone, the Capricornian, too, has his faults. At times, he can be over-critical of others. He expects others to live up to his own high standards. He thinks highly of himself and tends to look down on others.

His interest in material things may be exaggerated. The Capricorn man or woman thinks too much about getting on in the world and having something to show for it. He may even be a little greedy.

He sometimes thinks he knows what's best for everyone. He is too bossy. He is always trying to organize and correct others. He may be a little narrow in his thinking.

January 20–February 18

The Positive Side of Aquarius

The Aquarius man or woman is usually very honest and forthright. These are his two greatest qualities. His standards for himself are generally very high. He can always be relied upon by others. His word is his bond.

The Aquarian is perhaps the most tolerant of all the Zodiac personalities. He respects other people's beliefs and feels that everyone is entitled to his own approach to life.

He would never do anything to injure another's feelings. He is never unkind or cruel. Always considerate of others, the Aquarian is always willing to help a person in need. He feels a very strong tie between himself and all the other members of mankind.

The person born under this sign is almost always an individualist. He does not believe in teaming up with the masses, but prefers going his own way. His ideas about life and mankind are often quite advanced. There is a saying to the effect that the average Aquarian is fifty years ahead of his time.

He is broadminded. The problems of the world concern him greatly. He is interested in helping others no matter what part of the globe they live in. He is truly a humanitarian sort. He likes to be of service to others.

Giving, considerate, and without prejudice, Aquarians have no trouble getting along with others.

The Negative Side of Aquarius

The Aquarian may be too much of a dreamer. He makes plans but seldom carries them out. He is rather unrealistic. His imagination has a tendency to run away with him. Because many of his plans are impractical, he is always in some sort of a dither.

Others may not approve of him at all times because of his unconventional behavior. He may be a bit eccentric. Sometimes he is so busy with his own thoughts, that he loses touch with the realities of existence.

Some Aquarians feel they are more clever and intelligent than others. They seldom admit to their own faults, even when they are quite apparent. Some become rather fanatic in their views. Their criticism of others is sometimes destructive and negative.

February 19–March 20

The Positive Side of Pisces

The Piscean can often understand the problems of others quite easily. He has a sympathetic nature. Kindly, he is often dedicated in the way he goes about helping others. The sick and the troubled often turn to him for advice and assistance.

He is very broadminded and does not criticize others for their faults. He knows how to accept people for what they are. On the whole, he is a trustworthy and earnest person. He is loyal to his

friends and will do what he can to help them in time of need. Generous and good-natured, he is a lover of peace; he is often willing to help others solve their differences. People who have taken a wrong turn in life often interest him and he will do what he can to persuade them to rehabilitate themselves.

He has a strong intuitive sense and most of the time he knows how to make it work for him; the Piscean is unusually perceptive and often knows what is bothering someone before that person, himself, is aware of it. The Pisces man or woman is an idealistic person, basically, and is interested in making the world a better place in which to live. The Piscean believes that everyone should help each other. He is willing to do more than his share in order to achieve cooperation with others.

The person born under this sign often is talented in music or art. He is a receptive person; he is able to take the ups and downs of life with philosophic calm.

The Negative Side of Pisces

Some Pisceans are often depressed; their outlook on life is rather glum. They may feel that they have been given a bad deal in life and that others are always taking unfair advantage of them. The Piscean sometimes feel that the world is a cold and cruel place. He is easily discouraged. He may even withdraw from the harshness of reality into a secret shell of his own where he dreams and idles away a good deal of his time.

The Piscean can be rather lazy. He lets things happen without giving the least bit of resistance. He drifts along, whether on the high road or on the low. He is rather short on willpower.

Some Pisces people seek escape through drugs or alcohol. When temptation comes along they find it hard to resist. In matters of sex, they can be rather permissive.

THE SIGNS AND
THEIR KEY WORDS

		POSITIVE	NEGATIVE
ARIES	self	courage, initiative, pioneer instinct	brash rudeness, selfish impetuosity
TAURUS	money	endurance, loyalty, wealth	obstinacy, gluttony
GEMINI	mind	versatility	capriciousness, unreliability
CANCER	family	sympathy, homing instinct	clannishness, childishness
LEO	children	love, authority, integrity	egotism, force
VIRGO	work	purity, industry, analysis	fault-finding, cynicism
LIBRA	marriage	harmony, justice	vacillation, superficiality
SCORPIO	sex	survival, regeneration	vengeance, discord
SAGITTARIUS	travel	optimism, higher learning	lawlessness
CAPRICORN	career	depth	narrowness, gloom
AQUARIUS	friends	human fellowship, genius	perverse unpredictability
PISCES	confine-ment	spiritual love, universality	diffusion, escapism

THE ELEMENTS AND QUALITIES OF THE SIGNS

ELEMENT	SIGN	QUALITY	SIGN
FIRE....................	ARIES LEO SAGITTARIUS	CARDINAL.........	ARIES LIBRA CANCER CAPRICORN
EARTH................	TAURUS VIRGO CAPRICORN	FIXED.................	TAURUS LEO SCORPIO AQUARIUS
AIR.....................	GEMINI LIBRA AQUARIUS		
WATER..............	CANCER SCORPIO PISCES	MUTABLE.........	GEMINI VIRGO SAGITTARIUS PISCES

Every sign has both an element and a quality associated with it. The element indicates the basic makeup of the sign, and the quality describes the kind of activity associated with each.

Signs can be grouped together according to their *element* and *quality*. Signs of the same element share many basic traits in common. They tend to form stable configurations and ultimately harmonious relationships. Signs of the same quality are often less harmonious, but they share many dynamic potentials for growth as well as profound fulfillment.

THE FIRE SIGNS

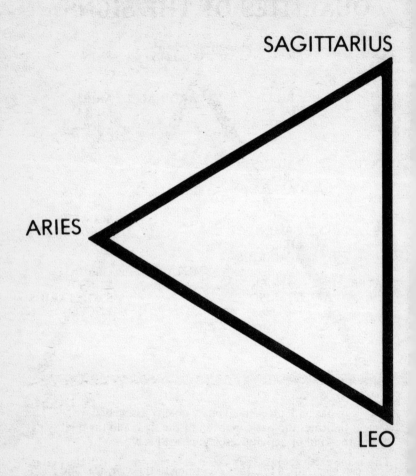

This is the fire group. On the whole these are emotional, volatile types, quick to anger, quick to forgive. They are adventurous, powerful people and act as a source of inspiration for everyone. They spark into action with immediate exuberant impulses. They are intelligent, self-involved, creative and idealistic. They all share a certain vibrancy and glow that outwardly reflects an inner flame and passion for living.

THE EARTH SIGNS

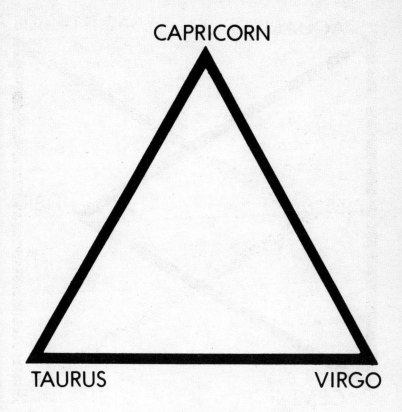

CAPRICORN

TAURUS   VIRGO

This is the earth group. They are in constant touch with the material world and tend to be conservative. Although they are all capable of spartan self-discipline, they are earthy, sensual people who are stimulated by the tangible, elegant and luxurious. The thread of their lives is always practical, but they do fantasize and are often attracted to dark, mysterious, emotional people. They are like great cliffs overhanging the sea, forever married to the ocean but always resisting erosion from the dark, emotional forces that thunder at their feet.

THE AIR SIGNS

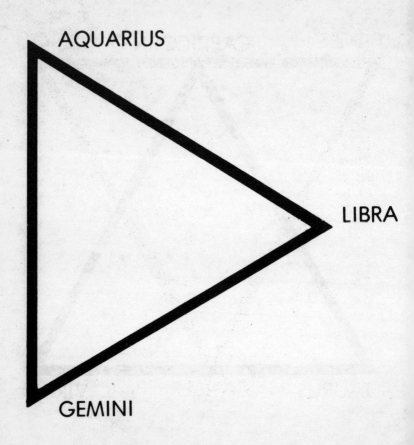

AQUARIUS

LIBRA

GEMINI

This is the air group. They are light, mental creatures desirous of contact, communication and relationship. They are involved with people and the forming of ties on many levels. Original thinkers, they are the bearers of human news. Their language is their sense of word, color, style and beauty. They provide an atmosphere suitable and pleasant for living. They add change and versatility to the scene, and it is through them that we can explore new territory of human intelligence and experience.

THE WATER SIGNS

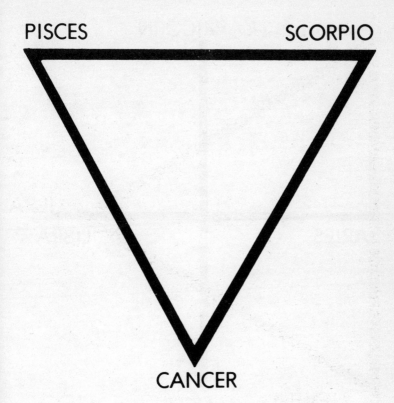

PISCES

SCORPIO

CANCER

This is the water group. Through the water people, we are all joined together on emotional, non-verbal levels. They are silent, mysterious types whose magic hypnotizes even the most determined realist. They have uncanny perceptions about people and are as rich as the oceans when it comes to feeling, emotion or imagination. They are sensitive, mystical creatures with memories that go back beyond time. Through water, life is sustained. These people have the potential for the depths of darkness or the heights of mysticism and art.

THE CARDINAL SIGNS

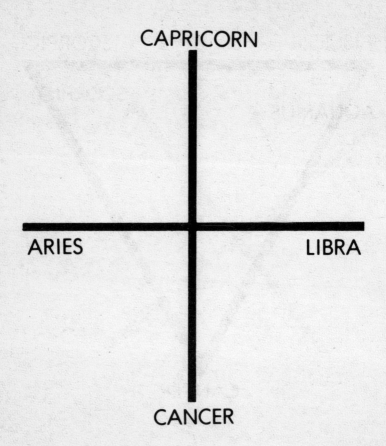

Put together, this is a clear-cut picture of dynamism, activity, tremendous stress and remarkable achievement. These people know the meaning of great change since their lives are often characterized by significant crises and major successes. This combination is like a simultaneous storm of summer, fall, winter and spring. The danger is chaotic diffusion of energy; the potential is irrepressible growth and victory.

THE FIXED SIGNS

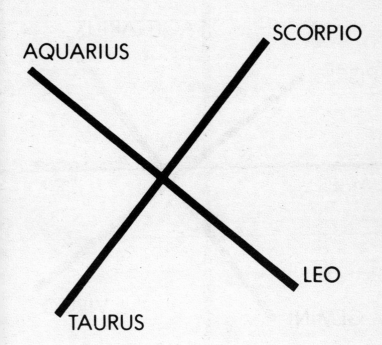

Fixed signs are always establishing themselves in a given place or area of experience. Like explorers who arrive and plant a flag, these people claim a position from which they do not enjoy being deposed. They are staunch, stalwart, upright, trusty, honorable people, although their obstinacy is well-known. Their contribution is fixity, and they are the angels who support our visible world.

THE MUTABLE SIGNS

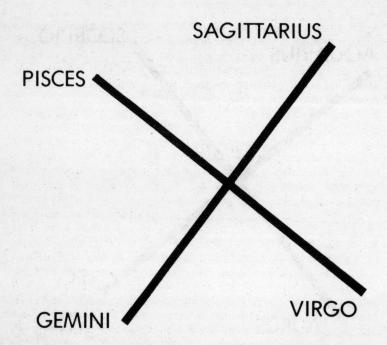

Mutable people are versatile, sensitive, intelligent, nervous and deeply curious about life. They are the translators of all energy. They often carry out or complete tasks initiated by others. Combinations of these signs have highly developed minds; they are imaginative and jumpy and think and talk a lot. At worst their lives are a Tower of Babel. At best they are adaptable and ready creatures who can assimilate one kind of experience and enjoy it while anticipating coming changes.

HOW TO APPROXIMATE YOUR RISING SIGN

Apart from the month and day of birth, the exact *time* of birth is another vital factor in the determination of an accurate horoscope. Not only do the planets move with great speed, but one must know how far the Earth has turned during the day. That way you can determine exactly where the planets are located with respect to the precise birthplace of an individual. This makes *your* horoscope *your* horoscope. In addition to these factors, another grid is laid upon that of the Zodiac and the planets: the houses. After all three have been considered, specific planetary relationships can be measured and analyzed in accordance with certain ordered procedures. It is the skillful translation of all this complex astrological language that a serious astrologer strives for in his attempt at coherent astrological synthesis. Keep this in mind.

The horoscope sets up a kind of framework around which the life of an individual grows like wild ivy, this way and that, weaving its way around the trellis of the natal positions of the planets. The year of birth tells us the positions of the distant, slow-moving planets like Jupiter, Saturn, Uranus and Pluto. The month of birth indicates the Sun sign, or birth sign as it is commonly called, as well as indicating the positions of the rapidly moving planets like Venus, Mercury and Mars. The day of birth locates the position of our Moon, and the moment of birth determines the houses through what is called the Ascendant, or Rising Sign.

As the Earth rotates on its axis once every 24 hours, each one of the twelve signs of the Zodiac appears to be "rising" on the horizon, with a new one appearing about every two hours. Actually it is the turning of the Earth that exposes each sign to view, but you will remember that in much of our astrological work we are discussing "apparent" motion. This *Rising Sign* marks the Ascendant and it colors the whole orientation of a horoscope. It indicates the sign governing the first house of the chart, and will thus determine which signs will govern all the other houses. The idea is a bit complicated at first, and we needn't dwell on complications in this introduction, but if you can imagine two color wheels with twelve divisions superimposed upon each other, one moving slowly and the other remaining still, you will have some idea of how the signs keep shifting the "color" of the houses as the Rising Sign continues to change every two hours.

The important point is that the birth chart, or horoscope, actually does define specific factors of a person's makeup. It contains a picture of being, much the way the nucleus of a tiny cell contains the potential for an entire elephant, or a packet of seeds contains a rosebush. If there were no order or continuity to the world, we could plant roses and get elephants. This same order that gives continuous flow to our lives often annoys people if it threatens to determine too much of their lives. We must grow from what we were planted, and there's no reason why we can't do that magnificently. It's all there in the horoscope. Where there is limitation, there is breakthrough; where there is crisis, there is transformation. Accurate analysis of a horoscope can help you find these points of breakthrough and transformation, and it requires knowledge of subtleties and distinctions that demand skillful judgment in order to solve even the simplest kind of personal question.

It is still quite possible, however, to draw some conclusions based upon the sign occupied by the Sun alone. In fact, if you're just being introduced to this vast subject, you're better off keeping it simple. Otherwise it seems like an impossible jumble, much like trying to read a novel in a foreign language without knowing the basic vocabulary. As with anything else, you can progress in your appreciation and understanding of astrology in direct proportion to your interest. To become really good at it requires study, experience, patience and above all—and maybe simplest of all—a fundamental understanding of what is actually going on right up there in the sky over your head. It is a vital living process you can observe, contemplate and ultimately understand. You can start by observing sunrise, or sunset, or even the full Moon.

In fact you can do a simple experiment after reading this introduction. You can erect a rough chart by following the simple procedure below:

1. Draw a circle with twelve equal segments.

2. Starting at what would be the nine o'clock position on a clock, number the segments, or houses, from 1 to 12 in a *counterclockwise direction*.

3. Label house number 1 in the following way: 4 A.M.-6 A.M.

4. In a counterclockwise direction, label the rest of the houses: 2 A.M.-4 A.M., MIDNIGHT-2 A.M., 10 P.M-MIDNIGHT, 8 P.M.-10 P.M., 6 P.M.-8 P.M., 4 P.M.-6 P.M., 2 P.M.-4 P.M., NOON-2 P.M., 10 A.M.-NOON, 8 A.M.-10 A.M., and 6 A.M.-8 A.M.

5. Now find out what time you were born and place the sun in the appropriate house.

6. Label the edge of that house with your Sun sign. You now have a description of your basic character and your fundamental drives. You can also see in what areas of life on Earth you will be most likely to focus your constant energy and center your activity.

7. If you are really feeling ambitious, label the rest of the houses with the signs, starting with your Sun sign, in order, still in a *counterclockwise direction.* When you get to Pisces, start over with Aries and keep going until you reach the house behind the Sun.

8. Look to house number 1. The sign that you have now labeled and attached to house number 1 is your Rising sign. It will color your self-image, outlook, physical constitution, early life and whole orientation to life. Of course this is a mere approximation, since there are many complicated calculations that must be made with respect to adjustments for birth time, but if you read descriptions of the sign preceding and the sign following the one you have calculated in the above manner, you may be able to identify yourself better. In any case, when you get through labeling all the houses, your drawing should look something like this:

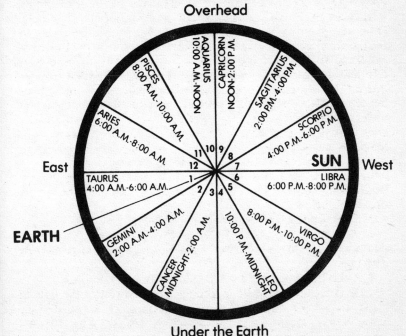

Basic chart illustrating the position of the Sun in Scorpio, with the Ascendant Taurus as the Rising Sign.

This individual was born at 5:15 P.M. on October 31 in New York City. The Sun is in Scorpio and is found in the 7th house. The Rising sign, or the sign governing house number 1, is Taurus, so this person is a blend of Scorpio and Taurus.

Any further calculation would necessitate that you look in an ephemeris, or table of planetary motion, for the positions of the rest of the planets for your particular birth year. But we will take the time to define briefly all the known planets of our Solar System and the Sun to acquaint you with some more of the astrological vocabulary that you will be meeting again and again. (See page 21 for a full explanation of the Moon in all the Signs.)

THE PLANETS AND SIGNS THEY RULE

The signs of the Zodiac are linked to the planets in the following way. Each sign is governed or ruled by one or more planets. No matter where the planets are located in the sky at any given moment, they still rule their respective signs, and when they travel through the signs they rule, they have special dignity and their effects are stronger.

Following is a list of the planets and the signs they rule. After looking at the list, go back over the definitions of the planets and see if you can determine how the planet ruling *your* Sun sign has affected your life.

SIGNS	RULING PLANETS
Aries	Mars, Pluto
Taurus	Venus
Gemini	Mercury
Cancer	Moon
Leo	Sun
Virgo	Mercury
Libra	Venus
Scorpio	Mars, Pluto
Sagittarius	Jupiter
Capricorn	Saturn
Aquarius	Saturn, Uranus
Pisces	Jupiter, Neptune

THE PLANETS
OF THE
SOLAR SYSTEM

Here are the planets of the Solar System. They all travel around the Sun at different speeds and different distances. Taken with the Sun, they all distribute individual intelligence and ability throughout the entire chart.

The planets modify the influence of the Sun in a chart according to their own particular natures, strengths and positions. Their positions must be calculated for each year and day, and their function and expression in a horoscope will change as they move from one area of the Zodiac to another.

Following, you will find brief statements of their pure meanings.

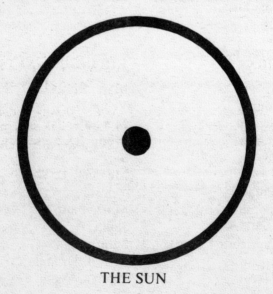

THE SUN

SUN

This is the center of existence. Around this flaming sphere all the planets revolve in endless orbits. Our star is constantly sending out its beams of light and energy without which no life on Earth would be possible. In astrology it symbolizes everything we are trying to become, the center around which all of our activity in life will always revolve. It is the symbol of our basic nature and describes the natural and constant thread that runs through everything that we do from birth to death on this planet.

To early astrologers, the sun seemed to be another planet because it crossed the heavens every day, just like the rest of the bodies in the sky.

It is the only star near enough to be seen well—it is, in fact, a dwarf star. Approximately 860,000 miles in diameter, it is about ten times as wide as the giant planet Jupiter. The next nearest star is nearly 300,000 times as far away, and if the Sun were located as far away as most of the bright stars, it would be too faint to be seen without a telescope.

Everything in the horoscope ultimately revolves around this singular body. Although other forces may be prominent in the charts of some individuals, still the Sun is the total nucleus of being and symbolizes the complete potential of every human being alive. It is vitality and the life force. Your whole essence comes from the position of the Sun.

You are always trying to express the Sun according to its position by house and sign. Possibility for all development is found in the Sun, and it marks the fundamental character of your personal radiations all around you.

It is the symbol of strength, vigor, wisdom, dignity, ardor and generosity, and the ability for a person to function as a mature individual. It is also a creative force in society. It is consciousness of the gift of life.

The underdeveloped solar nature is arrogant, pushy, undependable and proud, and is constantly using force.

MERCURY

Mercury is the planet closest to the Sun. It races around our star, gathering information and translating it to the rest of the system. Mercury represents your capacity to understand the desires of your own will and to translate those desires into action.

In other words it is the planet of Mind and the power of communication. Through Mercury we develop an ability to think, write, speak and observe—to become aware of the world around us. It colors our attitudes and vision of the world, as well as our capacity to communicate our inner responses to the outside world. Some people who have serious disabilities in their power of verbal communication have often wrongly been described as people lacking intelligence.

Although this planet (and its position in the horoscope) indicates your power to communicate your thoughts and perceptions to the world, intelligence is something deeper. Intelligence is distributed throughout all the planets. It is the relationship of the planets to each other that truly describes what we call intelligence. Mercury rules speaking, language, mathematics, draft and design, students, messengers, young people, offices, teachers and any pursuits where the mind of man has wings.

VENUS

Venus is beauty. It symbolizes the harmony and radiance of a rare and elusive quality: beauty itself. It is refinement and delicacy, softness and charm. In astrology it indicates grace, balance and the aesthetic sense. Where Venus is we see beauty, a gentle drawing in of energy and the need for satisfaction and completion. It is a special touch that finishes off rough edges. It is sensitivity, and affection, and it is always the place for that other elusive phenomenon: love. Venus describes our sense of what is beautiful and loving. Poorly developed, it is vulgar, tasteless and self-indulgent. But its ideal is the flame of spiritual love—Aphrodite, goddess of love, and the sweetness and power of personal beauty.

MARS

This is raw, crude energy. The planet next to Earth but outward from the Sun is a fiery red sphere that charges through the horoscope with force and fury. It represents the way you reach out for new adventure and new experience. It is energy and drive, initiative, courage and daring. The power to start something and see it through. It can be thoughtless, cruel and wild, angry and hostile, causing cuts, burns, scalds and wounds. It can stab its way through a chart, or it can be the symbol of healthy spirited adventure, well-channeled constructive power to begin and keep up the drive. If you have trouble starting things, if you lack the get-up-and-go to start the ball rolling, if you lack aggressiveness and self-confidence, chances are there's another planet influencing your Mars. Mars rules soldiers, butchers, surgeons, salesmen—any field that requires daring, bold skill, operational technique or self-promotion.

JUPITER

This is the largest planet of the Solar System. Scientists have recently learned that Jupiter reflects more light than it receives from the Sun. In a sense it is like a star itself. In astrology it rules good luck and good cheer, health, wealth, optimism, happiness, success and joy. It is the symbol of opportunity and always opens the way for new possibilities in your life. It rules exuberance, enthusiasm, wisdom, knowledge, generosity and all forms of expansion in general. It rules actors, statesmen, clerics, professional people, religion, publishing and the distribution of many people over large areas.

Sometimes Jupiter makes you think you deserve everything, and you become sloppy, wasteful, careless and rude, prodigal and lawless, in the illusion that nothing can ever go wrong. Then there is the danger of over-confidence, exaggeration, undependability and over-indulgence.

Jupiter is the minimization of limitation and the emphasis on spirituality and potential. It is the thirst for knowledge and higher learning.

SATURN

Saturn circles our system in dark splendor with its mysterious rings, forcing us to be awakened to whatever we have neglected in the past. It will present real puzzles and problems to be solved, causing delays, obstacles and hindrances. By doing so, Saturn stirs our own sensitivity to those areas where we are laziest.

Here we must patiently develop *method,* and only through painstaking effort can our ends be achieved. It brings order to a horoscope and imposes reason just where we are feeling least reasonable. By creating limitations and boundary, Saturn shows the consequences of being human and demands that we accept the changing cycles inevitable in human life. Saturn rules time, old age and sobriety. It can bring depression, gloom, jealousy and greed, or serious acceptance of responsibilities out of which success will develop. With Saturn there is nothing to do but face facts. It rules laborers, stones, granite, rocks and crystals of all kinds.

The Outer Planets

The following three are the outer planets. They liberate human beings from cultural conditioning, and in that sense are the law breakers. In early times it was thought that Saturn was the last planet of the system—the outer limit beyond which we could never go. The discovery of the next three planets ushered in new phases of human history, revolution and technology.

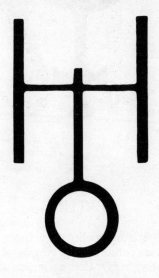

URANUS

Uranus rules unexpected change, upheaval, revolution. It is the symbol of total independence and asserts the freedom of an individual from all restriction and restraint. It is a breakthrough planet and indicates talent, originality and genius in a horoscope. It usually causes last-minute reversals and changes of plan, unwanted separations, accidents, catastrophes and eccentric behavior. It can add irrational rebelliousness and perverse bohemianism to a personality or a streak of unaffected brilliance in science and art. It rules technology, aviation and all forms of electrical and electronic advancement. It governs great leaps forward and topsy-turvy situations, and *always* turns things around at the last minute. Its effects are difficult to ever really predict, since it rules sudden last-minute decisions and events that come like lightning out of the blue.

NEPTUNE

Neptune dissolves existing reality the way the sea erodes the cliffs beside it. Its effects are subtle like the ringing of a buoy's bell in the fog. It suggests a reality higher than definition can usually describe. It awakens a sense of higher responsibility often causing guilt, worry, anxieties or delusions. Neptune is associated with all forms of escape and can make things seem a certain way so convincingly that you are absolutely sure of something that eventually turns out to be quite different.

It is the planet of illusion and therefore governs the invisible realms that lie beyond our ordinary minds, beyond our simple factual ability to prove what is "real." Treachery, deceit, disillusionment and disappointment are linked to Neptune. It describes a vague reality that promises eternity and the divine, yet in a manner so complex that we cannot really fathom it at all. At its worst Neptune is a cheap intoxicant; at its best it is the poetry, music and inspiration of the higher planes of spiritual love. It has dominion over movies, photographs and much of the arts.

PLUTO

Pluto lies at the outpost of our system and therefore rules finality in a horoscope—the final closing of chapters in your life, the passing of major milestones and points of development from which there is no return. It is a final wipeout, a closeout, an evacuation. It is a distant, subtle but powerful catalyst in all transformations that occur. It creates, destroys, then recreates. Sometimes Pluto starts its influence with a minor event or insignificant incident that might even go unnoticed. Slowly but surely, little by little, everything changes, until at last there has been a total transformation in the area of your life where Pluto has been operating. It rules mass thinking and the trends that society first rejects, then adopts and finally outgrows.

Pluto rules the dead and the underworld—all the powerful forces of creation and destruction that go on all the time beneath, around and above us. It can bring a lust for power with strong obsessions.

It is the planet that rules the metamorphoses of the caterpillar into a butterfly, for it symbolizes the capacity to change totally and forever a person's life style, way of thought and behavior.

FAMOUS PERSONALITIES

ARIES: Hans Christian Andersen, Pearl Bailey, Marlon Brando, Wernher Von Braun, Charlie Chaplin, Joan Crawford, Da Vinci, Bette Davis, Doris Day, W. C. Fields, Alec Guinness, Adolf Hitler, Billie Holiday, Thomas Jefferson, Nikita Khrushchev, Elton John, Arturo Toscanini, J. P. Morgan, Paul Robeson, Gloria Steinem, Lowell Thomas, Vincent van Gogh, Tennessee Williams

TAURUS: Fred Astaire, Charlote Brontë, Carol Burnett, Irving Berlin, Bing Crosby, Salvador Dali, Tchaikovsky, Queen Elizabeth II, Duke Ellington, Ella Fitzgerald, Henry Fonda, Sigmund Freud, Orson Welles, Joe Louis, Lenin, Karl Marx, Golda Meir, Eva Peron, Bertrand Russell, Shakespeare, Kate Smith, Benjamin Spock, Barbra Streisand, Shirley Temple, Harry Truman

GEMINI: Mikhail Baryshnikov, Boy George, Igor Stravinsky, Carlos Chavez, Walt Whitman, Bob Dylan, Ralph Waldo Emerson, Judy Garland, Paul Gauguin, Allen Ginsberg, Benny Goodman, Bob Hope, Burl Ives, John F. Kennedy, Peggy Lee, Marilyn Monroe, Joe Namath, Cole Porter, Laurence Olivier, Harriet Beecher Stowe, Queen Victoria, John Wayne, Frank Lloyd Wright

CANCER: "Dear Abby," David Brinkley, Yul Brynner, Pearl Buck, Marc Chagall, Jack Dempsey, Mildred (Babe) Zaharias, Mary Baker Eddy, Henry VIII, John Glenn, Ernest Hemingway, Lena Horne, Oscar Hammerstein, Helen Keller, Ann Landers, George Orwell, Nancy Reagan, Rembrandt, Richard Rodgers, Ginger Rogers, Rubens, Jean-Paul Sartre, O. J. Simpson

LEO: Neil Armstrong, Russell Baker, James Baldwin, Emily Brontë, Wilt Chamberlain, Julia Child, Cecil B. De Mille, Ogden Nash, Amelia Earhart, Edna Ferber, Arthur Goldberg, Dag Hammarskjöld, Alfred Hitchcock, Mick Jagger, George Meany, George Bernard Shaw, Napoleon, Jacqueline Onassis, Henry Ford, Francis Scott Key, Andy Warhol, Mae West, Orville Wright

VIRGO: Ingrid Bergman, Warren Burger, Maurice Chevalier, Agatha Christie, Sean Connery, Lafayette, Peter Falk, Greta Garbo, Althea Gibson, Arthur Godfrey, Goethe, Buddy Hackett, Michael Jackson, Lyndon Johnson, D. H. Lawrence, Sophia Loren, Grandma Moses, Arnold Palmer, Queen Elizabeth I, Walter Reuther, Peter Sellers, Lily Tomlin, George Wallace

LIBRA: Brigitte Bardot, Art Buchwald, Truman Capote, Dwight D. Eisenhower, William Faulkner, F. Scott Fitzgerald, Gandhi, George Gershwin, Micky Mantle, Helen Hayes, Vladimir Horowitz, Doris Lessing, Martina Navratalova, Eugene O'Neill, Luciano Pavarotti, Emily Post, Eleanor Roosevelt, Bruce Springsteen, Margaret Thatcher, Gore Vidal, Barbara Walters, Oscar Wilde

SCORPIO: Vivien Leigh, Richard Burton, Art Carney, Johnny Carson, Billy Graham, Grace Kelly, Walter Cronkite, Marie Curie, Charles de Gaulle, Linda Evans, Indira Gandhi, Theodore Roosevelt, Rock Hudson, Katherine Hepburn, Robert F. Kennedy, Billie Jean King, Martin Luther, Georgia O'Keeffe, Pablo Picasso, Jonas Salk, Alan Shepard, Robert Louis Stevenson

SAGITTARIUS: Jane Austen, Louisa May Alcott, Woody Allen, Beethoven, Willy Brandt, Mary Martin, William F. Buckley, Maria Callas, Winston Churchill, Noel Coward, Emily Dickinson, Walt Disney, Benjamin Disraeli, James Doolittle, Kirk Douglas, Chet Huntley, Jane Fonda, Chris Evert Lloyd, Margaret Mead, Charles Schulz, John Milton, Frank Sinatra, Steven Spielberg

CAPRICORN: Muhammad Ali, Isaac Asimov, Pablo Casals, Dizzy Dean, Marlene Dietrich, James Farmer, Ava Gardner, Barry Goldwater, Cary Grant, J. Edgar Hoover, Howard Hughes, Joan of Arc, Gypsy Rose Lee, Martin Luther King, Jr., Rudyard Kipling, Mao Tse-tung, Richard Nixon, Gamal Nasser, Louis Pasteur, Albert Schweitzer, Stalin, Benjamin Franklin, Elvis Presley

AQUARIUS: Marian Anderson, Susan B. Anthony, Jack Benny, Charles Darwin, Charles Dickens, Thomas Edison, John Barrymore, Clark Gable, Jascha Heifetz, Abraham Lincoln, John McEnroe, Yehudi Menuhin, Mozart, Jack Nicklaus, Ronald Reagan, Jackie Robinson, Norman Rockwell, Franklin D. Roosevelt, Gertrude Stein, Charles Lindbergh, Margaret Truman

PISCES: Edward Albee, Harry Belafonte, Alexander Graham Bell, Frank Borman, Chopin, Adelle Davis, Albert Einstein, Jackie Gleason, Winslow Homer, Edward M. Kennedy, Victor Hugo, Mike Mansfield, Michelangelo, Edna St. Vincent Millay, Liza Minelli, John Steinbeck, Linus Pauling, Ravel, Diana Ross, William Shirer, Elizabeth Taylor, George Washington

CANCER

CHARACTER ANALYSIS

The Cancerian is generally speaking a rather sensitive person. He is quite often a generous person by nature, and he is willing to help almost anyone in need. He is emotional and often feels sorry for persons less fortunate than he. He could never refuse to answer someone's call for help. It is because of his sympathetic nature that others take advantage of him now and again.

In spite of his willingness to help others, the Cancer man or woman may seem difficult to approach by people not well acquainted with his character. On the whole, he seems rather subdued and reserved. Others may feel there is a wall between them and the Cancerian while this may not be the case at all. The person born under this sign is careful not to let others hurt him; he has learned through hard experience that protection of some sort is necessary in order to get along in life. The person who wins his confidence and is able to get beyond this barrier will find him a warm and loving person.

With his family and close friends, he is a very faithful and dependable person. In his quiet way, he can be affectionate and loving. He is generally not one given to demonstrative behavior. He can be fond of someone without telling them so a dozen times a day. With people he is close to, the Cancerian is bound to be more open about his own need for affection, and he enjoys being made over by his loved ones. He likes to feel wanted and protected.

When he has made up his mind about something, he sticks to it, and is generally a very constant person. He knows how to hold his ground. He never wavers. People who don't know him may think him weak and easily managed, because he is so quiet and modest, but this is far from true. He can take a lot of punishment for an idea or a cause he believes in. For the Cancerian, right is right. In order to protect himself, the person born under this sign will sometimes put up a pose as someone bossy and domineering. Sometimes he is successful in fooling others with his brash front. People who have known him for a while, however, are seldom taken in.

Many people born under this sign are rather shy and seemingly lacking confidence. They know their own minds, though, even if they do not seem to. He responds to kindness and encouragement. He will be himself with people he trusts. A good person can bring out the best in this person. Disagreeable or unfeeling people can send him scurrying back into his shell. He is a person who does not appreciate sharp criticism. Some people born under this sign are worriers. They are very concerned about what others may think of them. This may bother them so much that they develop a deep feeling of inferiority. Sometimes this reaches the point where he is so unsure of himself in some matters that he allows himself to be influenced by someone who has a stronger personality. The Cancerian is sometimes afraid that people will talk behind his back if he doesn't comply to their wishes. However, this does not stop him from doing what he feels is right. The cultivated Cancerian learns to think for himself and has no fear of disapproval.

The Cancer man or woman is most himself at home. The person born under this sign is a real lover of domesticity. He likes a place where he can relax and feel properly sheltered. Cancerians like things to stay as they are; they are not fond of changes of any sort. They are not very adaptable people. When visiting others or going to unfamiliar places, they are not likely to feel very comfortable. They are not the most talkative people at a party. In the comfort of their own homes, however, they blossom and bloom.

The Cancer man or woman sticks by the rules, whatever the game. He is not a person who would ever think of going against an established grain. He is conventional and moderate in almost all things. In a way he likes the old-fashioned things; however, in spite of this, he is interested in new things and does what he can to keep up with the times. In a way, he has two sides to his character. He is seldom forgetful. He has a memory like an elephant and can pick out any detail from the past with no trouble at all. He often reflects on things that have happened. He prefers the past to the future, which sometimes fills him with a feeling of apprehension.

This fourth sign of the Zodiac is a motherly one. Even the Cancer man has something maternal about him. He is usually kind and considerate; ready to help and protect. Others are drawn to them because of these gentle qualities. People in trouble often turn to him for advice and sympathy. People find him easy to confide in.

The Cancer person in general is a very forgiving person. He almost never holds a grudge. Still, it would not be wise to anger him. Treat him fairly and he will treat you the same. He does not appreciate people who lose patience with him. The Cancerian is usually proud of his mind and does not like to be considered unin-telligent. Even if others feel that he is somewhat slow in some areas, he would rather not have this opinion expressed in his pres-ence. He's not a person to be played with; he can tell when some-one is treating him like a fool.

Quite often people born under this sign are musically inclined. Some of them have a deep interest in religious matters. They are apt to be interested in mystical matters, as well. Although they are fascinated by these things, they may be somewhat afraid of being overwhelmed if they go into them too deeply. In spite of this feel-ing of apprehension, they try to satisfy their curiosity in these mat-ters.

Health

For the person born under the sign of Cancer, the stomach is his weak point. Chances are that the Cancerian is very susceptible most of the time to infectious diseases. Sometimes his health is affected by nervousness. He can be quite a worrier; even little things eat at him from time to time and this is apt to lower his re-sistance to infectious illnesses. He is often upset by small matters.

The Cancerian as a child is sometimes rather sickly and weak. His physique during this period of growth can be described in most cases as fragile. Some develop into physically strong adults, others may have the remnants of childhood ailments with them for a good part of their adult lives. They are rather frightened of being sick. Illness is a word they would rather not mention. Pain is also a thing they fear.

They are given to quick-changing moods at times and this of-ten has an effect on their overall health. Worry or depression can have a subliminal effect on their general health. Usually their ill-nesses are not as serious as they imagine them to be. They some-times find it easy to feel sorry for themselves.

On the whole, the Cancer man or woman is a quiet person. He is not one to brag or push his weight around. However, let it not be thought that he lacks the force that others have. He can be quite purposeful and energetic when the situation calls for it. However, when it comes to tooting their own horn, they can be somewhat shy and reticent. They may lack the get-up-and-go that others have when it comes to pushing their personal interests ahead.

Some Cancerians are quite aware of the fact that they are not what one would call sturdy in physique or temperament, and often they go through life rather painfully trying to cover up the weak side of their nature.

The man or woman born under the sign of Cancer is not apt to be very vigorous or active. As a rule, they are not too fond of physical exercise, and they have a weakness for rich and heavy foods. As a result, in later life they could end up overweight. Some Cancerians have trouble with their kidneys and intestines. Others digest their food poorly. The wise Cancer man or woman, however, adheres to a strict and well-balanced diet with plenty of fresh fruit and vegetables. Moreover, they see to it that they properly exercise their bodies daily. The Cancer man or woman who learns to cut down on rich foods and worry, often lives to a ripe old age.

Occupation

The Cancer person generally has no trouble at all establishing himself in the business world. He has all those qualities that generally make one a success professionally. He is careful with his equipment as well as his money. He is patient and he knows how to persevere. Any job where he has a chance to use his mind instead of his body is usually a job in which he has no trouble succeeding. He can work well with people—especially persons situated in dire straits. Welfare work is the kind of occupation in which he usually excels. He can really be quite a driving person if his job calls for it. The Cancerian is surprisingly resourceful. In spite of his retiring disposition, he is capable of accomplishing some very difficult tasks.

The Cancerian can put on an aggressive front, and in some cases it can carry him far. Quite often he is able to develop leadership qualities and make good use of them. He generally knows how to direct his energy so that he never becomes immediately exhausted. He'll work away at a difficult chore gradually; seldomly approaching anything head on. By working at something obliquely he often finds advantages along the way that are not apparent to others. In spite of his cautious approach, the Cancerian is often taxed by work that is too demanding of his energy. He may put up a good front of being strong and courageous while actually he is at the end of his emotional rope. Risks sometimes frighten the person born under this sign. It is often this fear which exhausts him. The possible dangers in the world of business set him to worrying.

The Cancerian does not boast about what he is going to do; he just quietly goes ahead and does it. Quite often he accomplishes more than others in this quiet way.

The person born under this sign enjoys helping others. By nature, he is quite a sympathetic individual. He does not like to see others suffer or do without. He is willing to make sacrifices for someone he trusts and cares for. The Cancerian, as was mentioned before, has a maternal streak in him, which is perhaps why he works so well with children. People born under the fourth sign of the Zodiac often make excellent teachers. They understand young people well and do what they can to help them grow up properly.

Cancerians also are fairly intuitive. In business or financial matters, they often make an important strike by playing a strong hunch. In some cases they are able to rely almost entirely on their feelings rather than on reason.

Water attracts the Cancer person. Often they have connections with the sea through their professions. The Cancerian housewife may find herself working with various liquids quite successfully while at home. Trade and commerce often appeal to the person born under this sign.

The average Cancerian has many choices open to him as far as a career is concerned. There are many things that he can do well once he puts his mind to it. In the arts he is quite likely to do well. The Cancer man or woman has a way with beauty, harmony, and creativity. Basically, he is a very capable person in many things; it depends on which of his talents he wants to develop to a professional point. He has a rich imagination and sometimes can make use of it in the area of painting, music, or sculpture.

When working for someone else, the Cancerian can always be depended upon. He makes a loyal and conscientious employee.

It is important for the Cancerian that he select a job that is well suited to his talents and temperament. Although he may feel that earning money is important, the Cancerian eventually comes to the point where he realizes that it is even more important to enjoy the work he is doing. He should have a position which allows him to explore the recesses of his personality and to develop. When placed in the wrong job, the Cancer man or woman is apt to spend a good deal of time wishing he were somewhere else.

Cancerians know the value of money. They are not the sort of people who go throwing money about recklessly. The Cancer person is honest and expects others to be the same. He is quite modest in most things and deplores extravagance and unnecessary display. There are many rich Cancerians. They have a genius for making money and for investing or saving it. Security is important to the person born under this sign. He'll always see to it that he has something put away for that inevitable rainy day. He is also a hard worker and is willing to put in long hours for the money it brings him. Financial success is usually the result of his own perseverance and industry. Through his own need for security, it is often easy for the Cancerian to sympathize with those of like dispositions. He is a helpful person. If he sees someone trying to do his best to get ahead—and still not succeeeding—he is quite apt to put aside his own interests temporarily to help the other man. Sometimes the Cancerian worries over money even when he has it. He can never be too secure. It would be better for him to learn how to relax and not to let his worries undermine his health. Financial matters often cause him considerable concern—even when it is not necessary.

Home and Family

People born under this sign are usually great home-lovers. They are very domestic by nature; home for them spells security. The Cancerian is a family person. He respects those who are related to him. He feels a great responsibility toward all the members of his family. There is usually a very strong tie between the Cancer person and his mother that lasts through his whole life. Something a Cancerian will not tolerate is for someone to speak ill of a member of his family. This for him is a painful and deep insult. He has a great respect for his family and family traditions. Quite often the person under this sign is well-acquainted with his family tree. If he happens to have a relative who has been quite successful in life, he is quite proud of the fact. Once he is home for the weekend, he generally stays there. He does not particularly care for moving about. He is a born stay-at-home, in most cases.

The Cancerian is sentimental about old things and habits. He is apt to have many things stored away from years ago. Something that was dear to his parents will probably be dear to him as well.

Some Cancerians do travel about from time to time. But no matter what their destination, they are always glad to be back where they feel they belong.

The home of a person born under this sign is usually quite comfortable and tastefully furnished. The Cancerian is a bit of a romantic and usually this is reflected in the way his house is arranged.

The Cancer child is always attached to his home and family. He may not care to go out and play with other children very much but enjoys it when his friends come to his house.

The maternal nature of the Cancer person comes out when he gives a party. He is a very attentive host and worries over a guest like a mother hen—anxious to see that they are comfortable and lack nothing. He does his best to make others happy and at home, and he is admired and loved for that. People who visit Cancerians are usually deeply impressed by their out-going ways. The Cancer hostess prepares unusual and delicious snacks for her visitors. She is very concerned about them and likes to see to it that they are well-fed while visiting her.

Homebodies that they are, Cancerians generally do what they can to make their home a comfortable and interesting place for themselves as well as for others. They feel very flattered when a visitor pays them a compliment on their home.

Children play a very important part in the lives of people born under this sign. They like to fuss over their offspring and give them the things they feel that they need. They generally like to have large families. They like to see to it that their children are well-provided for and that they have the chances in life that their parents never had. The best mother of the Zodiac is usually someone born under the sign of Cancer. They have a strong protective nature. They usually have a strong sense of duty, and when their children are in difficulty they do everything they can to set matters right. Children, needless to say, are fond of their Cancerian parent, and do what they can to make the parent-child relationship a harmonious one.

Social Relationships

The Cancer person may seem rather retiring and quiet and this gives people the impression that he is not too warm or sympathetic. However, the person born under this sign is very sensitive and loving. His ability to understand and sympathize with others is great. He likes to have close friends—people who love and understand him as well as he tries to love and understand them. He wants to be well-liked—to be noticed by people who he feels should like him. If he does not get the attention and affection he feels he is entitled to, he is apt to become a little sullen and difficult to deal with.

The Cancer man or woman has strong powers of intuition and he can generally sense when he has met a person who is likely to turn into a good friend. The Cancerian suffers greatly if ever he should lose a friend. To him friendships are sacred. Sometimes the Cancerian sets his friends on too high a pedestal; he is apt to feel quite crest-fallen when he discovers that they have feet of clay. He is often romantic in his approach to friendship and is likely to seek people out for sentimental reasons rather than for practical ones.

The Cancerian is a very sensitive person and sometimes this contributes to making a friendship unsatisfactory. He sometimes makes the wrong interpretation of a remark that is made by a friend or acquaintance. He imagines something injurious behind a very innocent remark. He sometimes feels that people who profess to be his friends laugh at him cruelly behind his back. He has to be constantly reassured of a friend's sincerity, especially in the beginning of a relationship. If he wants to have the wide circle of friends he desires, the Cancerian must learn to curb these persecution fantasies.

LOVE AND MARRIAGE

The Cancer man or woman has to have love in his life, otherwise his existence is a dull and humdrum affair. When he loves someone, the Cancerian will do everything in his power to make her happy. He is not afraid to make sacrifices in order to make an important relationship work. To his loved one he is likely to seem uncertain and moody. The Cancer person is usually very influenced by the impression he has of his lover. He may even be content to let his romance partner have her own way in the relationship. He may not make many demands but be willing to follow those of his loved one. At times he may feel that he is not really loved, and draw away somewhat from the relationship. Sometimes it takes a lot of coaxing before he can be won over to the fact that he is indeed loved for himself alone.

The Cancerian is often possessive about people as well as material objects. This often makes the relationship difficult to accept for his partner.

His standards are sometimes impossibly high and because of this he is rather difficult to please. The Cancer man or woman is interested in finding someone with whom he can spend the rest of his life. He or she is not interested in any fly-by-night romance.

Romance and the Cancer Woman

The Cancer woman is usually a very warm and loving person. Her feelings run deep. She is sincere in her approach to love. Still and all, she is rather sensitive when in love and her lover may find her difficult to understand at times. The Cancer woman is quite given to crying and when she has been wronged or imagines she has, she is capable of weeping buckets. It may be quite a while before she comes out of her shell again.

Marriage is a union quite suited to the Cancer woman's temperament. She longs for permanence in a relationship and is not fond of flings or meaningless romantic adventures. Her emotions are usually very deep. She desires a man who is protective and affectionate; someone who can help and guide her through life.

She may be too possessive with her husband and this may cause discord. The demands she is likely to make on her family may be overbearing at times. She often likes to be reassured that she is loved and appreciated.

She makes a devoted and loving wife and mother who will do everything to keep her family life harmonious and affectionate.

Romance and the Cancer Man

Quite often the Cancer man is the reserved type. He may be difficult for some women to understand. Generally speaking, he is a very loving person; but sometimes he has difficulty in letting this appear so. He is a bit afraid of being rejected or hurt, so he is liable to keep his true feelings hidden until he feels that the intended object of his affection is capable of taking him seriously.

Quite often he looks for a woman who has the same qualities as his mother. He is more easily attracted to a woman who has old-fashioned traits than to a modern woman. He likes a woman who is a good cook; someone who does not mind household chores and a quiet life.

When deeply in love, the Cancer man does everything in his power to hold the woman of his choice. He is very warm and affectionate and may be rather extravagant from time to time in entertaining the woman he loves.

Marriage is something in which the Cancer man is seriously interested. He wants to settle down with a warm and loving wife—someone who will mother him to some extent. He makes a good father. He is fond of large families. His love of his children may be too possessive.

Woman—Man

CANCER WOMAN
ARIES MAN

Although it's possible that you could find happiness with a man born under the sign of the Ram, it's uncertain as to how long that happiness would last.

An Arien who has made his mark in the world and is somewhat steadfast in his outlooks and attitudes could be quite a catch for you. On the other hand, men under this sign are often swift-footed and quick-minded; their industrious mannerisms may fail to impress you, especially if you feel that much of their get-up-and-go often leads nowhere.

When it comes to a fine romance, you want someone with a nice, broad shoulder to lean on. You are likely to find a relationship with someone who doesn't like to stay put for too long somewhat upsetting.

The Arien may have a little trouble in understanding you, too . . . at least, in the beginning of the relationship. He may find you a bit too shy and moody. Ariens tend to speak their minds; he's liable to criticize you at the drop of a hat.

You may find a man born under this sign too demanding. He may give you the impression that he expects you to be at his beck-and-call. You have a barrelful of patience at your disposal and he may try every last bit of it. He is apt not to be as thorough as you are in everything that he does. In order to achieve success or a goal quickly, he is liable to overlook small but important details—and regret it when it is far too late.

Being married to an Arien does not mean that you'll have a secure and safe life as far as finances are concerned. Not all Ariens are rash with cash, but they lack that sound head you have for putting away something for that inevitable rainy day. He'll do his best, however, to see that you're adequately provided for—even though his efforts may leave something to be desired as far as you're concerned.

With an Aires man for a mate, you'll find yourself constantly among people. Ariens generally have many friends—and you may not heartily approve of them all. People born under this sign are more interested in "Interesting" people than they are in influential ones. Although there is liable to be a family squabble from time to time, you are stable enough to take it all in your stride. Your love of permanence and a harmonious homelife will help you to take the bitter with the sweet.

Aries men love children. They make wonderful fathers. Kids take to them like ducks to water. Their quick minds and behavior appeal to the young.

CANCER WOMAN
TAURUS MAN

Some Taurus men are strong and silent. They do all they can to protect and provide for the women they love. The Taurus man will never let you down. He's steady, sturdy, and reliable. He's pretty honest and practical, too. He says what he means and means what he says. He never indulges in deceit and will always put his cards on the table.

The Tauren is a very affectionate man. Being loved, appreciated, and understood is very important for his well-being. Like you, he is also looking for peace, harmony, and security in his life. If you both work toward these goals together, you'll find that they are easily attained.

If you should marry a Taurus man, you can be sure that the wolf will never darken your door. They are notoriously good providers and do everything they can to make their families comfortable and happy.

He'll appreciate the way you have of making a home warm and inviting. Slippers and pipe, and the evening papers are essential ingredients in making your Taurus husband happy at the end of the workday. Although he may be a big lug of a guy, you'll find he's pretty fond of gentleness and soft things. If you puff up his pillow and tuck him in at night, he won't complain. He'll eat it up and ask for more.

You probably won't complain about his friends. The Taurean tends to seek out friends who are successful or prominent. You admire people, too, who work hard and achieve what they set out for. It helps to reassure your way of life and the way you look at things.

Like you, the Taurus man doesn't care too much for change. He's a stay-at-home of the first degree. Chances are that the house you move into after you're married will be the house you'll live in for the rest of your life.

You'll find that the man born under this sign is easy to get along with. It's unlikely that you'll have many quarrels or arguments.

Although he'll be gentle and tender with you, your Taurus man is far from being a sensitive type. He's a man's man. Chances are he loves sports like fishing and football. He can be earthy as well as down-to-earth.

Taureans love their children very much but do everything they can not to spoil them. They believe in children staying in their places. They make excellent disciplinarians. Your children will be polite and respectful. They may find their Taurus father a little gruff, but as they grow older they'll learn to understand him.

CANCER WOMAN
GEMINI MAN

Gemini men, in spite of their charm and dashing manner, may make your skin crawl. They may seem to lack the sort of common sense you set so much store in. Their tendency to start something, then—out of boredom—never finish it, may do nothing more than exasperate you.

You may be inclined to interpret a Geminian's jumping around from here to there as childish if not downright neurotic. A man born under this sign will seldom stay put and if you should take it upon yourself to try and make him sit still, he's liable to resent it strongly.

On the other hand, the Gemini man is liable to think you're an old slowpoke—someone far too interested in security and material things. He's attracted to things that sparkle and dazzle; you, with your practical way of looking at things, are likely to seem a little dull and uninteresting to this gadabout. If your're looking for a life of security and permanence—and what Cancerian isn't—then you'd better look elsewhere for your Mr. Right.

Chances are you'll be taken in by his charming ways and facile wit—few women can resist Gemini-magic—but after you've seen through his live-for-today, gossamer facade, you'll most likely be very happy to turn your attention to someone more stable—even if he is not as interesting. You want a man who is there when you need him. You need someone on whom you can fully rely. Keeping track of a Gemini's movements will make you dizzy. Still, you are a patient woman, most of the time, and you are able to put up with something contrary if you feel that in the end it will prove well worth the effort.

A successful and serious Gemini could make you a very happy woman, perhaps, if you gave him half a chance. Although you may think that he has holes in his head, the Gemini man generally has a good brain and can make good use of it when he wants. Some Geminians who have learned the importance of being consequent have risen to great heights, professionally. President Kennedy was a Gemini as was Thomas Mann and William Butler Yeats. Once you can convince yourself that not all people born under the sign of the Twins are witless grasshoppers, you'll find you've come a long way in trying to understand them.

Life with a Gemini man can be more fun than a barrel of clowns. You'll never have a chance to experience a dull moment. He lacks your sense when it comes to money, however. You should see to it that you handle the budgeting and bookkeeping.

In ways, he's like a child himself; perhaps that is why he can get along so well with the younger generation.

CANCER WOMAN
CANCER MAN

You'll find the man born under the same sign as you easy to get along with. You're both sensitive and sensible people; you'll see eye-to-eye on most things. He'll share your interest in security and practicality.

Cancer men are always hard workers. They are very interested in making successes of themselves in business and socially. Like you, he's a conservative person who has a great deal of respect for tradition. He's a man you can depend on come rain or come shine. He'll never shirk his responsibilities as provider and will always see to it that you never want.

The Cancer man is not the type that rushes headlong into romance. Neither are you, for that matter. Courtship between the two of you will be a sensible and thorough affair. It may take months before you even get to that holding-hands stage of romance. One thing you can be sure of: he'll always treat you like a lady. He'll have great respect and consideration for your feelings. Only when he is sure that you approve of him as someone to love, will he reveal the warmer side of his nature. His coolness, like yours, is just a front. Beneath it lies a very affectionate heart.

Although he may seem restless or moody at times, on the whole the Cancer man is a very considerate and kind person. His standards are extremely high. He is looking for a girl who can measure up to his ideals . . . a girl like you.

Marriage means a lot to the Cancer male. He's very interested in settling down with someone who has the same attitudes and outlooks as he has. He's a man who loves being at home. He'll be a faithful husband. Cancerians never pussyfoot around after they've made their marriage vows. They do not take their marriage responsibilities lightly. They see to it that everything in this relationship is just the way it should be. Between the two of you, your home will be well managed; bills will be paid on time, there will be adequate insurance on everything of value, and there will be money in the bank. When retirement time rolls around, you both should be very well off.

The Cancer man has a great respect for family. You'll most likely be seeing a lot of his mother during your marriage, just as he'll probably be seeing a lot of yours. He'll do his best to get along with your relatives; he'll treat them with the kindness and concern you think they deserve. He'll expect you to be just as considerate with his relatives.

The Cancerian makes a very good father. He's very patient and understanding, especially when the children are young and dependent.

CANCER WOMAN
LEO MAN

To know a man born under the sign of the Lion is not necessarily to love him—even though the temptation may be great. When he fixes most girls with his leonine double-whammy, it causes their hearts to pitter-pat and their minds to cloud over.

But with you, the sensible Cancerian, it takes more than a regal strut and a roar to win you over. There is no denying that Leo has a way with women—even practical Cancerians—and that once he's swept a girl off her feet, it may be hard for her to scramble upright again. Still, you are no pushover for romantic charm when you feel there may be no security behind it.

He'll wine you and dine you in the fanciest places. He'll croon to you under the moon and shower you with diamonds if he can get a hold of them. Still, it would be wise to find out just how long that shower is going to last before consenting to be his wife.

Lions in love are hard to ignore, let alone brush off. Once mesmerized by this romantic powerhouse, you will most likely find yourself doing things you never dreamed of. Leos can be like vain pussycats when involved romantically. They like to be cuddled and curried, tickled under the chin and told how wonderful they are. This may not be your cup of tea, exactly, still when you're romantically dealing with a man born under the sign of Leo, you'll find yourself doing all kinds of things to make him purr.

Although he may be big and magnanimous while trying to win you, he'll let out a blood-curdling roar if he thinks he's not getting the tender love and care he feels is his due. If you keep him well supplied with affection, you can be sure his eyes will never stray and his heart will never wander.

Leo men often tend to be authoritarian—they are born to lord it over others in one way or another, it seems. If he is the top banana of his firm, he'll most likely do everything he can to stay on top. If he's not number one, he's most likely working on it and will be sitting on the throne before long. You'll have more security than you can use if he is in a position to support you in the manner to which he feels you should be accustomed. He's apt to be too lavish, though—at least, by your standards.

You'll always have plenty of friends when you have a Leo for a mate. He's a natural born friend-maker and entertainer. He loves to kick up his heels at a party.

As fathers, Leos tend to spoil their children no end.

CANCER WOMAN
VIRGO MAN

The Virgo man is often a quiet, respectable type who sets great store in conservative behavior and level-headedness. He'll admire you for your practicality and tenacity—perhaps even more than for your good looks. The Virgo man is seldom bowled over by glamour pusses. When looking for someone to love, he always turns to a serious, reliable girl.

He'll be far from a Valentino while dating. In fact, you may wind up making all the passes. Once he gets his motor running, however, he can be a warm and wonderful fellow—to the right girl.

The Virgo man is gradual about love. Chances are your romance with him will start out looking like an ordinary friendship. Once he's sure that you are no fly-by-night flirt and have no plans of taking him for a ride, he'll open up and rain sunshine all over your heart.

The Virgo man takes his time about romance. It may be many years before he seriously considers settling down. Virgos are often middle-age when they make their first marriage vows. They hold out as long as they can for that girl who perfectly measures up to their ideals.

He may not have many names in his little black book; in fact, he may not even have a little black book. He's not interested in playing the field; leave that to the more flamboyant signs. The Virgo man is so particular that he may remain romantically inactive for a long period of time. The girl he chooses has to be perfect or it's no go.

With your sure-fire perseverance, you'll most likely be able to make him listen to reason, as far as romance is concerned; before long, you'll find him returning your love. He's no block of ice and will respond to what he considers to be the right feminine flame.

Once your love-life with Virgo starts to bubble, don't give it a chance to die down. The Virgo man will never give a woman a second chance at winning his heart. If there should ever be a falling-out between you: forget about picking up the pieces. By him, it's one strike and you're out.

Once married, he'll stay that way—even if it hurts. He's too conscientious to back out of a legal deal of any sort. He'll always be faithful and considerate. He's as neat as a pin and will expect you to be the same.

If you marry a Virgo man, keep your kids spic-and-span, at least by the time he gets home from work. He likes children to be clean and polite.

CANCER WOMAN
LIBRA MAN

Cancerians are apt to find men born under the sign of Libra too wrapped up in their own private dreams to be romantically interesting. He's a difficult man to bring back down to earth, at times. Although he may be very careful about weighing both sides of an argument, he may never really come to a reasonable decision about anything. Decisons, large and small, are capable of giving a Libran the willies. Don't ask him why. He probably doesn't know, himself.

You are looking for permanence and constancy in a love relationship; you may find him a puzzlement. One moment he comes on hard and strong with declarations of his love; the next moment you find he's left you like yesterday's mashed potatoes. It does no good to wonder "what went wrong." Chances are: nothing, really. It's just one of Libra's strange ways.

On the other hand, you'll probably admire his way with harmony and beauty. If you're all decked out in your fanciest gown, you'll receive a ready compliment and one that's really deserved. Librans don't pass out compliments to all and sundry. If something strikes him as distasteful, he'll remain silent. He's tactful.

He may not seem as ambitious as you would like your lover or husband to be. Where you have a great interest in getting ahead, the Libran is often content just to drift along. It is not that he is lazy or shiftless; material gain generally means little to him. He is more interested in aesthetic matters. If he is in love with you, however, he'll do everything in his power to make you happy.

You may have to give him a good nudge now and again to get him to recognize the light of reality. On the whole, he'll enjoy the company of his artistic dreams when you're not around. If you love your Libran, don't be too harsh or impatient with him. Try to understand him.

Librans are peace-loving people. They hate any kind of confrontation that might lead to an argument. Some of them will do almost anything to keep the peace—even tell a little lie.

If you find yourself involved with a man born under this sign, either temporarily or permanently, you'd better take over the task of managing his money. It's for his own good. Money will never interest a Libran as much as it should; he often has a tendency to be generous when he shouldn't be.

Don't let him see the materialistic side of your nature too often. It's liable to frighten him off.

He makes a gentle and understanding father. He's careful not to spoil children.

CANCER WOMAN
SCORPIO MAN

Some people have a hard time understanding the man born under the sign of Scorpio; few, however, are able to resist his fiery charm. When angered, he can act like an overturned wasps' nest; his sting can leave an almost permanent mark.. If you find yourself interested in a man born under this sign, you'd better learn how to keep on his good side.

The Scorpio man can be quite blunt when he chooses; at times, he'll seem like a brute to you. He's touchy—more so than you—and it is liable to get on your nerves after a while. When you feel like you can't take it anymore, you'd better tiptoe away from the scene rather than chance an explosive confrontation. He's capable of giving you a sounding-out that will make you pack your bags and go back to Mother—for good.

If he finds fault with you, he'll let you know. He's liable to misinterpret your patience and think it a sign of indifference. Still and all, you are the kind of woman who can adapt to almost any sort of relationship or circumstance if you put your heart and mind to it.

Scorpio men are all quite perceptive and intelligent. In some respects, they know how to use their brains more effectively than most. They believe in winning in whatever they do; second-place holds no interest for them. In business, they usually achieve the position they want through drive and use of intellect.

Your interest in home-life is not likely to be shared by him. No matter how comfortable you've managed to make the house, it will have very little influence on him with regards to making him aware of his family responsibilities. He does not like to be tied down, generally, and would rather be out on the battlefield of life, belting away for what he feels is a just and worthy cause. Don't try to keep the homefires burning too brightly while you wait for him to come home from work—you may just run out of firewood.

The Scorpio man is passionate in all things—including love. Most women are easily attracted to him—and the Cancer woman is no exception . . . that is, at least before she knows what she might be getting into. Those who allow themselves to be swept off their feet by a Scorpio man, shortly find that they're dealing with a carton of romantic fireworks. The Scorpio man is passionate with a capital P, make no mistake about that.

Scorpio men are straight to the point. They can be as sharp as a razor blade and just as cutting. Always manage to stay out of his line of fire; if you don't, it could cost you your love-life.

Scorpio men like large families. They love children but they do not always live up to the role of father.

CANCER WOMAN
SAGITTARIUS MAN

Sagittarius men are not easy to catch. They get cold feet whenever visions of the altar enter the romance. You'll most likely be attracted to the Sagittarian because of his sun-shiny nature. He's lots of laughs and easy to get along with, but as soon as the relationship begins to take on a serious hue, you may feel yourself a little let-down.

Sagittarians are full of bounce; perhaps too much bounce to suit you. They are often hard to pin down; they dislike staying put. If he ever has a chance to be on-the-move, he'll latch on to it without so much as a how-do-you-do. Sagittarians are quick people —both in mind and spirit. If ever they do make mistakes, it's because of their zip; they leap before they look.

If you offer him good advice, he's liable not to follow it. Sagittarians like to rely on their own wits and ways whenever possible.

His up-and-at-'em manner about most things is likely to drive you up the wall at times. And your cautious, deliberate manner is likely to make him cluck his tongue occasionally. "Get the lead out of your shoes," he's liable to tease when you're accompanying him on a stroll or jogging through the park with him on a Sunday morning. He can't abide a slowpoke.

At times you'll find him too much like a kid—too breezy. Don't mistake his youthful zest for premature senility. Sagittarians are equipped with first-class brain power and know how to use it well. They are often full of good ideas and drive. Generally, they are very broad-minded people and very much concerned with fair play and equality.

In the romance department, he's quite capable of loving you whole-heartedly while treating you like a good buddy. His hail-fellow-well-met manner in the arena of love is likely to scare off a dainty damsel. However, a woman who knows that his heart is in the right place, won't mind it too much if, once in a while, he slaps her (lightly) on the back instead of giving her a gentle embrace.

He's not very much of a homebody. He's got ants in his pants and enjoys being on-the-move. Humdrum routine—especially at home—bores him silly. At the drop of a hat, he may ask you to whip off your apron and dine out for a change. He's a past-master in the instant-surprise department. He'll love keeping you guessing. His friendly, candid nature will win him many friends. He'll expect his friends to be yours, and vice-versa.

Sagittarians make good fathers when the children become older; with little shavers, they feel all thumbs.

CANCER WOMAN
CAPRICORN MAN

The Capricorn man is quite often not the romantic kind of lover that attracts most women. Still, with his reserve and calm, he is capable of giving his heart completely once he has found the right girl. The Cancer woman who is thorough and deliberate can appreciate these same qualities in the average Capricorn man. He is slow and sure about most things—love included.

He doesn't believe in flirting and would never lead a heart on a merry chase just for the game of it. If you win his trust, he'll give you his heart on a platter. Quite often, it is the woman who has to take the lead when romance is in the air. As long as he knows you're making the advances in earnest, he won't mind—in fact, he'll probably be grateful. Don't get to thinking he's all cold fish; he isn't. While some Capricorns are indeed quite capable of expressing passion, others often have difficulty in trying to display affection. He should have no trouble in this area, however, once he has found a patient and understanding girl.

The Capricorn man is very interested in getting ahead. He's quite ambitious and usually knows how to apply himself well to whatever task he undertakes. He's far from being a spendthrift. Like you, he knows how to handle money with extreme care. You, with your knack for putting pennies away for that rainy day, should have no difficulty in understanding his way with money. The Capricorn man thinks in terms of future security. He saves to make sure that he and his wife have something to fall back on when they reach retirement age. There's nothing wrong with that; in fact, it's a plus quality.

The Capricorn man will want to handle household matters efficiently. Most Cancerians have no trouble in doing this. If he should check up on you from time to time, don't let it irritate you. Once you assure him that you can handle this area to his liking, he'll leave it all up to you.

Although he's a hard man to catch when it comes to marriage, once he's made that serious step, he's quite likely to become possessive. Capricorns need to know that they have the support of their women in whatever they do, every step of the way.

The Capricorn man likes to be liked. He may seem like a dull, reserved person but underneath it all, he's often got an adventurous nature that has never had the chance to express itself. He may be a real dare-devil in his heart of hearts. The right woman, the affectionate, adoring woman, can bring out that hidden zest in his nature.

Although he may not understand his children fully, he'll be a loving and dutiful father.

CANCER WOMAN
AQUARIUS MAN

You are liable to find the Aquarious man the most broadminded man you have ever met; on the other hand, you are also liable to find him the most impractical. Oftentimes, he's more of a dreamer than a doer. If you don't mind putting up with a man whose heart and mind are as wide as the Missouri but whose head is almost always up in the clouds, then start dating that Aquarian who has somehow captured your fancy. Maybe you, with your good sense, can bring him back down to earth when he gets too starry-eyed.

He's no dumb-bell; make no mistake about that. He can be busy making some very complicated and idealistic plans when he's got that out-to-lunch look in his eyes. But more than likely, he'll never execute them. After he's shared one or two of his progressive ideas with you, you are liable to ask yourself "Who is this nut?" But don't go jumping to conclusions. There's a saying that Aquarians are a half-century ahead of everybody else in the thinking department.

If you decide to say "yes" to his "will you marry me", you'll find out how right his zany whims are on or about your 50th anniversary. Maybe the waiting will be worth it. Could be that you have an Einstein on your hands—and heart.

Life with an Aquarian won't be one of total despair if you can learn to temper his airiness with your down-to-earth practicality. He won't gripe if you do. The Aquarius man always maintains an open mind; he'll entertain the ideas and opinions of everybody. He may not agree with all of them.

Don't go tearing your hair out when you find that it's almost impossible to hold a normal conversation with your Aquarius friend at times. He's capable of answering your how-are-you-feeling with a run-down on the price of Arizona sugar beets. Always try to keep in mind: he means well.

His broadmindedness doesn't stop when it comes to you and your personal freedom. You won't have to give up any of your hobbies or projects after you're married; in fact, he'll encourage you to continue your interests.

He'll be a kind and generous husband. He'll never quibble over petty things. Keep track of the money you both spend. He can't. Money burns a hole in his pocket.

You'll have plenty of chances to put your legendary patience to good use during your relationship with an Aquarian. At times, you may feel like tossing in the towel, but you'll never call it quits.

He's a good family man. He understands children as much as he loves them.

CANCER WOMAN
PISCES MAN

The Pisces man is perhaps the man you've been looking all over for, high and low; the man you almost thought didn't exist.

The Pisces man is very sensitive and very romantic. Still, he is a reasonable person. He may wish on the moon, yet he's got enough good sense to know that it isn't made of green cheese.

He'll be very considerate of your every wish and whim. He will do his best to be a very compatible mate. The Pisces man is great for showering the object of his affection with all kinds of little gifts and tokens of his affection. He's just the right mixture of dreamer and realist that pleases most women.

When it comes to earning bread and butter, the strong Pisces man will do all right in the world. Quite often they are capable of rising to very high positions. Some do very well as writers or psychiatrists. He'll be as patient and understanding with you as you are with him.

One thing a Pisces man dislikes is pettiness. Anyone who delights in running another into the ground is almost immediately crossed off his list of possible mates. If you have any small grievances with any of your girl friends, don't tell him about them. He couldn't care less about them and will be quite disappointed in you if you do.

If you fall in love with a weak Pisces man, don't give up your job at the office before you get married. Better still: hang onto it until a good while after the honeymoon; you may need it.

A funny thing about the man born under this sign is that he can be content almost anywhere. This is perhaps because he is quite inner-directed and places little value on some exterior things.

In a shack or a palace, the Pisces man is capable of making the best of all possible adjustments. He won't kick up a fuss if the roof leaks or if the fence is in sad need of repair. He's got more important things on his mind, he'll tell you. Still and all, the Pisces man is not lazy or aimless. It's important to understand that material gain is never a direct goal for him.

Pisces men have a way with the sick and troubled. He'll offer his shoulder to anyone in the mood for a good cry. He can listen to one hard luck story after another without seeming to tire. Quite often he knows what is bothering someone before that person, himself, realizes what it is. It's almost intuitive with Pisceans, it seems.

As a lover, he'll be attentive and faithful. Children are often delighted with Pisces men. As fathers, they are never strict, always permissive.

Man—Woman

CANCER MAN
ARIES WOMAN

The Aires woman may be a little too bossy and busy for you. Generally speaking, Ariens are ambitious creatures. They can become a little impatient with people who are more thorough and deliberate than they are—especially if they feel such people are taking too much time. The Aries woman is a fast worker. Sometimes she's so fast she forgets to look where she's going. When she stumbles or falls, it would be nice if you were there to grab her. Ariens are proud women. They don't like to be told "I told you so" when they err. Tongue-wagging can turn them into blocks of ice. Don't begin to think that the Aires woman frequently gets tripped up in her plans. Quite often they are capable of taking aim and hitting the bull's-eye. You'll be flabbergasted at times by their accuracy as well as by their ambition. On the other hand, because of your interest in being sure and safe, you're apt to spot a flaw in your Arien's plans before she does.

You are somewhat slower than the Arien in attaining what you have your sights set on. Still, you don't make any mistakes along the way; you're almost always well-prepared.

The Aries woman is rather sensitive at times. She likes to be handled with gentleness and respect. Let her know that you love her for her brains as well as for her good looks. Never give her cause to become jealous. When your Aires date sees green, you'd better forget about sharing a rosy future together. Handle her with tender love and care and she's yours.

The Aires woman can be giving if she feels her partner is deserving. She is no iceberg; she responds to the proper flame. She needs a man she can look up to and feel proud of. If the shoe fits, put it on. If not, better put your sneakers back on and quietly tiptoe out of her sight. She can cause you plenty of heart ache if you've made up your mind about her but she hasn't made up hers about you. Aires women are very demanding at times. Some of them are high-strung; they can be difficult if they feel their independence is being hampered.

The cultivated Aires woman makes a wonderful homemaker and hostess. You'll find she's very clever in decorating and color-use. Your house will be tastefully furnished; she'll see to it that it radiates harmony. Friends and acquaintances will love your Aries wife. She knows how to make everyone feel at home and welcome.

Although the Aries woman may not be keen on burdening responsibilities, she is fond of children and the joy they bring.

CANCER MAN
TAURUS WOMAN

A Taurus woman could perhaps understand you better than most women. She is a very considerate and loving kind of person. She is methodical and thorough in whatever she does. She knows how to take her time in doing things; she is anxious to avoid mistakes. Like you, she is a careful person. She never skips over things that may seem unimportant; she goes over everything with a fine-tooth comb.

Home is very important to the Taurus woman. She is an excellent homemaker. Although your home may not be a palace, it will become, under her care, a comfortable and happy abode. She'll love it when friends drop by for the evening. She is a good cook and enjoys feeding people well. No one will ever go away from your house with an empty stomach.

The Taurus woman is serious about love and affection. When she has taken a tumble for someone, she'll stay by him—for good, if possible. She will try to be practical in romance, to some extent. When she sets her cap for a man, she keeps after him until he's won her. Generally, the Taurus woman is a passionate lover, even though she may appear otherwise at first glance. She is on the look-out for someone who can return her affection fully. Taureans are sometimes given to fits of jealousy and possessiveness. They expect fair play in the area of marriage; when it doesn't come about, they can be bitingly sarcastic and mean.

The Taurus woman is generally an easy-going person. She's

fond of keeping peace. She won't argue unless she has to. She'll do her best to keep a love relationship on even keel.

Marriage is generally a one-time thing for Taureans. Once they've made the serious step, they seldom try to back out of it. Marriage is for keeps. They are fond of love and warmth. With the right man, they turn out to be ideal wives.

The Taurus woman will respect you for your steady ways; she'll have confidence in your common sense.

Taurus women seldom put up with nonsense from their children. They are not so much strict as concerned. They like their children to be well-behaved and dutiful. Nothing pleases a Taurus mother more than a compliment from a neighbor or teacher about her child's behavior. Although children may inwardly resent the iron hand of a Taurus woman, in later life they are often quite thankful that they were brought up in such an orderly and conscientious way.

CANCER MAN
GEMINI WOMAN

The Gemini woman may be too much of a flirt ever to take your heart too seriously. Then again, it depends on what kind of mood she's in. Gemini women can change from hot to cold quicker than a cat can wink its eye. Chances are her fluctuations will tire you after a time, and you'll pick up your heart—if it's not already broken into small pieces—and go elsewhere. Women born under the sign of the Twins have the talent of being able to change their moods and attitudes as frequently as they change their party dresses.

Sometimes, Gemini girls like to whoop it up. Some of them are good-time girls who love burning the candle to the wick. You'll always see them at parties and gatherings, surrounded by men of all types, laughing gaily or kicking up their heels at every opportunity. Wallflowers, they're not. The next day you may bump into the same girl at the neighborhood library and you'll hardly recognize her for her "sensible" attire. She'll probably have five or six books under her arm—on five or six different subjects. In fact, she may even work there. If you think you've met the twin sister of Dr. Jekyll and Mr. Hyde, you're most likely right.

You'll probably find her a dazzling and fascinating creature— for a time, at any rate. Most men do. But when it comes to being serious about love you may find that that sparkling Eve leaves quite a bit to be desired. It's not that she has anything against being serious, it's just that she might find it difficult trying to be serious with you.

At one moment, she'll be capable of praising you for your steadfast and patient ways; the next moment she'll tell you in a cutting way that you're an impossible stick in the mud.

Don't even begin to fathom the depths of her mercurial soul—it's full of false bottoms. She'll resent close investigation anyway, and will make you rue the day you ever took it into your head to try to learn more about her than she feels is necessary. Better keep the relationship fancy free and full of fun until she gives you the go-ahead sign. Take as much of her as she is willing to give; don't ask for more. If she does take a serious interest in you, then she'll come across with the goods.

There will come a time when the Gemini girl will realize that she can't spend her entire life at the ball and that the security and warmth you offer is just what she needs to be a happy, fulfilled woman.

She'll be easy-going with her children. She'll probably spoil them silly.

CANCER MAN
CANCER WOMAN

The girl born under Cancer needs to be protected from the cold cruel world. She'll love you for your gentle and kind manner; you are the kind of man who can make her feel safe and secure.

You won't have to pull any he-man or heroic stunts to win her heart; she's not interested in things like that. She's more likely to be impressed by your sure, steady ways—the way you have of putting your arm around her and making her feel that she's the only girl in the world. When she's feeling glum and tears begin to well up in her eyes, you'll know how to calm her fears, no matter how silly some of them may seem.

The girl born under this sign—like you—is inclined to have her ups and downs. Perhaps you can both learn to smooth out the roughed-up spots in each other's life. She'll most likely worship the ground you walk on or place you on a very high pedestal. Don't disappoint her if you can help it. She'll never disappoint you. The Cancer woman is the sort who will take great pleasure in devoting the rest of her natural life to you. She'll darn your socks, mend your overalls, scrub floors, wash windows, shop, cook, and do anything short of murder in order to please you and to let you know that she loves you. Sounds like that legendary good old-fashioned girl, doesn't it? Contrary to popular belief, there are still a good number of them around and the majority of them are Cancerians.

Treat your Cancer mate fairly and she'll treat you like a king.

There is one ohing you should be warned about: never be unkind to your mother-in-law. It will be the only golden rule your Cancerian wife will probably expect you to live up to. Mother is something pretty special for her. You should have no trouble in understanding this, for your mother has a special place in your heart, too. It's always that way with people born under this sign. They have great respect and love for family-ties. It might be a good idea for you both to get to know each other's relatives before tying the marriage knot, because after the wedding bells have rung, you'll be seeing a lot of them.

Of all the signs in the Zodiac, the woman born under Cancer is the most maternal. In caring for and bringing up children, she knows just how to combine tenderness and discipline. A child couldn't ask for a better mother. Cancer women are sympathetic, affectionate, and patient with children. Both of you will make excellent parents—especially when the children are young; when they grow older you'll most likely be reluctant to let them go out into the world.

CANCER MAN
LEO WOMAN

The Leo woman can make most men roar like lions. If any woman in the Zodiac has that indefinable something that can make men lose their heads and find their hearts, it's the Leo woman.

She's got more than a fair share of charm and glamour and she knows how to make the most of her assets, especially when she's in the company of the opposite sex. Jealous men either lose their cool or their sanity when trying to woo a woman born under the sign of the Lion. She likes to kick up her heels quite often and doesn't care who knows it. She often makes heads turn and toungues wag. You don't necessarily have to believe any of what you hear—it's most likely just jealous gossip or wishful thinking. Needless to say, other women in her vicinity turn green with envy and will try anything short of shoving her into the nearest lake in order to put her out of commission.

Although this vamp makes the blood rush to your head and makes you momentarily forget all the things you thought were important and necessary in your life, you may feel differently when you come back down to earth and the stars are out of your eyes. You may feel that although this vivacious creature can make you feel pretty wonderful, she just isn't the kind of girl you planned to bring home to Mother. Not that your mother might disapprove of your choice—but *you might* after the shoes and rice are a thing of the past. Although the Leo woman may do her best to be a good wife for you, chances are she'll fall short of your idea of what a good wife should be.

If you're planning on not going as far as the altar with that Leo woman who has you flipping your lid, you'd better be financially equipped for some very expensive dating. Be prepared to shower her with expensive gifts and to take her dining and dancing to the smartest spots in town. Promise her the moon if you're in a position to go that far. Luxury and glamour are two things that are bound to lower a Leo's resistance. She's got expensive tastes and you'd better cater to them if you expect to get to first base with this femme.

If you've got an important business deal to clinch and you have doubts as to whether you can swing it or not, bring your Leo girl along to the business luncheon. Chances are that with her on your arm, you'll be able to win any business battle with both hands tied. She won't have to say or do anything—just be there at your side. The grouchiest oil magnate can be transformed into a gushing, obediant schoolboy if there's a charming Leo woman in the room.

Leo mothers are blind to the faults of their children. They make very loving and affectionate mothers and tend to spoil their offspring.

CANCER MAN
VIRGO WOMAN

The Virgo woman is pretty particular about choosing her men friends. She's not interested in just going out with anybody; she has her own idea of what a boyfriend or prospective husband should be—and it's quite possible that that image has something of you in it. Generally speaking, she's a quiet girl. She doesn't believe that nonsense has any place in a love affair. She's serious about love and she'll expect you to be. She's looking for a man who has both feet on the ground—someone who can take care of himself as well as her. She knows the value of money and how to get the most out of a dollar. She's far from being a spendthrift. Throwing money around turns her stomach—even when it isn't her money.

She'll most likely be very shy about romancing. Even the simple act of holding hands may make her turn crimson—at least, on the first couple of dates. You'll have to make all the advances—which is as it should be—and you'll have to be careful not to make any wrong moves. She's capable of showing anyone who oversteps the boundaries of common decency the door. It may even take quite a long time before she'll accept that goodnight kiss at the front gate. Don't give up. You are perhaps the kind of man who can bring out the warm woman in her. There is love and tenderness underneath Virgo's seemingly frigid facade. It will take a patient and understanding man to bring it out into the open. She may have the idea that sex is something very naughty, if not unnecessary. The right man could make her put this old-fashioned idea in the trunk up in the attic along with her great grandmother's woolen nighties.

She is a very sensitive girl. You can help her overcome this by treating her with gentleness and affection.

When a Virgo has accepted you as a lover or mate, she won't stint in giving her love in return. With her, it's all or nothing at all. You'll be surprised at the transformation your earnest attention can bring about in this quiet kind of woman. When in love, Virgos only listen to their hearts, not to what the neighbors say.

Virgo women are honest about love once they've come to grips with it. They don't appreciate hypocrisy—particularly in this area of life. They will always be true to their hearts—even if it means tossing you over for a new love. But if you convince her that you are earnest about your interest in her, she'll reciprocate your love and affection and never leave you. Do her wrong once, however, and you can be sure she'll call the whole thing off.

Virgo mothers are tender and loving. They know what's good for their children and will always take great pains in bringing them up correctly.

CANCER MAN
LIBRA WOMAN

The song goes: It's a woman's prerogative to change her mind. The lyricist must have had the Libra woman in his thoughts when he jotted this ditty out. Her changeability, in spite of its undeniable charm (sometimes), could actually drive even a man of your patience up the wall. She's capable of smothering you with love and kisses one day and on the next, avoid you like the plague. If you think you're a man of steel nerves then perhaps you can tolerate her sometimey-ness without suffering too much. However, if you own up to the fact that you're a mere mortal who can only take so much, then you'd better fasten your attention on a girl who's somewhat more constant.

But don't get the wrong idea—a love affair with a Libran is not all bad. In fact, it can have an awful lot of plusses to it. Libra women are soft, very feminine, and warm. She doesn't have to vamp all over the place in order to gain a man's attention. Her delicate presence is enough to warm the cockles of any man's heart. One smile and you're like a piece of putty in the palm of her hand.

She can be fluffy and affectionate—things you like in a girl. On the other hand, her indecision about which dress to wear, what to cook for dinner, or whether or not to redo the rumpusroom could make you tear your hair out. What will perhaps be more exasperating is her flat denial to the accusation that she cannot make even the simplest decision. The trouble is that she wants to be fair or just in all matters; she'll spend hours weighing both sides of an argument or situation. Don't make her rush into a decision; that would only irritate her.

The Libra woman likes to be surrounded by beautiful things. Money is no object when beauty is concerned. There will always be plenty of flowers in her apartment. She'd rather die than do without daisies and such. She'll know how to arrange them tastefully, too. Women under this sign are fond of beautiful clothes and furnishings. They will run up bills without batting an eye—if given the chance.

Once she's cottoned to you, the Libra woman will do everything in her power to make you happy. She'll wait on you hand and foot when you're sick, bring you breakfast in bed on Sundays, and even read you the funny papers if you're too sleepy to open your eyes. She'll be very thoughtful and devoted. If anyone dares suggest you're not the grandest man in the world, your Libra wife will give that person a good sounding-out.

Librans work wonders with children. Gentle persuasion and affection are all she uses in bringing them up. It works.

CANCER MAN
SCORPIO WOMAN

When the Scorpio woman chooses to be sweet, she's apt to give the impression that butter wouldn't melt in her mouth . . . but, of course, it would. When her temper flies, so will everything else that isn't bolted down. She can be as hot as a *tamale* or as cool as a cucumber when she wants. Whatever mood she's in, you can be sure it's for real. She doesn't believe in poses or hypocrisy.

The Scorpio woman is often seductive and sultry. Her femme fatale charm can pierce through the hardest of hearts like a laser ray. She doesn't have to look like Mata Hari (many of them resemble the tomboy next door) but once you've looked into those tantalizing eyes, you're a goner.

The Scorpio woman can be a whirlwind of passion. Life with a girl born under this sign will not be all smiles and smooth-sailing. If you think you can handle a woman who can purr like a pussycat when handled correctly but spit bullets once her fur is ruffled, then try your luck. Your stable and steady nature will most likely have a calming effect on her. You're the kind of man she can trust and rely on. But never cross her—even on the smallest thing; if you do, you'd better tell Fido to make room for you in the dog-house—you'll be his guest for the next couple of days.

Generally, the Scorpio woman will keep family battles within the walls of your home. When company visits, she's apt to give the impression that married life with you is one big joy-ride. It's just her way of expressing her loyalty to you—at least, in front of others. She believes that family matters are and should stay private. She certainly will see to it that others have a high opinion of you both. She'll be right behind you in whatever it is you want to do. Although she's an individualist, after she has married she'll put her own interests aside for those of the man she loves. With a woman like this behind you, you can't help but go far. She'll never try to take over your role as boss of the family. She'll give you all the support you need in order to fulfill that role. She won't complain if the going gets rough. She knows how to take the bitter with the sweet. She is a courageous woman. She's as anxious as you are to find that place in the sun for you both. She's as determined a person as you are.

Although she may love her children, she may not be very affectionate toward them. She'll make a devoted mother, though. She'll be anxious to see them develop their talents. She'll teach the children to be courageous and steadfast.

CANCER MAN
SAGITTARIUS WOMAN

The Sagittarius woman is hard to keep track of: first she's here, then she's there. She's a woman with a severe case of itchy feet. She's got to keep on the move.

People generally like her because of her hail-fellow-well-met manner and her breezy charm. She is constantly good-natured and almost never cross. She is the kind of girl you're likely to strike up a palsy-walsy relationship with; you might not be interested in letting it go any farther. She probably won't sulk if you leave it on a friendly basis, either. Treat her like a kid-sister and she'll eat it up like candy.

She'll probably be attracted to you because of your restful, self-assured manner. She'll need a friend like you to help her over the rough spots in her life; she'll most likely turn to you for advice frequently.

There is nothing malicious about a girl born under this sign. She is full of bounce and good cheer. Her sunshiny dispositon can be relied upon even on the rainiest of days. No matter what she says or does, you'll always know that she means well. Sagittarians are sometimes short on tact. Some of them say anything that comes into their pretty little heads, no matter what the occasion. Sometimes the words that tumble out of their mouths seem downright cutting and cruel; they mean well but often everything they say comes out wrong. She's quite capable of losing her friends—and perhaps even yours—through a careless slip of the lip. Always remember that she is full of good intentions. Stick with her if you like her and try to help her mend her ways.

She's not a girl that you'd most likely be interested in marrying, but she'll certainly be lots of fun to pal around with. Quite often, Sagittarius women are outdoor types. They're crazy about things like fishing, camping, and mountain climbing. They love the wide open spaces. They are fond of all kinds of animals. Make no mistake about it: this busy little lady is no slouch. She's full of pep and vigor.

She's great company most of the time; she's more fun than a three-ring circus when she's in the right company. You'll like her for her candid and direct manner. On the whole, Sagittarians are very kind and sympathetic women.

If you do wind up marrying this girl-next-door type, you'd better see to it that you take care of all financial matters. Sagittarians often let money run through their fingers like sand.

As a mother, she'll smother her children with love and give them all of the freedom they think they need.

CANCER MAN
CAPRICORN WOMAN

The Capricorn woman may not be the most romantic woman of the Zodiac, but she's far from frigid when she meets the right man. She believes in true love; she doesn't appreciate getting involved in flings. To her, they're just a waste of time. She's looking for a man who means "business"—in life as well as in love. Although she can be very affectionate with her boyfriend or mate, she tends to let her head govern her heart. That is not to say that she is a cool, calculating cucumber. On the contrary, she just feels she can be more honest about love if she consults her brains first. She wants to size-up the situation first before throwing her heart in the ring. She wants to make sure it won't get stepped on.

The Capricorn woman is faithful, dependable, and systematic in just about everything that she undertakes. She is quite concerned with security and sees to it that every penny she spends is spent wisely. She is very economical about using her time, too. She does not believe in whittling away her energy on a scheme that is bound not to pay off.

Ambitious themselves, they are quite often attracted to ambitious men—men who are interested in getting somewhere in life. If a man of this sort wins her heart, she'll stick by him and do all she can to help him get to the top.

The Capricorn woman is almost always diplomatic. She makes an excellent hostess. She can be very influential when your business acquaintances come to dinner.

The Capricorn woman is likely to be very concerned, if not downright proud, about her family tree. Relatives are pretty important to her, particularly if they're socially prominent. Never say a cross word about her family members. That can really go against her grain and she'll punish you by not talking for days.

She's generally thorough in whatever she does: cooking, housekeeping, entertaining. Capricorn women are well-mannered and gracious, no matter what their backgrounds. They seem to have it in their natures to always behave properly.

If you should marry a woman born under this sign, you need never worry about her going on a wild shopping spree. They understand the value of money better than most women. If you turn over your paycheck to her at the end of the week, you can be sure that a good hunk of it will go into the bank and that all the bills will be paid on time.

With children, the Capricorn mother is both loving and correct. She'll see to it that they're polite and respectful.

CANCER MAN
AQUARIUS WOMAN

The woman born under the sign of the Water Bearer can be pretty odd and eccentric at times. Some say that this is the source of her mysterious charm. You're liable to think she's just a plain screwball; you may be 50 percent right.

Aquarius women often have their heads full of dreams and stars in their eyes. By nature, they are often unconventional; they have their own ideas about how the world should be run. Sometimes their ideas may seem pretty weird—chances are they're just a little bit too progressive. There is a saying that runs "The way the Aquarian thinks, so will the world in fifty years."

If you find yourself falling in love with a woman born under this sign, you'd better fasten your safety belt. It may take some time before you know what she's like and even then, you may have nothing to go on but a string of vague hunches.

She can be like a rainbow: full of dazzling colors. She's like no other girl you've ever known. There is something about her that is definitely charming—yet elusive, you'll never be able to put your finger on it. She seems to radiate adventure and optimism without even trying. She'll most likely be the most tolerant and open-minded woman you've ever encountered.

If you find that she's too much mystery and charm for you to handle—and being a Cancerian, chances are you might—just talk it out with her and say that you think it would be better if you called it quits. She'll most likely give you a peck on the cheek and say "Okay, but let's still be friends." Aquarius women are like that. Perhaps you'll both find it easier to get along in a friendship than in a romance.

It is not difficult for her to remain buddy-buddy with an ex-lover. For many Aquarians, the line between friendship and romance is a pretty fuzzy one.

She's not a jealous person and while you're romancing her, she won't expect you to be, either. You'll find her a pretty free spirit most of the time. Just when you think you know her inside-out, you'll discover that you don't really know her at all. She's a very sympathetic and warm person; she is often helpful to those in need of assistance and advice.

She'll seldom be suspicious even when she has every right to be. If the man she loves makes a little slip, she's liable to forget it.

She makes a fine mother. Her positive and big-hearted qualities are easily transmitted to her offspring.

CANCER MAN
PISCES WOMAN

The Pisces woman places great value on love and romance. She's gentle, kind, and romantic. Perhaps she's that girl you've been dreaming about all these years. Like you, she has very high ideals, she will only give her heart to a man who she feels can live up to her expectations.

She'll never try to wear the pants in the family. She's a staunch believer in the man being the head of the house. Quite often, Pisces women are soft and cuddly. They have a feminine, domestic charm that can win the heart of just about any man.

Generally, there's a lot more to her than just her pretty face and womanly ways. There's a brain ticking behind that gentle facade. You may not become aware of it—that is, until you've married her. It's no cause for alarm, however; she'll most likely never use it against you. But if she feels you're botching up your married life through careless behavior or if she feels you could be earning more money than you do, she'll tell you about it. But any wife would, really. She will never try to usurp your position as head and bread winner of the family. She'll admire you for your ambition and drive. If anyone says anything against you in her presence, she'll probably break out into tears. Pisces women are usually very sensitive. Their reaction to adversity or frustration is often just a plain good old fashioned cry. They can weep buckets when inclined.

She'll have an extra-special dinner waiting for you when you call up and tell her that you've just landed a new and important contract. Don't bother to go into the details at the dinner table, though; she probably doesn't have much of a head for business matters. She's only too glad to leave those matters up to you.

She's a wizard in decorating a house. She's fond of soft and beautiful things. She's a good housekeeper. She'll always see to it that you have plenty of socks and underwear in the top drawer of your dresser.

Treat her with tenderness and your relationship will be an enjoyable one. Pisces women are generally fond of sweets and flowers. Never forget birthdays, anniversaries, and the like. She won't.

Your talent for patience and gentleness can pay off in your relationship with a Pisces woman. Chances are she'll never make you sorry you placed that band of gold on her finger.

There's a strong bond between a Pisces mother and her children. She'll try to give them all the things she never had as a child. Chances are she'll spoil them a little.

CANCER

CANCER

YEARLY FORECAST: 1987

Forecast for 1987 Concerning Business and
Financial Matters, Job Prospects,
Travel, Health, Romance and Marriage
for Those Born with the Sun
in the Zodiacal Sign of Cancer.
June 21–July 20

Look forward to a year of opportunity that can bring the fulfillment of your highest aspirations. The Moon, the ruler of your sign, endows you with the sensitivity essential to common-sense acceptance of the promise offered by conditions and events. For those of you in business this should be a key year. While you will, as ever, have to apply yourself if you are to succeed, there will be ample opportunity for so doing. Conditions for those at the top of the tree will be good and for those yet aspiring to reach the top, this is the year to make the most of your chances. Pressure is still being applied in working conditions. This is not necessarily a bad thing. You should realize that good luck alone will not see you to the top. It is essential to be positive and work with a goal in mind. Look after your health, since your capability is limited by the time and purpose you can give to effort. There will, of course, be days when you will feel depressed and think that the effort needed is too much. Your natural resilience should lift you out of such depths, especially if you appreciate that you should be heading for the top whether through your career or other avenues of social recognition. Travel of any importance or distance will most probably be undertaken in the first two months of the year. Relationships are always, with you, a sensitive consideration. As was the case last year, you will need to use your intuitive gifts to a large extent in order to keep your personal and intimate life under reasonable control. For some the high point could be marriage, while for others there could be disappointment.

Material conditions always depend to a large extent on the way you apply yourself to whatever task is in hand. This year continues the pattern of last, to some extent, by keeping you aware that industry is not only essential but is praiseworthy. It follows that you should be able to consolidaate your position financially through your determination to work productively. Up till March 1st, the going may be precarious. You may be tempted to take more chances than are good for you. This could mean extra work because of mistakes. Speculative efforts are not likely to pay off. Hard work can reward those who take examinations for future career opportunities. Disruption of working harmony can be caused by having to take on more than usual during January and February. After that you should see some return for your work or studies. Be prepared to display originality and inventiveness. For this you could receive recognition. Between November 22 and December 21 you should find that employers and others who influence your working life can be particularly helpful and can promote your ideas. The period between January 8 and February 19 could be most active and you should then keep a clear and positive view of your target. Between April 5 and June 20 you may be better keeping a low profile or concentrating on private preparation for some personal project.

Take care of your health, since so much depends on your ability to function properly. You may overextend yourself in the attempt to succeed. If you do not judge pace and distance properly you can fall short. So be prudent and aware of your limitations. It will be wise to insure yourself well in preparation for any failure of health. This could mean putting spare cash by for eventualities, seeing that someone else can cover for you in case of a problem, or just keeping yourself in proper trim for whatever you have to do. Be careful not to let any minor ailment grow into a more serious illness. If you suffer from any chronic ailment, be patient and do not push your luck. Because you are sensitive you can overdramatize and blow things out of proportion. Do not take life too seriously if you feel you are not coping. You can achieve all you need if you keep health, like everything else, in perspective. A short change of scenery always helps if you are feeling depressed. In the first week of the year, again between April 5 and May 20, and then between August 22 and October 7, your judgment could be a bit haywire. In these periods try to avoid being careless, but expect all others, such as drivers, to be inconsiderate.

A busy working or business life may keep you more at home than overseas. Preparatory travel may be most useful in January and February. From then on, however, with some possible exceptions, you seem likely to appreciate your own neck of the woods. The two-month period may be extended to March 20 in some cases where there is a need to travel. Between August 22 and October 7 there could be some pressure on you to make full use of local or daily travel. This has both positive and negative possibilities. If you are particularly anxious to finish whatever you have in hand locally, you may take chances. Your good luck is likely to carry you through reasonably well, but be ever on your guard, particularly between September 23 and October 7. Speeding or careless driving can hinder your progress rather than aid it.

For you who are happily married, this can be a year of some ups and downs. Intimate life is an essential to Cancer happiness. The maternal instincts, so often attributed to you, may be put to full use in order to sustain the partnership. You are well aware that the secret of marriage is sharing and you have a great deal to give. If the return is not what you expect, try to understand why this should be. You may have to give more than you receive in order to find true balance for this year. Remember that a lot is going for you as an individual and be sure you are not concentrating too much on personal prestige. Your partner could feel neglected if you spend too much time attending to business. Obviously you must again use your well-known common sense and good judgment to see that this vital area of life experience is not the loser. In some cases, there may be special reasons to care for your partner, who may need all the support and comfort you can give. It seems very much a year when you can reach a much deeper understanding of the value of married life through sharing and caring.

Emotional young people could find this a perplexing or ecstatic year to be in love. You find it difficult at the best of times to keep emotions under control and are never slow to demonstrate your feelings. Many of you will be fully extended in your romantic life. The first week of the year will be highly emotional for many. Between July 5 and 29 and October 20 and November 2, you should feel the urge to love and be loved most inspiring. Those who are looking for a life partner will be particularly sensitive to Cupid's arrows. The prospect of marriage will loom large and important to many as a superattraction. To some others it may seem a little disconcerting. Only when you are in love do you fully appreciate the need for a partner who is also a soulmate. Marriage will therefore fall into place quite nicely for some and leave others in midair. Try to be practical as well as romantic, if that is possible. Marriage could be a practicality for some in the first three weeks of the year and after December 22. You could meet a loved one almost anywhere this year. As you are not apt to be traveling a great deal it is most likely to be an everyday situation that leads on to greater things. Love and marriage mean much to you and this is your year of success, so look out for events.

Relatives will play an important part in your relationships from August 23 to September 22. This is also the time you may find the neighborhood attractions far outweigh anything else in the field.

Business prospects this year look better than they did for many in the past. Up to the beginning of March you could have loose ends to tie up. Travel in pursuit of contracts or overseas business will most likely be undertaken during January and February. Any publicity should be attended to in these two months as another precursor to a most active year ahead. Attend to as much detail as you can in the first week of the year when you may be finishing leftover personal details. After February 19 you can turn your activities to more positive business initiatives. Your positive attitude should settle problems and satisfy difficult people with whom you have to deal. From March 21 to April 19 you could be in a position to appreciate advice and help offered by influential people in your sphere of business activity. Take full advantage of this positive gesture. You should by now be seeing the road ahead more clearly and a helping hand should be grasped. There could be another period between June 21 and July 20 when your efforts attract the attention of people in high places who can add to your future prosperity. July should be a particularly harmonious month, so you should feel ready to grasp any help being tendered. Productivity and reward can depend a great deal on labor. You will have the reminder of last year's conditions and efforts to guide you in your labor relations. Be prepared for some hitches, especially in the first two months or so. Should you be on the move at this time your absence could be exploited. Unrest can be stirred up all too easily. After March 2 you should be in a much stronger position to handle business and gain the positive cooperation of staff. Consider joint sharing if the staff are really cooperative. It may not be particularly wise to accept all the offers you get from potential business partners. Sharing with someone who is not prepared to pull a fair share of weight is not to your advantage. While you are making constructive progress through hard work and innovation in one direction, you can let this asset flow out the back door because of an unreliable or wasteful partner. Equally, be careful you do not take on too much because a partner lets you down. Use your judgment and have plans well laid before March 2. Be active in increasing business assets between February 22 and April 5.

Whatever you choose to do to make your mark, this year should be well starred from early on. You should approach life in a positive manner, using all the intuition and sensitivity at your command in order to make this a super year. A great deal will depend on the manner in which you coordinate your life between constructive effort and work, and in cooperating with partners and loved ones. This will be the key to realizing your ambitions that should be fulfilled before the year is out. It is not the year to sit back and expect everything to fall in your lap. Make hay while the sun shines if you really want to enjoy 1987.

DAILY FORECAST
January—December 1987
JANUARY

1. THURSDAY. Quiet.   Start the New Year on a quiet note. You may need to be at peace in order to catch up on a bit of rest. Most of your friends will doubtless feel the same. There is little chance of getting involved, even if you are up and about. There may be cause to look at the family bank account. It will not be a pleasant job so soon after the holidays. The picture presented could be disheartening. Do not worry too much. Entertaining may have been a little more expensive than you thought. Keep a sense of proportion. An old flame could have come back into your life over the holiday. Think of the resolutions you have made a few hours ago and try to avoid breaking any of them today.

2. FRIDAY. Good.   Fully refreshed, you should make this a positive day. Working conditions will seem much more lively and to your liking. Bright ideas that have been developed over the months can be introduced. If you play your cards right you could gain deserved recognition for services rendered. It is a day to be considerate of your partner. Much can be achieved through a close liaison that has a bit of feeling. Make arrangements to meet a loved one early in the day. Artistic interests can be jointly enjoyed with someone you appreciate as a close friend. An unexpected new working arrangement can boost the family funds and relieve you of some of your earlier worry.

3. SATURDAY. Exciting.   Head for the country. If you want to make the most of this weekend break, you could do so by traveling with your loved one to see friends. Make an effort not to spend too much time, if any, on weekend chores. Use your imagination to devise some distraction that will appeal to all concerned. The studious types will meet others who can share their interests and perhaps develop into some long-standing relationships. Since traveling votes strongly in your pattern this month, make good use of any opportunity to spread your wings and gain a bit more knowledge. What you experience today may be useful in the future for both business and pleasure.

4. SUNDAY. Splendid. Make the most of your lovelife. All systems are go for those of you who are in love and unattached. It is probable that you have been attracted to someone at a distance. Try heading somewhere that takes you into new surroundings. Some will be making plans for this year's vacation. Harmony between partners should lead to a good choice of resort. Look after the small things if you are trying to please someone. Every little bit counts. Anything that allows you to make maximum use of your natural talents should be practiced. It is a day to do your own thing without upsetting anyone. Company is a necessity if you want to really enjoy yourself.

5. MONDAY. Variable. Be gentle with your partner. The last few days have been enjoyable and relaxing. The return to work and business worries may put you or your partner somewhat on edge. It is essential to look after career interests, but try to avoid cutting yourself off completely from the domestic scene. Those who are traveling a great deal at this time may find this separation puts a strain on marriage. Be as understanding as you can and all will work out well. You will need to practice some independence or show initiative before the day is out. Someone is likely to feel upset. Be honest with yourself and everyone with whom you are involved. Look after work prospects.

6. TUESDAY. Sensitive. Do what you can to strengthen working ties. Business prospects will survive or perish according to the way you apply yourself to the work in hand. It is a day to stabilize and consolidate. You will not have things go all your own way. Partnership could be tested. Quite important people may have ideas that do not match your own. It is no time to doubt your ability to carry through what you have started. Look after your reputation. Try not to keep unreliable company or company that is not working happily with you. There could be problems that could affect your prospects and your social standing. Trust your own judgment and the advice you get from older people.

7. WEDNESDAY. Lucky. Keep your eyes open for any chance to make a quick killing. Events early in the day are likely to change the established pattern of work. Be prepared to innovate. If you are on the ball you can be ahead of all the competition when the news does eventually break. Self-employed people should be prepared to get away from their normal practice in order to get business. You have a good business mind and can spot a bargain when you see it. There can be some reward at the end of the day. Partners will understand what you have been through and will show their affection. Business finances could look healthier. But it is still early in the year and too soon to predict the outcome.

8. THURSDAY. Satisfactory. Handle cash with care. You can take in with one hand and give away with the other. This is fine as long as one hand knows what is happening with the other. Pleasurable pursuits can be expensive. Be careful that company money is not wasted on injudicious speculation. A partner can give you good advice and keep you on the right track. Make a deal with someone you trust who has joint interests at heart. But keep away from those who are tempting or challenging you. Partnership arrangements should be made. This seems like a good time to spend the evening with your loved one at some social engagement. Your feelings for children may be stirred happily.

9. FRIDAY. Excellent. You should find this will be a very friendly day. Those you meet will be eager to agree and will act positively. Influential people will be cooperative and enthusiastic about your plans. Such social interests that you enjoy will find enthusiastic support among those who count and are influential. Legal advice should come freely if you need it. Take this opportunity to develop and use any means of publicity. Business profits should increase because you can attract interested parties who have much to offer. Students should have a particularly good day. Good fortune will assist any who are about to take examinations. Travelers will find what they seek at the end of their journeys.

10. SATURDAY. Fair. You may feel like keeping your own company today. There is a chance that a previous engagement with someone you admire is broken. This could be upsetting and you could retreat into your shell for a little while. Do not expect too much from relationships. Your opposite number could have problems. If you are positive you will soon recognize an opportunity that will propel you into the social limelight. Take the bull by the horns and do what you can to assist. A new relationship may be formed, though it may not have romantic connotations. Be considerate of those who need private attention. This is a good day to make family plans for future travel.

11. SUNDAY. Disturbing. It may be necessary to comfort someone you know who is in difficulty. A way for making positive advances to bring about a solution is not yet clear. Accept a delay. Should your own health give you cause for concern, be patient. It will get straightened out later, but not today. Arrangements may have to be postponed if someone you were to meet in private does not arrive. All secret actions will be suspect. While it is to your advantage to do whatever you have to do in private, be sure your actions are honorable. All will be revealed in due course and you should have a firm footing for any arrangement made today. Accept responsibility cheerfully.

12. MONDAY. Mixed.   Watch your actions and do only that which seems to be right. Someone may try to overturn your work and efforts. This may be only half the battle. Others in business may have a particular line of action to press and will try to keep you out of the action. Get yourself organized early in the day and you will be able to cope with whatever comes you way. Partners could let you down if they are not kept up to date with your activities. Influential people with your interests at heart will also appreciate information. They should be willing to help ou. You may feel like going it alone. Consider whether this is the wisest course and whether or not you are not being overly sensitive.

13. TUESDAY. Deceptive.   All is not what it may seem. Those you normally trust with your every confidence may seem a little distant. There will be good reason for this, but you will not know for a day or two. So, act with discretion in all your personal dealings. Give away only that which is necessary and follow your own hunches. Romantic developments are likely. A dear friend from the past can come again into your life. This could be a regular monthly arrangement if you wish it that way. Seek pleasure from long-standing interests. You may be restricted in the time available this year for pleasure, so stick to what you know well.

14. WEDNESDAY. Variable.   You face a challenge. A decision could be made today that will have lasting repercussions. Joint acceptance of responsibilities will need to be considered. You can either take on an individual role for a while or come to a satisfactory agreement after all the cards are on the table. Legal advice can be a great help in any difficulty. Some of you will travel far and enjoy the change. Getting away from immediate personal responsibilities and problems can be a huge relief. Try to keep your emotions under control if you are in a sticky position. Use your intuition to make an important choice. This has worked for you in the past and you should have every confidence in it.

15. THURSDAY. Challenging.   Put your best foot forward. There can be some challenge to accept if you are to make the most of the day's work. Business presents problems that you gladly accept. It will mean more money in the bank if you get cracking and make progress with various projects. Working conditions are also favorable. Rewards from work should be greater than usual. Work colleagues are particularly cooperative. Look after your career prospects, which may need active attention. Otherwise, your talents could go unrecognized. Keep an eye on your personal output as well as your social possibilities if you want to make the right sort of impression. Money isn't everything, but it makes life easier.

16. FRIDAY. Good. Persevere with your main interest. This is no time to change your plans. A little later in the day, you may possibly be in a better position to start something quite new. At first, it is the reliable and long-standing practice that will be tops. Rely on the support of older people. Responsibility will do you no harm and should be fully rewarded. You are not one to avoid your fair share of work, so you can cope adequately with all that is presented today. Anything you earn should be salted away till you can find an appropriate type of investment. You may be given good news about a health matter that had caused previous worry. This is not necessarily your own, but could be that of a family member.

17. SATURDAY. Adverse. Active business engagements can bring problems. For those who own or manage a store on the weekend, this can be an upsetting day. The public may be very fickle and you could have quite a job getting them to part with their money. Look out for devious business tactics. If you're in a market, keep a weather eye open for pickpockets and other such cunning people. Associates with whom you try to do business or make arrangements with can be unsure of their ground. There is no hope of making a bargain under such conditions. Apply your energies to things that concern the good working order of your affairs. You will get far enough today to satisfy yourself.

18. SUNDAY. Sensitive. Relatives may let you down over your weekend arrangements. There could be a family matter developing that somewhat puts a damper on local activities. Journeys undertaken today may be necessary, but they will not be very inspiring. Some need can arise for a serious look at basic relationships. Home studies may be necessary to clear up a problem that is bothering you. Get your books and accounts into good order. There seems little hope of having a day of rest or one in which you can relax with a pleasant hobby. It may prove to be expensive if you insist on looking for adventure or the bright lights. It would perhaps be best to take things as easy as conditions permit.

19. MONDAY. Demanding. Problems at work greet you at once. You may be asked to travel some considerable distance on business. Local matters may need immediate attention, but you cannot be in two places at once. This is a day when you must get your priorities and your schedule absolutely right. And that will not be easy. Unexpected developments at your place of work can cause production machinery to break down or to be so unreliable as to be useless. Take all the hindrances as they come and cope with them one at a time, in the correct priority. Only by being organized are you going to make a success of this day. Eventually you may get off on your trip, if it is essential.

20. TUESDAY. Tricky. Domestic conditions can be fluid. You may have your own plans for the day. Business interests must come first with some, while domestic affairs take priority with others. The family scene can become confused. When partners go in opposite directions without keeping the other advised of their aims and schedules, there will be friction. Try to be informative and honest in your dealings. Should those you deal with be vague, encourage them to be more communicative. It will be too easy to get hold of the wrong end of the stick. You can make this day a helpful one for joint resources if you are careful to keep your partner on the ball. Do this by setting a good example.

21. WEDNESDAY. Productive. Enjoy your home life. This means so much to you at any time. Today you may be inclined to bring a friend home to meet the family. For the single and unattached, this could be a friend you have met at work who is likely to become more than just a co-worker. You will be looking for something substantial in relationships at this time. Bring to a satisfactory conclusion any business concerning property that still requires completion. It is a good day to do some work on the house if you can find time. Older people will take some work off your shoulders if you want to quit early in the day. Listen to the advice they may give you about responsibility and dependability.

22. THURSDAY. Disturbing. Be careful how you proceed with partnership affairs. Opposition can come from your partner, with support from influential people. If there is anything of family interest that needs to be settled, be prepared to negotiate. Do not expect to get support from any quarter. All is not against you, but you do need to be careful if you are handling property matters. Make no agreement at this stage. If you are unsure or unsettled, leave final arrangements until a later date. This is not the time to contemplate rearranging the home or redecorating. There are bound to be differing points of view about nearly everything. After all, everyone is entitled to his own opinion.

23. FRIDAY. Manageable. You are inclined to be very sure of your pleasure needs. There is no possibility of your being thrown off course if you make up your mind to get your way. Try to avoid being too forthright or dogmatic. It may upset someone. Romantic interests can occupy your whole attention. You could be completely mesmerized by someone you meet or have met on a previous occasion last month. If you go all out to please someone it could be an expensive proposition. Agreement can be reached on a business proposal. Put yourself out, if you must, to settle the deal. This is no time for pussyfooting. Take positive steps to get your family finances straightened out.

24. SATURDAY. Disquieting. You may be concerned about your own health or that of a dear one. This is not the time to worry, but like everyone else, you will have your fears for the future. Something of importance could crystallize today. A settlement can be reached and an important matter finalized. Work should bring a reward that has taken some time to mature. A relationship can finally be understood for its true value. This should give you considerable satisfaction. You may be a bit worried about your ability to cope. Perhaps you have too much time on your hands at the moment. If you were fully employed you would probably not have time to worry nearly as much as you now do.

25. SUNDAY. Variable. Take time to unwind if the past few days have got you down. Today a good many things are going your way, but you may not yet realize this. Responsibilities connected with work may keep you from relaxing. If you feel that way, be logical and consider all the possibilities. You will find that the situation is in no way as bad as you had first thought. You can only live one day at a time and this is not the right time to be impulsive. Your intuition should tell you that everything will turn out right in the long run. You have more security than you realize and you should be thankful for this blessing.

26. MONDAY. Disquieting. Business routine returns with the Monday rush. Take everything as it comes. You undoubtedly gained some benefit from a weekend respite, away from the hurly-burly. But you will now need all your energy to cope with the unexpected that seems to occur when you are not back into the working swing. Try to avoid getting emotional. If your colleagues are a bit odd, take it all with a pinch of salt. Do not get exasperated and throw up a good job. There is no need to jeopardize your opportunities because someone else is having problems. Aggravation is likely to set off stomach problems. This is no time to have to embark on a miserable diet. Nor is it a time to look for new jobs.

27. TUESDAY. Useful. Someone may think you are a soft touch. You may be feeling sensitive and cooperative, but anyone who hopes to take advantage could be surprized. A business colleague may try to put one over on you. There is no possibility of being cooperative with such a person, so just ignore that attempt. You may feel like taking on all opposition if you are emotionally aroused. Cool it. Relax with someone whose company you appreciate. Look for recreation rather than work if the atmosphere in the office is too lively and aggressive. Self-employed people should be able to work a deal that will boost finances. Family funds can be increased, if you get full cooperation from all.

28. WEDNESDAY. Uneventful. Get personal relationships into good working harmony if there is any need for such measures. This is a day to concentrate on whatever you feel is worthy of attention. Everything will appear clear and manageable if you give yourself time to contemplate. There appears to be no reason why you should not take life easy today. Take your partner into your full confidence if there is any family or mutual matter that needs discussion. All kinds of problems will appear very minor when you put your heads together. Remember the maxim that a trouble shared is a trouble halved. Equate family income with work prospects and see what this means in practical terms.

29. THURSDAY. Sensitive. This should be a good day for business projects. There should be no difficulty in getting something off the ground quite easily and with a boost. Relationships with workers who share your daily routine may be somewhat strained. You may all be feeling the pressure of work. But it would be well to remember the long-term advantages that come with reliable and constructive occupations. Your job should be quite secure and is your best investment for the future. Look after family prospects by putting a little away for a rainy day. Family insurance and pension rights are matters you should not neglect at this time.

30. FRIDAY. Good. Put yesterday's thoughts into practice. Look after the family resources in a practical manner and see that insurance matters are dealt with. Your partner may have as much to contribute as you do and this will be mutually satisfying. It is particularly heartening to reach the end of the month with a healthy bank balance. Think of family needs such as what the children will require and the more long-term essentials for the family future. A sudden turn of events can be to your advantage. There is a possibility that your recent consideration of responsibility will mean a change of job. Look to the future for what good it can bring. Set yourself goals with time limits for achieving them.

31. SATURDAY. Sensitive. Changes may continue to affect your working life and bring useful financial rewards. It will be helpful, therefore, to accept such alterations in your work schedule as are to your advantage. You could be in a very sensitive state of mind at the moment. Traveling may be a major part of your present lifestyle. There is a danger that you may be too much on the go to appreciate all the alterations that are constantly taking place around you. Make the most of the opportunity to be yourself. Sensitivity is your strong point, provided you use it in the right way. Be creative and loving. This is where you shine. And both attributes come easily for you so don't hold back.

FEBRUARY

1. SUNDAY. Active. This could be a very busy Sunday. There will be little chance of your taking it easy or relaxing away from everyday involvement. You could travel and see the sights somewhere out of town. The possibility of this depends a great deal on your friends. Take care of arrangements and you should be all right. But do not expect everything to go smoothly all the time. An unexpected event may upset your plans at some point in the day. This could throw the whole family into a spin. Try to avoid getting uptight. Cooperation with family and friends can straighten out a lot of the possible problems. You could express interest in visiting places that have educational worth.

2. MONDAY. Rewarding. Cooperative action may be a bit shaky early in the day. Later on you will feel more positive and able to do your own thing with the conviction of know-how. There seems to be a chance to improve the family fortunes if you are observant enough to draw someone with influence into your sphere of operations. A senior member of the family, or someone well versed in tax matters, can put you on the right track. It is a day to attend to business matters with gusto. Let nothing stand in your way if you feel you are onto a good thing. Remember that the early indications are not necessarily those you should accept as being an accurate guide to the day's potential.

3. TUESDAY. Promising. You could be strongly attracted to someone who works with you. This is likely to come as a surprise. It is amazing how someone can turn you on quite unexpectedly. Business, also, could be full of surprises. Partners could be more cooperative and this could signify a change of tune. Keep your eyes open for changes of mood and conditions. These may give you a business opening to do yourself some good. Someone is likely to make a quick switch of plans. This can work to your advantage. Innovate and change your work schedule if you think this will improve output. Fellow workers are most cooperative. With these conditions holding, you can go places.

4. WEDNESDAY. Challenging. You may have to choose between work and play. A heavy love attraction could put you on the spot. You are well aware that business pressures should claim your attention. So you must make up your mind. It is difficult to please everyone, but look after that which is most important. Your partner will be feeling tender and romantic. Perhaps it is best to wait until soft lights and sweet music are appropriate before you react. Do what you have to do during the day with vigor. Social life can be most entertaining later on, provided you have the right company. You must be fully in tune with your partner for the evening. Avoid confrontations with jealous people.

5. THURSDAY. Confusing. Friends could let you down today. They could be extremely self-centered and not at all inclined to cooperate. This is just when you were feeling the need for friendship. Family interests are likely to conflict with social activities. You could upset someone of importance by deciding to take on a public role. Do not expect senior family members to go along with you all the way. This could give you the urge to go it alone. If so, tread with much caution. Do nothing out of pique. Business is likely to produce some problems. Financial matters are not as straightforward as you had thought. Prepare your ground or do a little planning, rather than taking the initiative.

6. FRIDAY. Worrisome. News in general could make you depressed. But your inborn sympathies are stirred by word from afar that someone you know is in trouble. Students will find it difficult to concentrate on their work. Although they are well aware that quiet is needed, there is a temptation to be out and about in their area. Private consultation with a legal person is not likely to produce what you are seeking. You could need more time to get things in order. So be content to accept a quiet period when you can collect your thoughts. It may be necessary to visit someone you know in a hospital. You could be more concerned with the troubles of others than your own.

7. SATURDAY. Mixed. Tidy up loose ends and attend to personal matters that demand privacy. Self-employed people will find it appropriate to do some office work well away from their usual place of employment. Those who have to do business today will achieve much more by dealing on a private level or by appointment than by announcing their wares in advertisements and by flyers. It will be a day when you can choose, to a large extent, what is best for you to do. Being a good business person you are not likely to strike out. Be prepared to accept or to argue against the opposite point of view, but even more important, listen to the opposition's beliefs. Hard bargaining could be necessary.

8. SUNDAY. Disappointing. A quiet day would have great appeal for you. You and your partner may find it pleasant to get away from your familiar surroundings for a day out of town. The unexpected, however, could upset your plans for the day. Do not put too much faith in a firm schedule. At some future time, you may appreciate the limelight. You could gain some personal or private satisfaction from a task well done in public. Your partner could be the mainstay if events disturb the harmony of the weekend. Health problems might interfere with arrangements. You seem ready to consider others' needs to some degree. You may well find yourself going in many directions before the day is over.

9. MONDAY. Changeable. Partners can be very demanding. You may feel obliged to attend to their interests. You have a soft spot for someone who is very close to you. But even so, demands can become a bit wearing. For the unattached, it will be a day to remember. Enjoy your romance and do not settle down too readily. It is a good day to stay on the move or seek relationships that are good but not binding. Travel around a bit. The change of scene will do you good. It will be interesting to meet a variety of people, rather than just the few you are accustomed to seeing. Students should find all systems go. Personal aims can be achieved without bother. If you have a legal matter to settle, why not do it now?

10. TUESDAY. Reassuring. Visit distant relatives to follow up a romantic affair. You could be feeling very sensitive toward someone you wish could be more meaningful in your life. Be prepared to travel in order to make your point. It is a good day to develop any creative talent or interest. Be clever and purposeful. You can go a long way toward making a hobby or interest much more important in your life. Imagination should be working well. You will feel in tune with most things around you, so you are unlikely to make a false move. With emotions running free, you seem ready to develop a relationship that will mean much to you.

11. WEDNESDAY. Challenging. Be on the lookout for a chance to make your mark. Opportunity is with you today, so no matter whatever you have on your mind, be optimistic. Finances will be of importance during the day. You could find that someone who carries a bit of weight in the money market can be of help. Get out and about when you can. There is much going on in the wide world and you need to be prepared to seize any financial opportunity if your resources are to match your future requirements. Friendly people abound. Because you feel loving and optimistic you will radiate harmony and attract nice people. It should be a good day for taking examinations.

12. THURSDAY. Disquieting. You will find few bargains today. Some pressure appears to being exerted where you are likely to be hurt. Do not be tempted to go overboard on anything. Too much is at stake for you to be careless or a spendthrift, no matter what the cause. There may be some need to travel on the spur of the moment. Take as much precaution as possible. But do not expect conditions to be comfortable when your preparations for the trip have been so sketchy. Someone is likely to have great ideas for expanding work production. Take no step to put such plans into action. Sleep on everything that appears out of the blue. Romantic affairs can be expensive and emotionally disturbing.

13. FRIDAY. Sensitive. Some of you will be planning weddings or engagement parties. This seems a good time to finalize a courtship and get the essentials sorted out. It will also be a day to do things on your own. So you can make your mind up and be positive in all your decisions. Working conditions seem settled. Finances should be good and you should feel that you are getting where you want to go. A decision may not please everyone. You could meet opposition from a parent or senior member of the family. Consider all the basic factors and be realistic. It is essential that you stand on your own feet, and also that you win the support of people who matter.

14. SATURDAY. Good.   Relatives and friends will make you welcome. You may feel very loving toward a partner and want to become involved in whatever interests are his or hers. This is a day for joint festivities. Romance is never far away. You are not in the mood to travel far to seek a companion. Perhaps you have traveled enough on business lately to suit you. A bit of business initiative can uncover an unknown asset. Work changes are possible. Do not be afraid to examine very thoroughly any new project that is proposed. You are in a position to find out the economics and basic particulars. Do your research thoroughly. When you know exactly what you hold in your hand you can ask a true price.

15. SUNDAY. Mixed.   It will be better to stay near home today than travel afar. If you are to appreciate Sunday as a day of rest, you will find the local scene much more to your liking. Means of transport are not up to par. You are likely to meet delays or hindrances, even at local levels. A long journey would really be out of the question. Look after your health. You may have gone a little too far with partying last night and feel like a dish rag. Take it easy. Some of you will be looking forward to the future. This is the time to confer with someone who carries a bit of influence in financial circles. Look for good sound backing if you are ambitious and have a workable scheme.

16. MONDAY. Easygoing.   You would appreciate a quiet day at home. If conditions and duties allow for this, take advantage of an opportunity to accomplish little chores. They usually constitute much of the domestic scene. Business will carry on quite well without you. A ramble through the family photograph albums never goes amiss when you have a spare moment. Your antique collection, while a burden at times, can also be a source of quiet joy. Opportunity plays a large part in your life during the year. So you should spend some time thinking how best to use it when career and business affairs are stimulated in the spring. Property transactions should be considered if you have plans to move soon.

17. TUESDAY. Sensitive.   You may find it difficult to share your joys or worries. Partners are a bit under the weather and may not be seeing things in the same light as yourself. Tactful handling can overcome almost any problem. Perhaps your loved one feels somewhat neglected. Be gentle and talk to anyone who is feeling this way in the household. It will be advisable to get involved in company in order to brighten things up. Travel around a bit if this will relieve any possible boredom or feeling of loss. There are interesting people you can meet if you get out of the house and seek a change of company. There is also a possibility that you may expect too much of a good thing and overdo it.

18. WEDNESDAY. Satisfactory. Cater to major family interests. All members of the family could be involved in any property transactions today. Senior family members will be full of praise for your interest in home affairs. Business interests clash with family responsibilities. Match one with the other and get your priorities right. You have plenty of backing and support in whatever you consider to be right. Take advice given by an important person who understands the legal side of investment for the future. Family fortunes are important, as is anything connected with home and family. A rearrangement of responsibilities at work will fit in with your domestic plans.

19. THURSDAY. Fair. You will have a chance to renew contact with an old flame. Enjoy a monthly reunion. Some will be thinking seriously of future relationships of a more settled nature. Traveling should open up some opportunities for pleasure. Booking accommodations for travel for vacations in the future can now be undertaken with confidence. You could enter wholeheartedly into sporting activities. Involvement with others will give you pleasure. It may be necessary to travel out of town to really appreciate how much the countryside has to offer. A letter from someone dear to you who lives far from your home will be most welcome. Keep in touch with this person.

20. FRIDAY. Lucky. Your luck could shine. If you feel the urge, go out and look for opportunity. Seldom does anything drop right into your lap, so you should be ready to spot a winner when you see it. A relationship can be developed, if given enough encouragement. A legal arrangement can bring happiness into someone's life. You will meet outspoken people on your travels and should be prepared to be equally broadminded. A worthwhile business venture could be started. There should be no fear of getting the right sort of challenging conditions if you are feeling adventurous. Speculation should not be risky. Your judgment is good and this will keep you from taking any bad risks.

21. SATURDAY. Disconcerting. Attend to all your regular weekend duties before you consider tomorrow. It could be a bit boring, but essentials must be attended to. Distant attractions may distract you. Try to avoid getting involved with too many people who will hold different views as to what is a priority. If you keep your nose to the grindstone you will accomplish all that has to be done. Health may be worrisome. There could be changes afoot at your workplace. Thoughts of this possibility may make you rather nervous or at least somewhat anxious. In consequence, you could be snappy. News generally is not likely to cheer you up. It seems like a day for you to keep to yourself insofar as is feasible.

22. SUNDAY. Unsettling. Though you realize this is a day of rest, you might find it beneficial to meet someone with professional know-how before the day is through. You could be torn between duty and pleasure. While your natural inclination is to get out and about for a much-needed change, you may be obliged to look after someone's needs. Try to moderate your activities. There is a possibility that unexpected events can upset your schedule. This will try your temper and your patience. But you must be honest with yourself and take any appropriate action to deal with events. Do not overdramatize any situation. It may not be as bad as you imagine. There will be a logical answer to any problem.

23. MONDAY. Misleading. Try to avoid being too rational. You work much better when you react to true emotion and intuition because you are a sensitive person. Today you are likely to find yourself in a highly sensitive mood. You could be either very romantic or you may be feeling sorry for yourself. Do not push yourself, but allow everything to take its natural course. In this way you can enjoy a certain amount of peace and quiet or pleasant company who will appreciate your sensitivity. Initiative is not your scene today. Nor is it the day to make positive decisions, especially with respect to permanent relationships. So try to relax and enjoy the freedom of mind and body that gives you so much pleasure.

24. TUESDAY. Buoyant. You should be able to handle your relationships more easily today. Something will have fallen into place and you can feel more secure about a personal issue. Some of you will accept a proposal of marriage. Others will actually tie the knot, knowing this is the end of one great phase in life and the beginning of another. For those with business on their minds this will be a day to settle a deal. All details should have, by now, been agreed upon, and there is no need to quibble over settlement. It is a fine day for those with artistic talent. Take every opportunity to develop and promote those talents so that everyone will be aware of your gift. Publicity should be greatly to your advantage.

25. WEDNESDAY. Worrisome. Ill-judged actions are likely to rebound and upset the family. Be particularly careful in all matters connected with the family fortunes. This applies to people as well as money. Someone may try to badger you into buying an investment or insurance policy you do not really need. Resist all such advances, even if you have to be blunt. Any such approach deserves an equally impolite rebuff. Avoid like the plague all quick investment proposals which will indeed be pure speculation. Business money could be placed at risk. Do not encourage spending at this time, though it may seem to be necessary. It is far better to sit back and take stock before committing yourself.

26. THURSDAY. Rewarding. Now you can feel more comfortable in handling joint finances. Cooperation is freely available, especially in influential quarters. The mechanics and use of investment will be much clearer after you have had time to think about a new proposal. This one has a lot to offer and incorporates advanced concept. Workers will notice a different attitude on the part of management. Advantageous proposals regarding pension benefits could be announced. Be prepared to get down to hard, constructive work today. Those who are self-employed should be able to make solid progress in building up business. Invest in the future while the opportunity lasts.

27. FRIDAY. Successful. Today is a red-letter day. There appears little to cloud the horizon. For some, this will mean marriage. Others will start out on a great journey that will take them far from their native land. You love your home, but are also known as a great traveler. This will be the year you will fulfill a travel plan you have been contemplating for some time. Enjoy the sense of satisfaction and accomplishment. Do not attempt to make light of it, for many will envy you. For the actor or actress, this is a day to make the most of the limelight. For those in love, it will be a highpoint of the year. Be loving and emotional. It is a day to be your natural self, so let all know who and what you are.

28. SATURDAY. Mixed. Take time, if you can, to sort out the ups and downs of the day. You could be fortunate in some ways. This could give you extra confidence to cope with anything, or it could make you careless. At some stage you are likely to come up against an awkward situation or an unusual person who can gum up the works. Be considerate. Don't fly off on a tangent. Older people will have ideas and opinions different from yours. Someone is likely to say that you are eccentric. Use your sensitive gifts to get things into the right proportion. Your judgment is not lacking. Events seem bent on throwing you off course, but you should not let them do so. Maintain your sense of direction and balance.

MARCH

1. SUNDAY. Fair.   A change of air and scene will do you good. The weekend should be suitable for travel and you should make full use of the day. Get off to an early start before traffic gets heavy. You should have some good fortune that will start the day off well. Some may be unable to travel, but they should make travel arrangements for the future. There may be some uncertainties later in the day. A partner may let you down, or some mutual arrangement could fall through. Do not put too much trust in joint affairs. This is a better day to handle your own business affairs. Something helpful in the line of business could be developing, but there could also be some trouble.

2. MONDAY. Good.   Get off to a good start this first working day of the week. Be firm in all your dealings. You should consolidate or hold your ground if you have any dealings to complete. Make the most of a working relationship that can be good for your reputation. Business prospects are as good as you can expect until the end of the month. Take advantage of your chances while you can. You could win some recognition that will be lasting. It is most important this year to look after essentials. Today you should be aware of the responsibility and potential reward that lies in doing a good job. Exercise authority where this is necessary.

3. TUESDAY. Useful.   It should be a nice day to enjoy with someone you love. Provided you have a full wallet, there are great possibilities for sharing pleasure. If you are somewhat short of money, do not be too ambitious with your romantic plans. It could be all too easy to get out of your depth. However, an understanding partner can make this a most enjoyable day and one to remember. Business finances are best left alone for the day. You could waste money or perhaps put it at risk. All ventures may not be as profitable as you are led to think. Expense accounts should be reviewed if this is part of your workaday routine. Friends can get you into trouble if you take them too seriously later on.

4. WEDNESDAY. Sensitive.   Social affairs could attract your attention to a charitable cause! A new venture can appeal to your better nature if it benefits children. Start a friendly relationship if you feel there is a future in it. Be positive if you wish to succeed today. You could be aware of developments overseas that should be to your benefit. Someone with influence in the legal profession could help you with humanitarian interests. Use such backing to make progress that will benefit many people you know. Personal relationships may cause you a few problems. You cannot be in two places at once, so may have to disappoint someone who relies on you for support. This is no crisis.

5. THURSDAY. Quiet. Take full advantage of a quiet period to be with friends who appreciate your company. It should be a private sort of day. That does not mean you will be out of circulation. It is rather that you tend to seek the right people to share your privacy and enjoyment. You should have plenty of cooperation. Partnership finances could seem to be much more settled than previously. Traveling could be irksome. You will not want to be drawn out of your seclusion. A business opportunity may come up late in the day. You will want to deal with it quietly, so you will not be likely to disturb anyone. Make appropriate arrangements for later action.

6. FRIDAY. Difficult. Someone may resent your success. An attempt can be made to upset your social plans. Do not expect to have everything your own way if you have plans for a public venture. Young lovers could find romantic plans completely over-turned without warning. If someone is aggressive you may have to call for help from friends. Pleasures could be expensive. Consider this before you get involved in any social occasion. There could be arguments among friends that might break up a pleasant evening. For those whose pastime is competitive sport, this could be a challenging evening; no quarter asked and none given.

7. SATURDAY. Manageable. The break from work should do you good. If you are obliged to be on duty, you could resent it. A good idea would be to keep yourself fully employed, nose to the grindstone. Time on your hands could easily lead to brooding over missed chances or past mistakes. What's gone is gone. Look to the future and make plans whenever you have a quiet moment. You could be concerned for someone's health. Do what you can to help. You are at your best when looking after others. This will help to keep you from worrying about your own problems. They will not be improved by negative thoughts in any event.

8. SUNDAY. Sensitive. Do what you feel is right for you. Your partner may be undecided, so do not bother too much trying to persuade anyone to share your day. Travel seems to be good for you. It is not necessary to go very far, but at least you can be diverted from the weekday concerns. You could be tempted to take a risk. This may come in the way of a wager or challenge. Think before you take up the gauntlet. So much time could be wasted and your reputation could be lost if you do the wrong thing. Think about a proposition you received today from a distant place. This could be helpful, but the time is not yet ripe for judicious action.

9. MONDAY. Rewarding. Put your personal plans to the test. Fortune should favor you if you are direct in your dealings. You should find support from friends and recognition from people with influence. Do not waste your time on trivialities. Be prepared to get around and to enjoy some traveling. Professional people have your interests at heart. Look for some personal reward if you are engaged in studies or examinations. Use your energies constructively to promote some social venture that has public backing. You should get good publicity today, so why not make hay while the sun shines? Make your point both loud and clear. You should have little trouble in winning people over to your way of thinking.

10. TUESDAY. Uneventful. This could be a lull before great activity. You should be feeling quite content in some ways. Business prospects are likely to be good. Things could now be picking up noticeably after earlier preparations. Tidy up any personal loose ends. You will be considering money matters soon, so you should have your books in order. This assumes that you want to make progress in the right way. Joint finances should be considered in relation to outlays for pleasure and personal savings. Be prepared for upsets if you have not yet made adequate preparations for the days ahead. Relationships can be disturbed if someone is too materialistic.

11. WEDNESDAY. Difficult. You have reached a financial crossroads. It will be essential to get yourself organized. Pressure could be applied from all directions. You must be prepared to take action in order to remain solvent. Consider expense as it applies to joint resources, social involvement, and entertainment. Have you been pushing too far in one direction? Do you think you have the mixture right? Whatever conclusions you arrive at, today must offer you some serious considerations. It is not the day to take any action you cannot fully support. What is good for one aspect of interest could be bad for another.

12. THURSDAY. Challenging. Problems will take some time to clear up today. Serious matters need serious attention and action. You may not make a lot of headway, but at least you will have a better idea of the whole situation. Take things slowly. Avoid making any arrangements that cannot be sustained. Be prepared to work hard for all you get. Instead of worrying as you were before, you will soon be achieving and gaining experience and expertise. Older and more reliable people should be able to help you out at work. A responsible attitude is always the safest when you are in any doubt about procedure. Keep your health under consideration. You cannot function properly if you are under par.

13. FRIDAY. Strenuous. Don't expect to settle down for long. It seems that everyone will want you to be on the go. Local matters should really take priority, but there could be bad news that will take you out of town. Try to arrange a schedule if you have to keep in touch with home base. You are likely to improvise, but it is better to have some kind of plan rather than none at all. Poor publicity can give you a headache. A script could be rejected. You do not seem to hit it off with legal advisors either. Perhaps you should settle down to do your homework better. Relatives have problems. You are likely to be let down if you decide to make a visit.

14. SATURDAY. Enjoyable. This is a day to attend to essentials and then to enjoy good company. The weekend is always interesting, since it provides an opportunity to do some stock taking and also to get yourself organized. If you are looking forward to the social attractions later in the day, you may find routine matters are somewhat boring. But this need not spoil your day or the evening. You will have a lot of energy to spare for whatever you decide to do. Enthusiastic friends will soon have you fully engaged in activities you enjoy. Relatives are cooperative and glad to enjoy a weekend get-together. Some may be a little annoyed if they feel they have been overlooked. Be considerate of everyone.

15. SUNDAY. Disconcerting. There is no question of your having a quiet weekend. Any plans you make can be shattered early in the day. Something is likely to break down and leave you in a jam. Do not put your trust in anything that is not well tried and dependable. Instant friendship is risky. Family quarrels can arise if relatives try to interfere in intimate family matters. Some sort of priority system will have to be devised if you are to avoid future squabbles. Traveling is unwise. You could find it difficult to concentrate on one thing at a time. People you meet can be eccentric or scatterbrained. Try to keep cool and avoid extremes.

16. MONDAY. Disappointing. You may leave home under a cloud. Conditions there can be unsatisfactory, for no particular reason. Perhaps you will be able to clear the air and your head at work. Joint decisions should not be made. If you are uncertain about something, sleep on it. Discuss with your partner any problem that needs to be shared. But do not take any steps, as yet, to resolve a problem. There is every chance you do not know the full story. Someone could be kidding you along. A lovers' tiff in the home is probable. Give a soft shoulder to any one of the family who needs to unburden. It is much better to get things out of your system, too, if you are disappointed.

17. TUESDAY. Mixed. It could be difficult to patch up a relationship quarrel. Someone who means a lot to you can cause an upset. Because of distance between you, there can be misunderstandings that will get out of proportion. You may be called upon to travel. This will not suit you at all. Much can be achieved by staying where you are and attending to matters close to home. Real estate deals should give satisfaction. Property overseas is not a good investment at the moment. Look after your health if you are traveling abroad. A change of climate could be upsetting. Working projects should bring reward. For the handy person, this is a good day to look into home alterations.

18. WEDNESDAY. Variable. You can expect a day that brings emotional ups and downs. A regular engagement with someone you love can be upsetting. This is not the situation you imagined. However, something seems likely to go wrong which may mar the day. Do not be disheartened. Make what you can of your chances. Nothing will be gained by being fainthearted. For some, a creative venture will give a new interest to life. Be positive when exhibiting your talents. Imaginative cooperation can come from a partner. Look ahead and be idealistic. Romance can bloom for many who have marriage in mind. You could make your mind up today, though you may keep it to yourself for a while.

19. THURSDAY. Demanding. It will be a difficult day to keep your cool. Pressure can build up. You may feel like letting off steam and enjoying yourself, but some of your friends may not be cooperative. Conditions recently could have disturbed you. Try to put this out of your mind and concentrate on today's business and interests. If you are to make progress, you must react positively to opposition. You will feel you have to make a stand. In the process, you could lose friends, but perhaps that is not such a bad thing. Business assets should not be jeopardized. Avoid speculation or investment that has not been fully investigated. Advisers who advocate immediate action should be ignored.

20. FRIDAY. Strenuous. Be guided by your own sensitive intuition. If you are looking for opportunity, it is out there. You are entirely likely to have problems. Accept both and make the best of your chances. Your reputation can be enhanced through work or your commonsense approach to an important question. Career prospects should blossom and this could mean money in the bank. Legal matters are not likely to be straightforward. Avoid making business deals with people you cannot meet in person. Communications can be disrupted and this could easily lead to misunderstanding. Mischievous people could upset your schedule, so you will need to be philosophical and use good judgment.

21. SATURDAY. Uneventful. The past week should have been productive. This may be apparent from the state of the family accounts. In consequence, you may be tempted to go shopping with your partner. Bargains can be found if you are systematic. But as you will not be particularly eager to get rid of your hard-earned cash, you will probably use it wisely. An old friend you met at work can make the day pleasant for you. You will feel somewhat restricted. Perhaps your present commitment does not allow you all the freedom you would like. Responsibilities, nevertheless, are for your own good. You may feel protective toward a loved one who is having emotional difficulties.

22. SUNDAY. Sensitive. Relax with your partner if you want to enjoy your hard-earned Sunday. There could be an early change of plans that would leave you out on a limb. Let it pass and look for peace and quiet. A pleasant journey to see distant relatives can take you away from familiar local scenes for a nice change. It may be best to keep a low profile in order to make your partner happy. It might also be difficult to know what is going on, so let things develop and do not force an issue. This can be a very sensitive day. Being the person you are, you will soon catch on and will be able to adapt to the emerging scene. Whatever happens, do not talk business. You will upset all hopes of cooperation if you do.

23. MONDAY. Demanding. Tread with caution. You may feel everything is coming up roses, but this is not necessarily the case. Beware! Friends may have an influence on whatever happens today. You may have to choose between business and personal interests. At some time, you will not please everyone, so you should try to be tactful. Considerable force or forthrightness may have to be used if you are to do what you want. You will naturally arouse some opposition, so you must be prepared to do battle, especially in the business and financial arena. Try to avoid being too aggressive, but do not flinch from a verbal battle if you are right.

24. TUESDAY. Good. You may win recognition from your friends in high places. That could be a pleasant change if you have been struggling to get ahead for a while. Bureaucratic intervention can make things a bit smoother for you. Take this opportunity to get your taxation problems straightened out at the highest level. This will be a big help to you. Business prospects should be good. Look for the cooperation of corporate bodies who set the pattern for industry. This is the time to consider big issues. An opportunity may arise to increase family resources by wise investment. You should get good advice from a senior business friend. Look after the future of your loved ones.

25. WEDNESDAY. Important. Consolidate your recent gains. A productive and rewarding day will result if you are prepared to take on whatever comes your way. Work can give a lot of satisfaction which will be appreciated by your family. They will enjoy knowing you are happy. Something of lasting value will be forged, giving you great peace of mind. Be content with what you do or gain today. For the person who is self-employed, this is a time to come to some lasting or long-term arrangement. Cooperation will be to your advantage. You may feel able to take on someone who will ease your work load. The end of a period of pressure can improve your health. You feel strong enough for any responsibility.

26. THURSDAY. Challenging. Fortune favors the brave. It could be all systems go if you recognize your opportunities. A very great deal depends on your keeping an open mind and rising to the occasion at the appropriate time. Your reputation can be enhanced. It is a day for enjoying the limelight. Be prepared to start some business project on a high note of expectation for the future. Look ahead and be optimistic as well as up to date. Some will reach a high point in their lives. It is a day to change your social status for the better. Get organized on a legal matter. You could be tying up the loose ends of an arrangement. Traveling should be to your advantage, if you have an asset to sell.

27. FRIDAY. Easygoing. Slow down to a gentle pace. Now you should sit back and compare notes or take stock of your progress. Any attempt you may make to keep up your latest initiative will meet frustration. You will probably feel ready for a rest. Some may be tired out. So take it easy, rather than let yourself become frustrated. It could be a little difficult to concentrate. With the help of a positive friend, however, you should be able to get down to the serious consideration of your next move. Students could find this a helpful day if they are prepared to be thankful for small mercies. Contact with distant friends can be to your advantage.

28. SATURDAY. Mixed. You will feel you have achieved something and will be looking for recognition. Make the most of your public appearances, but take care to avoid hasty or erratic actions. Do not get carried away by the excitement of the moment. Expect to meet some people who will try to catch you off guard. Or they try to get you involved in something that is not as honest as you may think. There could be a great temptation to take on all comers. You could be walking on air, figuratively speaking. Think of the practicalities as well as the future possibilities and you will be able to judge everything right. The year is now beginning to blossom and you could feel as though you have a new lease on life.

29. SUNDAY. Sensitive. This should be a good day if you have nothing very energetic on your schedule. Early hours can be a bit confusing if you allow others to interfere with your weekend peace. A partner can become rather a nuisance. Perhaps there are underlying worries of which you know nothing. It is a day to get out. You may be expected to make repairs around the house, or attend to some necessary chores. If you do have to handle such tasks, try to leave them till later in the day. By then, the misunderstandings can have been cleared up. It is best not to get involved till you feel happier and have had a breath of fresh air.

30. MONDAY. Challenging. Be on the lookout for advancement. Promotion is possible if you are prepared to make your presence felt. But be prepared to back it up with productivity and sound ideas. Start the week with enthusiasm. You have a lot to gain this year and should always be aware of the opportunities open to you. Apply yourself right from the beginning of the day. Make a resolution to start work on time for the rest of the year. Be prepared to tell your superiors about ideas you have had for some time. You will get a good hearing. It is not the day to rely too heavily on the actions of others. While you have the ball in your court, take every opportunity possible to make it work for you.

31. TUESDAY. Variable. Someone near you could be extremely sensitive. You will understand how they feel, since you are such a sensitive person yourself. It could be to your advantage to

slow down a little at this point. You have been having quite a busy
time in public and at business. Try a bit of social relaxation for a
change. Involvement in some club activity where reputations are
not at stake will be good for you. It will also ease the strain that
may have developed between you and your partner. There is a
strong bond of love between you and someone close to you. Love
is something we should all foster. There is never enough.

APRIL

1. WEDNESDAY. Quiet.   Go about your business quietly today and question nothing. This is not the time to look for trouble
or expect any favors. This is just a run-of-the-mill day when you
should face no upsets, nor will you welcome anything that takes
you off the beaten track. Make the most of friendship. You should
make time to enjoy social involvement that gives you nothing extra
to do, yet interests you enough to make the day worthwhile. Look
into business finances quietly when you have the time and are not
observed. You will want to keep your own company to a large extent, or perhaps, choose your companions. Emotional ties should
not be put under pressure. Treat all as friends if you are to relax.

2. THURSDAY. Variable.   A relationship may become over-
sensitive and you could try to keep out of the way. You certainly
seem to need privacy and will be a little shy for some reason.
Rather than cause trouble you should keep to yourself. Business
prospects could be quite good. Handle any arrangments or deals
quietly behind closed doors. This will get much farther than publicity will. News from overseas could be bad. It may be difficult to
balance fact with the information you receive. Try to keep things
in balance, though this will be difficult. It is a bad day to expect
help from a private source if you are studying for the future. Take
any opportunity to promote your reputation.

3. FRIDAY. Mixed.   Complete all background work that winds
up the working week pattern. It may be a case of keeping a low
profile and carrying on with menial tasks. Problems may have to
be solved at your place of work. No one is likely to know what you
have to put up with, so tighten your belt and get on with it. Try to
avoid contact with distant places. You have no time to spare. At
some stage you could have to look after someone who is in

trouble. Your partner's health may be causing you worry. Do something to help if this is so. There is nothing like being positive. Dubious business deals should be avoided.

4. SATURDAY. Uncertain. A decision may have to be made. This can give you butterflies inside, since all emotional and nervous problems fly to your stomach. Be as honest as you can. If you are prepared to accept changes, you will probably avoid a great deal of soul searching. It may be necessary to visit someone who has had a sudden illness. Do whatever you can to help. Do not doubt your ability to cope with whatever comes your way. Even though you may wish to take a back seat, this does not mean you are not capable of undertaking a job. You will be asked if you are needed. Later on in the day, you could meet someone very dear to you who has come a long way to see you.

5. SUNDAY. Enjoyable. Try to stay completely away from business. Someone at the top could try to involve you in office affairs that would be better left till tomorrow. Rather than cause an argument that might hurt your reputation, it would be wise to hit the road. Find and enjoy the company of someone who has anything but business in mind. Partners are likely to be vague. You should be positive and take the lead if you want to get anything done at all. The unattached will find it a grand day for a trip to quiet, secluded areas. Lovers without ties can make this a really happy day. Personal ties can grow in strength.

6. MONDAY. Difficult. If you have to travel far to the place where you work, there can be some frustrations. Little may go right, so you will need to exercise great restraint and patience if you are to hold your ground. Personal matters may be important, but they may have to take second place before the day is over. Cooperation with staff will be difficult. Bad news can influence the attitude of co-workers generally. Mischievous publicity can undermine previous good relationships and make more work for someone in the future. Stick to your guns. You have your own targets for today. Try to achieve them even if there are disagreeable people trying to hold you up.

7. TUESDAY. Demanding. A new love affair may cause you trouble. Someone could try to push things a little too far and this would upset you. Stand on your dignity. It may serve to put any offender in his or her place. Financial resources can be totally depleted, if you plunge headlong into some luxury spending. Consider what you can afford before committing yourself. Opportunities abound in business if you are willing to consider work before pleasure. Get your priorities right today. A lot depends now on your sticking to your goals and making the right decisions at the right time. Something that has been hanging fire for a few days can now come to a head.

8. WEDNESDAY. Good. You should put everything in the right perspective. All systems can be go if you accept cooperation from all quarters. People in responsible positions will see things your way. Fellow workers will also be in agreement. This is the time to make hay and to feather your nest. You will meet with little opposition. Material resources need to be replenished now. See to it that you waste no opportunity for building up your reserves. Your reputation will be high if you are determined to succeed. It is only by seeing what you can achieve through hard work that you can tell whether you are going in the right direction.

9. THURSDAY. Sensitive. Keep an open mind if management suggests modernization. This is a day to look for a new lead or new approach to improve marketing. It is essential to keep ahead of the field. Personal finances could be made more secure if you look far enough ahead. A different kind of employment could add to your resources. There is no real need to be too adventurous. Just look ahead and plan for the developing future. Later in the day you could be tied up and this might make you irritable. Local affairs are likely to be topsy-turvy. An argument can cause delays. Be optimistic. If someone is making derogatory remarks about you in private, wait until they come out in the open to challenge them.

10. FRIDAY. Satisfactory. You have a great deal to be thankful for. Accept all that is regular and reliable in your daily life as a bonus. This is something you can depend on and will give you security. Your lovelife can be interesting, to say the least. You are naturally emotional, and are therefore used to ups and downs. A partner or loved one can make this a day to remember. If you are at loose ends, however, you could be led astray. Or you find that a relationship turns out differently than you had expected. Well-known and trusted relationships can be fulfilling, but casual acquaintances lead to disappointment. If you must travel a long way to meet a loved one there could be problems.

11. SATURDAY. Disturbing. This is a poor day for business if you are working today. It's not very good, either, if you are having to go around the markets. Bargains are not always what they seem. Everyone seems to be trying to put one over on their neighbor. Traveling in search of a better locale is out of the question. It would be far better to stay where you know the devil for his true value. Relatives may call for assistance. You should be ready to help, though this may not be easy or even practicable in some cases. Someone could be leaving your neighborhood who will be a loss to you. Working conditions or arrangements about future work should be pigeonholed till a later date.

12. SUNDAY. Confusing. A private family get-together can make this a happy day. Public affairs are better avoided, even if your partner is somewhat puzzled or doubtful about your motives. There could be some mismanagement, as the schedule may be a bit hazy. But in the end, you should be able to enjoy home comforts and privacy with friends. They not only have something to say but they also have ideas about making progress. Do not get involved with those who are looking for a stronger tie than friendship. Intimate partnership is not a sensible consideration at the moment. You need to think a while and should have private advice or support. You are inclined to be absentminded.

13. MONDAY. Sensitive. Consider family interests first. You could be under pressure from outside business, and so may be obliged to take note of the views of a superior at times. Seek the support of colleagues who work with you if you feel that your employer is being unfair. You will have to arrive at a solution. Your work record will stand up to any fair appraisal. Older people seem to have good advice for you. Senior members of the family will want to see you making progress. Property maintenance should be undertaken. Pressure of business can make this a bit difficult. There is good news that a family health problem is disappearing.

14. TUESDAY. Good. You could have a relationship problem early in the day. Someone could disappoint you at work. Colleagues could be a bit depressed about something. Emotional harmony will develop as the day progresses. You should find romance in the air and are likely to be deeply involved before the day is over. A lasting relationship can develop for many. For others this can be a day when old and trusted relationships demonstrate they can stand the test of time and prove their worth. Partners can be extra loving. You should be happy to share all you have to offer. Enjoy doing what gives you pleasure, but you might get even more enjoyment by sharing.

15. WEDNESDAY. Enjoyable. It is a great day if you do not have any work to do. It is not the day to attend to essentials. Romance is in the air and you should get away from everyday restrictions. A friend who lives some distance from you will consider your company worth the trip. You are feeling very sensitive, so are open to any suggestion that will prevent your suffering from boredom. It's an ideal day for those who display their talents. You will be appreciated in the best circles. Students and young people interested in furthering career prospects should feel free to follow their own ideas. Individual talents are at a premium.

16. THURSDAY. Challenging. Keep in close touch with outside affairs. Some good news could give working people a boost. Arrangements should be made to improve conditions. If you are in management, you can rely on efficiency from the floor staff if you maintain good relations. Now is the time for ambitious workers to let the top brass know who produces the things that count. Carry out changes in your daily routine if you feel like making the day brighter. Health can be boosted by variety in diet, or trying a new form of exercise to improve the figure. Be prepared to improvise. It can make life so much more interesting and lively. If you are looking for a job change, keep an eye on the classified ads.

17. FRIDAY. Upsetting. Use your charm, tact, and diplomacy today to good advantage. It may be difficult to run with the hare and hunt with the hounds, but you could probably succeed. Difficulties can arise with publicity. This could throw a monkey wrench in the works. Behind the scenes, there seems to be progress being made in the right direction. Positive management arrangements will be successful. Make private arrangements for a public engagement later on this evening. Above all, it is essential to keep your cool. With so many things going on before the weekly schedule is completed, you could feel dizzy. Allow no one to think they know your mind. Keep them all guessing.

18. SATURDAY. Sensitive. Seek recognition for your good works. You should be respected by people with influence for the contribution you have made toward production goals. You may be a little bit bored by some things in the early part of the day. This is likely to change quite quickly with the arrival of a stranger. You may be upset, or you may enjoy the change of tactics. A rest could do you good after the unusual excitement. Find a loving partner and enjoy sharing your interests. It can be an emotional day one way or another, full of ups and downs. Do not put too much credence in joint arrangements made later in the day.

19. SUNDAY. Disquieting. Rely on your own judgment. Even that could be a bit off the mark. But at least you will know you have yourself to blame. Relationships are best left alone if you start the day off on the wrong foot. You could have problems with someone who is a resident in a college or university. Do not push this issue at the moment. Relatives overseas can make life difficult. Partners are not clear-headed. Cooperation will be risky if you have joint schemes in mind for today. This may be an unavoidable restraint, so be gentle with those who share your life. There can be some pressure on you to go all-out or to take a chance. This might pay off, but consider your reputation.

20. MONDAY. Sensitive. Look out for squalls at business. Top brass is likely to be on the warpath. See to it that you have all your responsibilities well under control. Be prepared to use a bit of charm if you think this will ease the tension. Publicity should be more helpful. Let everyone know only the good news and keep the bad news out of earshot. It is not the time to further antagonize a future parent. If you are thinking of marriage, keep away from your fiancés parents who may be in an uncooperative frame of mind at the moment. Your future is important and you must consider your partner if you wish to start out on the right foot.

21. TUESDAY. Productive. Take positive action immediately to make the family funds more secure. Unknown benefits can come from private sources. You could become aware of a definite boost in your prestige. Keep in touch with all that goes on in the boardroom. What you learn can be kept secret, but it will give you a secure background knowledge of business affairs. Take steps to increase insurance for your dependents. Business ventures should be unusually productive. Something that makes you feel good can have an equally beneficial effect on the family as a whole. You should be feeling so sure of yourself that you are unlikely to make a faulty judgment. You should achieve success.

22. WEDNESDAY. Rewarding. Put working assets to good use for your dependents. This is an ideal time to put away as much as you possibly can for later use. Working relationships should be good, as long as you are prepared to show initiative and not be too restricted by routine. Inventiveness should be rewarded in tangible ways. Social activities will become more important and more diverse. Keep in touch with learned people who may be able to give you support in a civic venture. Take professional advice if that is necessary. You have two days or so to get your affairs in order. Social activities will not necessarily lead to a waste of resources, as so often happens. Team up with others for a joint operation.

23. THURSDAY. Important. This is a day to put your best foot forward. Make your presence felt so that you keep in the public eye. It could be disastrous for your image if you live too privately. If anyone has fault to find, let it be made openly and aboveboard. You may be shot down by someone who prefers not to reveal his or her identity. This will be better than your turning to deceitful tactics. Should you feel that your confidence is ebbing, remember the hard work and long hours you have put in to get where you are. That should sway you to go on with your good work. You will have a little bit of privacy that may do good. Travel should be good for you.

24. FRIDAY. Useful. Take the opportunity to strike a bargain. This should be a private undertaking that will, in due course, be good for your reputation. A welfare project you are interested in gets a boost from a public source. This is very good news. Long-distance travel can be subject to disruption. Rather than waste time try to rearrange your schedule, you should try another mode of transportation. An arrangement can be made between management and work groups that will be satisfactory to all concerned. Those in responsible positions will feel more secure. Health plans can be made. Long-term changes of diet should be to your advantage. You should feel very cooperative and understanding.

25. SATURDAY. Strenuous. There may be a conflict of interests today. Partnership misunderstandings are likely to arise if you do not give your mate almost undivided attention. This may not appeal to you, however. You will have to talk yourself out of a tight situation by being very shrewd. Opportunities abound. This could be a gala day that you can enjoy. It will be fine if you are unattached. If not, there are weekend chores to undertake, or you could find yourself in the doghouse. Perhaps you can use a bit of back-door diplomacy to finesse your problems. It may mean a few white lies, but consider something more entertaining for later on.

26. SUNDAY. Buoyant. Get out and about with children, if possible. The young folk should be in the limelight and you can give them full support. Much can be done and there will be plenty of variety to interest you and the family. Relatives can add to the happy throng in which you can become fully involved. Show your prowess and your skills if you get the chance. It is not often you can combine work with play on the weekend. Arts and crafts you have learned and developed through daily use can be displayed to advantage. You can entertain others in a totally different kind of setting to that which you usually do. The unexpected may happen at any time during a lively and nonstop day of public pleasure.

27. MONDAY. Satisfactory. It's a good time to consider marriage seriously. This could also be a good day for taking the major initiative. Some will be inclined to put all their eggs in one basket. Others may recognize that this could be the start of something big. A friendly meeting when you have stars in your eyes may lead to more important developments later on. Today is for friendship and tomorrow, who knows? Imagination can be strong. Important advances can be made in group activities. Put all your goodwill into anything that you feel deserves support. Your sympathies can be aroused to do something tangible for your fellows, but there are some things you will not be able to get away with.

28. TUESDAY. Exciting. You may have high hopes for making progress in social affairs. Some project you wish to prosper should have the full support of influential people. They understand the importance of partnerships and unselfish cooperation. It is a day for high ideals and great hopes. Give yourself as much opportunity as you can to participate in an interesting group activity. You will appreciate who your friends are. It could be quite an emotional day. You may get yourself in a bit of a tangle if friendly relationships get out of line. But your tact and common sense should keep you from getting out of your depth. Be aware of the many sensitive friends around you whose feelings can be hurt.

29. WEDNESDAY. Easygoing. Take the weight off your feet and unwind. Settle down to a bit of reflective thought prior to making a fresh assault on all fronts. It may be difficult to plan ahead very far. People with some influence in the entertainment world are having problems and these could spawn repercussions later. Keep a low profile. Prepare any paperwork or other essential background information that may be needed shortly. Recent community affairs will have left you with some loose ends to tie up. You may wish to work on your accounts. You may feel there are duties that need attention, relating to someone who is deprived or lonely. A lot can be accomplished on a so-called quiet day.

30. THURSDAY. Useful. Progress should be made today in business. Far more will be achieved by working behind closed doors than will ever be accomplished in public. A government official can be of assistance. Put all your efforts into getting adequate preparations made for next month's activities. Plans will have been made, but many of the details will need attention today. You may be aware of mounting opposition. Weigh this against the goodwill you have in public and do not rate your chances too poorly. You are naturally a conservative person, so you are not going to be caught unawares. See that you have considered all aspects of a work project you think should be encouraged.

MAY

1. FRIDAY. Disturbing.   Be careful that you don't overdo it. If the pressure gets too high, bow out. You really need some peace and quiet, but a sense of duty can keep you on the treadmill. Try to be philosophical. By all means do what you can, but avoid taking over the troubles of others, as well. They are only going to be a drag. An older member of the family can be helped with a little sympathy and show of caring. There could be some changes in your schedule you will not be in the mood to appreciate. Never mind. Something will turn up to make up for the inconvenience. A separation could make you feel isolated or ignored. Stand up for your rights if they are threatened. Be honest with yourself.

2. SATURDAY. Disconcerting.   A problem shared is a problem halved. This may be the case if you can get the full and undivided attention of a partner. Tread with caution, nevertheless, or you could get out of your depth. Spending could easily overcome your normal caution. You and your loved one may be in a relaxed mood. You might show pleasure by being hospitable and friendly to all and sundry. Compromise if you feel this is the right move. But know also that your needs are important. Should you push your luck, you can disappoint someone dear to you who had other plans. Give a lead, but be diplomatic. Crudity can lead to tears.

3. SUNDAY. Tedious.   Don't expect a lot of cooperation. You may be on the wrong wavelength for most of your colleagues and associates. Stick to friendly relationships insofar as possible. Relationships are much too casual to get intimate. You are likely to say the wrong thing and perhaps ruin a reputation. It is not going to be an exciting day, so you may as well accept it. Just relax where you will not be buttonholed by people who know you too well. New friends can make it pleasant. Avoid getting too deeply involved emotionally. You need to look after your own interests, so be friendly without being inquisitive or aloof. If an old flame tries to get you interested again, do not take the bait. It is just a tease.

4. MONDAY. Useful. A business acquaintance could be in a generous mood. Enjoy whatever you have to do in public. This is not the day for action or excitement, but you can get a good deal of satisfaction out of it. You should try to recognize an opportunity to do yourself some good, or else enjoy comfort and pleasant surroundings. You should be popular and you may meet well-known people before the day is through. There will be less pressure on you to make a good impression. Something helpful can fall in your lap. Most people are in friendly moods. Dress up if you are going to a show. It is always fun to show off your best clothes.

5. TUESDAY. Sensitive. Use your money wisely. Opportunities abound for making progress in business. Prospects are high. You should be respected where it matters most, so should not go wrong if you keep a firm grip on priorities. Business finances should not be touched. Make no arrangement or commitment involving this money. While your own finances can be improved through business and hard work, it is a poor day to spend company money. Friends may try to get you involved in a scheme that will only waste your time and your money. Take the advice of an old friend at work. Long memories can be an advantage at times.

6. WEDNESDAY. Challenging. Do some private business to boost your income. An inspiration can lead to better things. Work changes should be to your advantage. A new broom sweeps clean and this will help. Do not let everyone know what you are up to. As far as money is concerned, you have to keep an ace up your sleeve. Play one person off against another if you feel there is some tension building up. You can help sort out a problem at work by being realistic and considerate to both people involved. You have everything to gain by such action. Take note of good advice from seniors and administrators. They should know what is going on, despite some provocation from behind the scenes.

7. THURSDAY. Happy. Relatives can show their feelings and affection. It is a happy day for couples. Partners will be particularly cooperative. Everyday affairs can be most important. Though this may not be a notable day for the nation it could be a red-letter day for you. Appreciative comments come from all the people you meet on this average day. If you stay in your own neighborhood you will find all the love you need. The friend you have next door can become someone much more important than you had expected. Love is likely to grow in this happy climate. A milestone may eventually be reached. However, you may not realize the importance of the moment at the time. That will be clear later.

8. FRIDAY. Uncertain. Listen to good advice from friends. You could be a little impatient or feel frustrated, but there is no need to be like this. You are among friends who will look after you. A health problem can emerge if you do not relax. Do not listen to idle gossip, nor should you encourage it. Traveling to and from work can be a bore. The return journey is likely to be even more upsetting. If you are getting to work under your own steam, have your car in good condition. Take note of poor information or other bad news, but do not base any action on it. Business will prosper in some way despite the mistakes or indecision of other people at work. Take the day as it comes.

9. SATURDAY. Good. Show that you have potential. Do not hide your light. Be practical and you will earn public approval. A project that will be demonstrated in public will prove to be a winner. Lovers should feel secure if they have to ask permission from parents. They should know their social responsibilities so will not be denied by any reasonable elder. Cooperation between young and old at work will be productive. Business reputations can blossom from such admirable common sense. Consolidate any gains. Think of the future as you introduce someone special. Go out on the town with a feeling of security and enjoy yourself.

10. SUNDAY. Tricky. Don't burn the candle at both ends. Enough is enough. Ask your parents if you are in any doubt about priorities. They will give you the right perspective. Think primarily of basic security and do not confuse this with ambitious hopes and dreams. Consider carefully before you undertake to do too much. Should you feel like exercising your authority or your knowledge, remember where you are and to whom you are talking. Family affairs can be in a state of flux. A decision may need to be made about real estate offers. Give it a bit of time to settle down. There is a danger of making too quick a move at the present.

11. MONDAY. Quiet. A property bargain is possible if you keep your ear to the ground. Private information and guidance should be heeded. Make improvements to the home while you are in the mood. Modern methods can make this much more interesting and less time consuming. Family members should lend a hand.

With a bit of luck and some broad hints, you could supervise. If you have a problem to straighten out with someone at work, don't hold back. There is no need to make a fuss. A quiet word in the right place will be quite enough. Be considerate in anything that affects the security of the home. You may find a hidden defect that can be remedied right away. You could be entering a new phase.

12. TUESDAY. Fair. A regular reunion gives great pleasure. Emotions are strong at this time. You will need to concentrate on one person who means a great deal to you. Waste no time or effort on other things. If you can manage to control your attention in this single-minded way, you will feel happier. Keep your business to yourself and the person you understand. For some, this can be a difficult situation if taken too literally. Taken in an emotional way, you will be able to cope. This is because you understand feelings and the strength of emotional ties. Allow yourself to be resilient enough to take as much as you give.

13. WEDNESDAY. Upsetting. This is the morning after the night before. Little seems likely to go your way. Traveling has its problems. Minor hitches seem to be the order of the day. Do not attempt too much if you want to take your chances with someone of the opposite sex. You might be too sure of yourself or may find the response somewhat disappointing. It will be unwise to think you can buy your pleasure. Someone could take you for a jerk if you seem too anxious. It may be wise to share things for now or to compare notes with a close friend. It would be better to plan your own pleasures so that you will have less chance of being frustrated. Start to take more interest in your work. That will keep you busy.

14. THURSDAY. Disquieting. Concentrate on whatever job you have at hand. Someone seems likely to tempt you away from the straight and narrow. Avoid any secret arrangement. A blind date will be a letdown. You should know better. If you are a bit depressed, look at your situation honestly. Do not seek some panacea offered by a secretive adviser. All your problems can be dealt with quite adequately if you have patience. A change of circumstances should liven up the day later on. This can be a relief or an upset. Accept it as the former and react positively. Do not take risks at work. Your health could be a problem.

15. FRIDAY. Mixed. Combine pleasure with business. This could be achieved by entertaining business friends, or through acceptance of an invitation. Take advantage of any such opportunity. Lovers should make this an evening for going out on the town. Show up in the right places and let someone you want to impress appreciate your attributes. Early reactions may be a bit hasty. Try to avoid clutching at straws. There is no reason to be anxious. You are well liked and must be composed if you want to impress someone. An acquaintance may intrigue you. It should be a sensational end to the day if you are a late person.

16. SATURDAY. Sensitive. If you have a hangover sleep it off. Lovers will be on top of the world while late revelers will be suffering. It is one of those days, as you know so well, that can affect your stomach in different ways. A lot depends on the company you keep. A partner can be very calm and comforting. Should you display aggression or forcefulness, your mate may quite well become withdrawn or tease you in a playful manner. It would be best to be guided by intuition and to react to whatever the circumstances dictate. A deeply romantic day can be a pleasure for both of you. You will want to please your partner, whose wishes may be difficult to guess.

17. SUNDAY. Important. If you have something to achieve, turn to influential friends for support. This sounds rather business-like. General fraternization at the club level is not really of much use. But if you can get hold of someone with a bit of clout, you are on the right track. Entertain only if you include your partner in the festivities. This is a time for joint consideration for a joint approach to anything with important possibilities. A business partner may confide in you about the company's financial projects. Respect the confidence. You should be able to participate better after you know what is in the wind. Restrict social activities to only the most important engagements.

18. MONDAY. Variable. Keep your private affairs in order. At some time during the day you may have an opportunity to shine in public. Much depends on the way you have done your homework if you are to achieve success. Family finances look good. Do some background research into making them even better. Adjustments made where necessary could increase their value considerably. Secretarial assistance would be welcomed and would serve to take some worries off your shoulders. Resist all advice to speculate. Despite possible gains, this is not the time to play the market. The advice of someone behind the scenes might be worth investigation. All is not as rosy as it looks.

19. TUESDAY. Uncertain. You will have to work for all you get. Favors are not easy to come by. Superiors think about the company's profits before your family's income. A great deal can be accomplished if you accept limitations and are prepared to forge ahead until you can see light at the end of the tunnel. Think of long-term prospects. There could be a rapid change of tempo before the day is very old. React positively. Friends are likely to part you from your money, although you could get some pleasure in the process. Active cooperation with a private partner will be to your advantage. If you are thinking ahead to vacation, you could make some advance inquiries.

20. WEDNESDAY. Good. You can now let your partner know what holiday plans you have been cooking up. Arrangements should have been made. There could be hitches later on in the day, so immediate travel may not be suitable. However, make the most of good relations early in the day. Some may be setting off on a honeymoon trip. A visit from a loved one will make the day a winner for many. Distance is no object when the heart is full. Students should benefit from research in depth. Legal questions affecting marriage and children should be handled without delay. Your understanding of security will be put to good use.

21. THURSDAY. Disturbing. Make sure your means of transport is reliable if you are traveling any distance. A sense of duty may drive you on in order to keep an appointment. Cool down a bit. You will make little progress if you are all keyed up. Watch out for signs of stress. Let some bright spark produce the ideas to help release tension. What you have to say could upset some others. If you cannot get away from everyday worries, try to be constructive in what you do. You will eventually find some private support from people with influence. The danger is that you may blow your top before the issue is settled and spoil your prospects.

22. FRIDAY. Manageable. Personal ambition can decide how you act today. No doubt you will please some and upset others. This is often the case when you get the bit between your teeth. Try to avoid being egotistical or aggressive. Your stock will rise if you retain your poise and act with dignity. It is better to remain aloof at the top of the pile than harangue everyone you see in order to make your point. Your ambitions will confuse a partner. Perhaps you have forgotten to put someone in the picture. It will be very difficult to resist rising to the bait if you are provoked. But you should try to be resilient and, above all, diplomatic.

23. SATURDAY. Challenging. This is a day to be remembered. All systems are go and the devil take the hindmost. Reputations can be made today. There is no chance of your pulling out, as you will feel you can cope with anything. Neither is there any question of your popularity. All eyes may be focused on you. Those in show biz will have a great opportunity. For many it will mean a walk up the aisle to future happiness. On such occasions it is best to keep something in reserve, just for unforeseen emergencies. You will have a full supporting cast and will be sustained by a good and cooperative work force of helpers. Make good use of any background information or help you have.

24. SUNDAY. Good. You will feel friendly today and will probably appreciate the help of friends before the day is out. Some disappointed or resentful people may envy your happiness. You should not let this disturb your mind. They can get lost. Since you feel good, you certainly do not want a quarrel. Seek the pleasant company of reliable friends who share your interests and aims in life. Enjoy the social atmosphere and get a kick out of following your personal inclinations for activities. Try hard to assert yourself and give some meaning to life. Look ahead to a full month when you can put personal plans into action. Prove your worth despite any objections by uninformed people.

25. MONDAY. Good. Put your best foot forward. It's a day to dress up because you feel the need to attract attention. Be friendly and diplomatic, because you will get nowhere by being overbearing. Everything in its proper place is the order of the day. You may meet charming people so do your best to be equally attractive in order to be welcomed. Friendship will mean a great deal. There is always the possibility of romance. If this proves to be the case, keep it under wraps just in case it does not work out well for you for one reason or another. But there should be a good party atmosphere wherever you go. People can be extremely pleasing and attentive at times. See you get to know those kinds of people.

26. TUESDAY. Disquieting. Expect few favors if you have to cooperate with fellow workers. Someone could be stirring up trouble behind your back. Do not accept changes in schedule readily unless there is a logical reason. In such a case, it should be made known to you. If you knuckle down too meekly you could later feel sorry for yourself. It is possible to do a bit of investigation on the side and state your case quietly. Should opposition be irrational, leave it till another day. But you should make it known firmly that you are no fool. Someone may need your support. Your partner could be in poor health or in the hospital.

27. WEDNESDAY. Important. This is a day of mixed blessings. Only two things are sure. You will know where you are going and what you will be able to achieve. Do not make a song and dance about your activities proposed for the future. Lay your plans and start the ball rolling privately. Take into your confidence only those, or perhaps only one you can trust. Use your initiative as quietly as you know how. Tactics are important once you are quite sure of your goal. A little mystery never did any harm. You know the value of keeping your own counsel and are naturally security-minded. You may have a slight tendency to let your imagination run wild. Keep your feet on the ground.

28. THURSDAY. Variable. This will be a good chance to take a breather. You could be feeling shattered if you have spent long hours preparing for something important, due later on. Should you forge ahead at this point you are bound to meet stiff opposition. Older people will not see eye-to-eye with you. Your reputation will be enhanced if you remain aware of the responsibilities you carry. Be optimistic, despite any setback. Try to be philosophic. This is a year of opportunity in business and one stoppage is not the end of the world. Get things into perspective and quit feeling sorry for yourself.

29. FRIDAY. Demanding. Complete your arrangements today. Clinch any deal still outstanding. You are now ready for the fray and should be in good trim. The relatives who have been in your confidence should be informed that there is no longer need for much secrecy. You will want to take the initiative before the day is through. Earlier in the day you had felt frustrated at delays. Changes in schedule will erode your patience. This is not like you, nor is it good for you. So try to think more about others than about yourself and this may help you cool down. Be careful when you do take the initiative. You may still be misunderstood by a partner.

30. SATURDAY. Happy. Dress up and be sociable this evening. Earlier in the day, you should carry on with whatever you think is important. See to it that everyone knows where you stand. Romantic ties can be strengthened. It may be a very emotional day. You should be well aware of the attractions around you and of the way you can attract attention to yourself. Without being selfish, consider personal priorities first of all. You will enjoy company and will appreciate sharing. A relationship may develop from a social encounter or a dance. Foster any artistic interest. You are a notorious collector, so you must have a keen eye for beauty.

31. SUNDAY. Quiet. What more fitting way to end the month than by relaxing? A hectic evening may have floored you, so rest and quiet will be welcome. You may still be in a romantic or friendly mood. Join friends who are also looking for a quiet corner to converse or pass the time of day. A gentle companion will be appreciated. Before you get around to counting the cost of yesterday's entertainment, let the world pass by. Reflect on the week ahead if the spirit moves you in that direction. You have a lot going for you and any initiative taken earlier must show a return quite soon. Do not disturb anyone else who may have ideas different from your own. In return you may remain undisturbed.

JUNE

1. MONDAY. Uncertain. A partner can disappoint you. Straightforward action may be impossible if you are looking for cooperation. You are tempted to go your own way and take the consequences. Take any help offered privately by someone you know who holds a responsible position in the world of finance. Prospects can blossom in this area. It will be most unwise to risk money at this time. Advice you may receive will probably encourage you to stabilize rather than seek expansion. Romance may play a large part in your evening schedule. You are feeling the need to take the initiative. But you are likely to start something that will be difficult to control.

2. TUESDAY. Variable. Build up your resources. Productivity will insure a return on capital. Constancy and hard work will be rewarded. Take whatever opportunity is afforded to make a profit through business. Your judgment should be good. You will know precisely when the time is ripe to take positive action involving money and productivity. Employers should find their work force fully in support of joint effort. This will have a three-way effect that brings reward for all concerned. Put something away for a rainy day. Make yourself popular in the right public places. All this will help you in your old age and give you confidence.

3. WEDNESDAY. Buoyant. Make hay while the sun shines. So much is going your way now that it would be unwise to let it pass. Cooperation comes from all quarters. Partners are in the same frame of mind as are you. Sweethearts will be extra loving.

Ideas you propose will be greeted with enthusiasm. Do not waste time wondering if you are dreaming. Good news can add to the day's pleasure. Relatives will have heard of your progress and wish to congratulate you. Accept any support you can raise, just in case you need to fall back on it in the future. Renew old ties that may have become loosened during the past years. As ever, family ties are important to you.

4. THURSDAY. Tricky. You may tend to overdo it. Time could run out on you or you can waste too much effort in discussion rather than constructive work. Try to avoid being led into a wasted argument with a partner or others you have to deal with. Interruptions are likely to cause enough problems, without encouraging opposition from those who should be giving you support. Aggravation will occur where you work. Interference in schedules and general obstruction will make you impatient. Expect no help from superiors who will keep a low profile till the trouble dies down. So why put your reputation on the line?

5. FRIDAY. Mixed. Follow up any new social relationship struck yesterday. Make another date for the weekend. A connection with someone close at hand can become very attractive. Since you are rather a homebody at heart, this should please you. Look forward to the end of the working week. So much trouble and upset recently may have made life miserable. Discontented people always cause dissension all along the line. Traveling problems cannot help the situation. So you may be relieved to make life more pleasant without having to travel far. Local information gathered in the last two days should be useful in business. Profit can be made from this, and local trading is thus boosted.

6. SATURDAY. Deceptive. Home and family can be very demanding today. You normally do not mind giving your all for the benefit of domestic harmony. But with other fish to fry, you may be hard pressed to please everyone. It is essential to do personal things because your time is usually limited. Sharing is going to be a bit of a problem, if not a downright waste. Your heart is not in it at the moment. Security may be worrying. You may fear for the safety of property. If this is the case, do something about it rather than worry. A family gathering cannot get off the ground because of lack of enthusiasm. Do your own thing, after all.

7. SUNDAY. Uncertain. A visit may have to be canceled. This may not bother you very much, since you usually feel happier at home. Do not press the point too much if you are asked to put yourself out. Expectations could far exceed events. A property deal is likely to fall through, or perhaps never get off the ground. Inflated costs put many agreements on hold. Avoid business if you possibly can. More important matters may need attention. Property could be maintained much more economically, given a bit of foresight and expert advice. Take note of opinions from older members of the family or experts who know their business. A public servant or commercial agent can help you.

8. MONDAY. Fair. Employment can be risky because of a power struggle. Private war behind the scenes may cause a holdup that affects many. Take-over negotiations are not easily settled. Keep your ear to the ground for any information that can keep you one jump ahead. It is essential to keep the initiative and not be caught short by conniving and intrigue. Away from such, you should be in a romantic mood. You will have no difficulty in talking your way through any problem or tricky situation. You can be charming and will be strongly attracted to someone you know very well. This is a part of the month you can truly appreciate.

9. TUESDAY. Disconcerting. Background conditions remain clouded. You would dearly wish to enjoy a break away from work routine, but opportunities fade away. Put up with the uncertainty and possible frustration of work. A health problem may be worrisome. Expert advice will help clear things up, one way or another. Take no positive action until you are quite sure of the conditions. Though it may be difficult, try to avoid doing too much. You could be loaded with responsibility and getting very little thanks at the moment. Be prepared to take the place of a superior whose health is not up to par at present. Young folk may be taking on some of the responsibilities of their elders.

10. WEDNESDAY. Disquieting. Make a clean break from a friend who is not what he or she seemed to be. Love is something you cannot buy. Be straightforward in your decision so that afterwards no one can say you cheated. Secret agreements are not good enough at this stage. Be careful with your diet. Some may have been overdoing it and let things get out of balance. Get cracking with that planned nutrition course before you have problems. Someone you love may be taken into the hospital. You will try hard to visit, despite work schedules. Think first of your bread and butter, but be your usual sympathetic self in true need. Expect little things to put you off. Be considerate of pets.

11. THURSDAY. Challenging. You are up and down like a seesaw. Working conditions can cause you concern. Unexplained absence of senior staff members may put you once more in the hot seat. Take responsibility and make good use of it. You should be recognized for your versatility and reliability in the upper echelons. This is where it really matters. Opportunity is there to be taken. Encourage those who work with you to give you support. Be prepared to improvise. You have a lot of responsibility and are not going to have an easy day. Take it all as an adventure and you can end up enjoying the action. Even so, you could be exhausted by evening and need a pick-me-up.

12. FRIDAY. Deceptive. Treat your partner gently and with consideration. Relationships can be very sensitive. For some this day will be lovely. You will fly on cloud nine for most of it. For others it can be a day of uncertainty. Take it as you find it. Don't risk taking chances if there has to be a practical answer at the end of the day. Partnership is not a reasonable proposition, so business colleagues may be unreliable. For those of you who are in love, dream your dreams. Make your plans and think of the future, but postpone a firm commitment. If you want to go ahead with a personal project, find someone with imagination to help.

13. SATURDAY. Disconcerting. You will not get it all your own way. The weekend lull puts you on the spot in some ways. All sorts of things have to be done to keep the peace at home. Do all you are obliged to do in the way of sharing, since it will make light work of weekend chores. Personal inclinations will be difficult to neglect. You could have a stand-up argument to make your point, but that is not very diplomatic. You can do better. Avoid taking too many risks. Do not put any trust in a business friend who says he or she will help. If you have to compromise, do it gracefully. Prepare for better things tomorrow when the pressure is less.

14. SUNDAY. Easygoing. Commit yourself to no one. Be friendly to all, but keep your options open. This will make some of your friends sit up and take notice. You will even gain the admiration of quite a few. Never mind those who are jealous or envious. Let them get on with their own affairs. Take everything lightly. Family interests may come first with many. Others will seek a quiet rendezvous with the boy or girl of their dreams, well away from inquisitive people. Privacy can be very important if you are to have a peaceful day. Those with an ear and eye for future financial security may find a friend who gives good advice about personal and family investment. But follow your own hunches as well.

15. MONDAY. Good. A medical checkup will result in the all-clear for you. This good news will give you added zest. Take advantage of an opportunity to get public recognition. Family interests should benefit from the intervention or advice of a public figure. A pay raise is possible. After all the holdup and problems with your superiors, your past endeavors should be rewarded financially. Put all you can spare into a safe investment. Let money work for you. With good advice you and your partner can look around for a joint project that will engage dual interest. Listen attentively to the views of influential people behind the scenes.

16. TUESDAY. Mixed. A long journey may have to be delayed. If you have to travel far, let all who depend on you know your plans. Undertake nothing in secret. Trust no one who wishes to strike a private bargain. Secret rendezvous are out. You have little hope of hiding anything and can be prey to mischievous gossip if you try anything out of the ordinary. Trust your partner who will know how you feel and will give understanding support. Children, too, have a warmth for you and a depth of understanding you may not realize. Rely on those ties that originate in family and the past. The ties from casual relationships of friends and acquaintances may prove to be somewhat flimsy.

17. WEDNESDAY. Exciting. If the time is right, get away from it all. Holiday plans can be executed or arrangements made now. Should you feel it necessary to travel, do so with confidence. Personal plans and hopes may depend on overseas contact. A legal argument can be resolved to your advantage. Initiative will pay off. If you do not get started quickly enough, more responsibility could fall on your shoulders. Older people may have health problems that you can help to solve. But since you want to be on the move, this is not exactly to your taste. The early bird catches the train or plane today. The late riser is likely to be burdened with problems not of his making nor to his liking.

18. THURSDAY. Quiet. Sit back quietly and take stock. Most of the tension is past. You could be feeling a bit worn out and ready for a rest. Consider your public position. Is your reputation what you think it should be? Are you getting the private support you need? Is a partnership really working? You could have a few gripes and perhaps some concern about your progress to date. Very soon you will have to take personal initiative as your birthday approaches. Think out what new measures you can start and the direction and speed of your future progress. You are now in a position to look both backward and forward from a superior position.

19. FRIDAY. Useful. Impatience can get you into trouble. Your reputation can be jeopardized if you do not calm down and show a bit of tolerance. Realize that you cannot go two ways at once. Public presentation is vital to the success of any operation. Get thoughts and action into harmony with conditions or you will get precisely nowhere. Application to essentials will win you permanent favor. A great deal of value is placed on your capacity to take on responsibility and cope with everyday situations that are never constant. You can go with the current when appropriate and recognize your limitations at the right time.

20. SATURDAY. Good. It's a relief to have the day to yourself. Get together with your friends who have been out of touch for days. Someone in authority may give you a helping hand on the quiet. This is something you appreciate sincerely. Keep your private arrangements confined to those people who are likely to help you in a personal way. Friends fall into another category. They are always there to fall back on for pleasure and amusement. Personal plans are important today and for some weeks to come. You should be quite sure you have the right backing. For those who have to consider business, it will be a day when the public will spend, so you should make a profit.

21. SUNDAY. Sensitive. A date may be unexpectedly broken. This could be a blessing in disguise. Very close, intimate ties somehow have little to appeal to you today. You will resent anyone who wants to take you over and run your lovelife. You feel much more free among casual friends who are less demanding. In the main people are cooperative. You will find someone else will give you comfort if you have to clear the air early in the day. Later on, you can count on a ready audience among your friends for personal ideas and plans. Make arrangements to undertake some social task that will involve the community at large. Intelligent initiative will be appreciated. Friends can be very talkative.

22. MONDAY. Rewarding. Put plans made earlier into action. All that talking yesterday will be wasted if you do not act now. No one is going to oppose your initiative, though there will always be many who just pass by on the other side. Ignore them and get on with the job at hand. Get organized on a social type of undertaking. This will consume a great amount of your time, but it will be time and energy well spent. It's no good listening to others or expecting them to do the right thing. At the moment it is a matter of principle that you make a strong personal effort to help others and show your public spirit. Those with a birthday will have a busy and enjoyable day with their many friends.

23. TUESDAY. Easygoing. Keep right out of circulation. It should be an ideal day for those who need to study or meditate. After the party, some may be in need of a quiet, dark room, free from street noise. Recent events have been pretty hectic and this is one of the few days you will have the opportunity to get away without being noticed. Do not look for publicity or public involvement. No doubt there is some preparation to be done before Friday when activities will begin to heat up again. It may be necessary for someone to take care of a friend who is under the weather. If you are singled out, appreciate this opportunity to use your inborn skills.

24. WEDNESDAY. Confusing. Something that has been pending could come to a head. Yesterday could have been the forerunner of an event in your private life. Be sensitive to a friend. Loving care may be needed to comfort someone close to you who is in need. You may feel rejected and tend to feel sorry for yourself. There is really no need for such thoughts. It is essential to attend to practicalities and not shut yourself away from everyday activity. If, for some good reason, you cannot achieve all you would like to do, be philosophical. At some point you may have to make a decision that is not to your liking.

25. THURSDAY. Disappointing. Some long-planned action could turn out to be nonexistent. As observed by Robert Burns, the best laid schemes of mice and men gang aft a-gley. If that is the case, let it pass. Tomorrow could be a better day to take initiative. Perhaps what you have in mind is not yet ready for the acid test. Partners, who you would normally expect to add their weight, may be unenthusiastic about your proposals. If you are not prepared to go it alone this could be the last straw. Avoid making any agreements. You are likely to be left holding the bag, with no possibility of finding a legitimate backer. It is probably a good idea to keep your own company.

26. FRIDAY. Good. You can now get a clearer view of the road ahead. Yesterday's indecision will have passed and you are again in the driver's seat. Support and loving interest can come from a friend of the family. Deep and lasting ties should give you the confidence to do what you want to do. Creative enterprise can be purposefully directed early during the day. Personal arrangements should be made. Use all communicative means at your disposal to put your points across. Minor details should not be ignored in the rush to make progress. See what the mail has to offer. A last-minute arrangement can make a great deal of difference to an important situation. Get around to attending to details.

27. SATURDAY. Confusing. Safeguard your reputation. It could be too easy to jump out of the frying pan into the fire. Any ingenious ideas you have should be tempered with practicality and consideration of the current climate. Hasty action is all too likely. You may be easily aroused to argument. This would prove to be unwise. Judgment flies out the window when you are emotionally aroused. Concentrate on putting personal plans into operation. You have all the energy necessary. But do not put your career in jeopardy or expect to receive public acclaim all at once. Consider whether your plans are selfish or are beneficial to others as well as yourself. Much will depend on the latter qualification.

28. SUNDAY. Deceptive. You are not likely to get very far today. A partnership will prove to be a letdown. Energetic people are few and far between. What was seen as a day for personal initiative can become a flop. There is no remedy for this in entertaining. Whatever you try as a palliative can be expensive. True love is not likely to run smooth and a fat wallet will not fill the gap left by escaping love. Do not trust other people too much. You could be far better off on your own, making your own amusement and spending money on yourself. You may still be feeling a bit adventurous and in need of excitement. You are therefore likely to be careless with your resources. It's not worth taking any risks.

29. MONDAY. Mixed. The exercise of discretion and tact are duly recommended. Look hard at any proposal affecting your pocket. There is a lot to be gained if you are direct and to the point. This is no time to bother with nonessentials. For the hardworking person, this is a day to remember. Reward should meet with delight. A senior member of the family could give approval to a young person's project. Those in love should seek the personal acceptance of some, and the forthright agreement of a parent if they wish to go ahead with marriage plans. People with influence are usually amenable to suggestions for entertainment.

30. TUESDAY. Uncertain. Be on your guard for mischief makers. Scandal and innuendo can ruin an arrangement planned for today. Financial measures may be needed to keep things in perspective. Do not get involved with any back-room wizards who think they know all the answers. In the long run, they are most unreliable. Work prospects can be endangered by erratic actions of subversives. Treachery can be expected in some instances. Opportunity abounds for those with an eye for a bargain. Wise spending can reap great rewards. Stock up the larder if you see extra-special bargains in the market. Public approval can be awarded for your efforts on behalf of civic projects.

JULY

1. WEDNESDAY. Special.   Let your hair down with relatives and neighbors for a change of pace. It seems like a good time and chance to be sociable in your own little circle. Expansive plans are not for you today. Bigwigs of the neighborhood should be glad to join in the fun. Get around a bit in order to meet someone you admire. Make your presence felt through taking an interest in local arts. You should be able to enter your own particular contribution. Information you receive should give you encouragement to take personal initiative. Use your talents wisely. Entertain friends with a view to enlisting their support. Explain what your cause is about. It may be necessary to educate some people.

2. THURSDAY. Disquieting.   This could be a gossipy time. Someone may be trying to stir up trouble. Try to keep out of any differences of opinion, though you are likely to be caught up in a controversy. If you allow yourself to be worried you will probably have stomach trouble. It is not worth the trouble and discomfort. So seek the help of a strong friend who will encourage you and help you combat all problems. Traveling may be subject to delays. Underhand action can disrupt communications. Mail may be delayed. A sudden strike could cause disruption for some. Employers may be hard pressed to keep up production. Trust no one who wants to give you secret information.

3. FRIDAY. Deceptive.   Concentrate all your faculties on personal plans. It is time you started to get yourself organized to take constructive action in the days ahead. You should be able to shut your mind to outside activities. This may be misconstrued in the home. You are bound to offend your partner and other members of the family if you are not paying attention to them and their needs. Property matters can be confusing. Do not attempt any trading in real estate today. Prices could not only be out of your reach but you could also be stuck with inferior property. Someone could be trying to pull the wool over your eyes.

4. SATURDAY. Good. Make up your mind to settle down to do house repairs. It is time you did something constructive on a free Saturday. Now that you have the time, you may be inclined to go at it full speed ahead. This may lead to poor workmanship, but is likely to keep you happy. It would be a pity to risk your reputation for craftsmanship, though. You feel able to cope and are encouraged by the support you get from zealous members of the family. They are only too happy to join in. A new opening may appear at your place of work. You might get someone in the family interested. This seems a good time to test family loyalties. Attractions outside your home can disturb some of your concentration.

5. SUNDAY. Manageable. Someone is in the mood to have an argument. Try hard to keep the peace if you value family harmony. There are sensitive folk around who would be offended by a brawl. Seek gentle company if you wish to have a more pleasant day. Romantic interests should be well taken care of, despite envy in some quarters. Be sincere if you want to grab the brass ring. This is a situation you regularly encounter, as you well know. You should surely recognize the depth of your feelings by now and be able to master opposition from rivals. Press your attention without being forceful. You know there is no need to push, but someone may have managed to get under your skin.

6. MONDAY. Good. Impress someone of importance with your talents. If you wish to exhibit something in the future it will be essential to get authoritative support and consent. An official can help out in this connection right now. You must do something in the next few weeks to enhance your reputation. It could be your birthday time about now. It would be a good time to look back, then make plans for the coming year or even longer. Some will be thinking seriously of marriage. Develop all skills that are creative. You do not have nearly as much time to develop your artistic talents. Work at improving this drawback.

7. TUESDAY. Rewarding. Spare no effort to make progress today. You should have the active cooperation of people who have your personal welfare at heart. Combined efforts can add to your achievements and help the bank balance. Artistic endeavors and other works that reflect your talents in general will be snapped up. A relationship may develop quite quickly with someone who shares your sporting interests. As you may wish to show off your strength or skill, you are likely to get attached to a lively partner for the day. A combined effort can win a prize. You will be feeling strong and competitive. Put everything you have into the last lap.

8. WEDNESDAY. Strenuous. Stick to your guns. Ignore all distractions. This could be either a miserable day or a productive one. It is largely up to you. The one sure thing is that you will not be able to avoid your responsibilities. By now, you are well aware of the current pressures. You should, therefore, be able to make solid progress in whatever direction you think appropriate. Working conditions can be hard. Old people may bore you with talk of the past and the bright days of their youth. Be patient. Needless to say, you will be old yourself one day. Look after any poor health condition. Chronic problems can start early in life if you are careless. But creating a firm, healthy foundation will lead to a long life.

9. THURSDAY. Challenging. Try to get off to a bright start. The early hours bring hopes of progress. Public activity should inspire you to put in an early appearance, ready to grasp any opportunity for getting ahead. Business needs foresight today. Competitors have to be outsmarted and you must deal with this situation before yesterday's dust settles. Be original. Use your common sense and trust your own judgment. You should be able to keep one step ahead without any trouble as long as you realize the other fellow is probably thinking like you. Pay an unexpected visit to a government office. You may find some cooperation there that you had not anticipated. The unexpected is likely to pay off today.

10. FRIDAY. Disturbing. Tread very carefully if you want a quiet kind of day. You can be feeling sorry for yourself, or you may be living with someone else who is. One of you must get out of this rut if any progress is to be made. Be gentle, by all means, but not submissive. Opposition can come from someone who holds an important position. If you are trying to promote a partnership you must first consider all the personal implications. It seems you can best be served by letting a professional look after these interests. In your present state of mind, you could give up all your assets and let someone walk all over you. Try to be constructive.

11. SATURDAY. Demanding. Be diplomatic and compromise. You need to share your fortunes, whether good or bad. Take your partner into your confidence. There may be very little of importance to share, but at least you are retaining an essential relationship. Lovelife may be somewhat unpredictable. You may be faced with a challenge. Do not fly off the handle, as this will only cause you more trouble. Stay cool, calm, and collected. Let no one see you are rattled and you will eventually get your own way. Be prepared to spend some money for a good cause, either friendship or peacekeeping. Above all, look after your best friend.

12. SUNDAY. Good.   Today is good for constructive major projects. Look into any financial matter that affects the whole family. You could consolidate a deal or make a substantial gain that will strengthen future prospects. Some of you may benefit from a family inheritance. Consider financial conditions in some depth. There is little need to look at the current situation, but the long-term prospects have great possibilities. A joint interest in work affairs should be made more profitable. Partners in business will find this a good day for making the most of current trading and firm contracts. Take on anything that will give a steady income and regular work, even though it may not seem spectacular now.

13. MONDAY. Challenging.   Follow up your initiative. If you spent most of yesterday in uncharacteristic Sunday business discussions, see that your work is not wasted today. You should look on the bright side and will find most things come your way. Consider all possibilities. There could be unexpected developments that need a bit of good judgment and expertise to bring them to full flower. Your reputation can be enhanced if you are on the ball and prepared to take a chance. You are not really putting anything in jeopardy, since you did your groundwork yesterday. Snap up any business that is offered. Adjust your work schedule to meet emergencies. All this will pay off in the long run.

14. TUESDAY. Mixed.   Make an early start if you are traveling far. Conditions then will be favorable, but there could be delays later in the day. Take a pleasant companion with you if you are not planning to meet someone. Good company makes a long, tedious journey much more agreeable. If traveling does not attract you, romance can be a good substitute. Combine studies with self-expression if you are in a university or college. Do not depend solely on reading, but find out for yourself how something functions. Use your talents in a realistic way. It will increase the interest. Serious study can follow. An old friend from afar may be in trouble. Send loving thoughts if nothing else and keep in touch.

15. WEDNESDAY. Active. Explore new horizons. Personal prospects should benefit from your inquiries outside the usual perimeters. It is a time to be a bit more adventurous. There will be some hitches. You may have to amend a schedule. Traveling may be necessary, although full of surprises, especially early in the day. There seems to be a financial incentive to your activities. Business takes up most of your time and there is not a lot of scope for entertainment. This is what suits you at the moment. Look ahead and also pursue immediate career priorities. Colleagues should recognize your enthusiasm and give you encouragement.

16. THURSDAY. Variable. You could feel a little self-conscious today. A relationship problem may occur that throws you off balance. Do not take it to heart. Concentrate on practical matters. Work is far more important at the moment. Health problems may emerge. A minor upset may get you in an uproar. Perhaps it's a matter of lost balance or a diet variation. This will soon right itself and you will be back to your routine again quite happily. Do not look for cooperation. You are in no need of support at the moment. It could cramp your style and possibly slow you down. You travel faster on your own. Keep your eyes open.

17. FRIDAY. Challenging. Aim for the top. You are not going to please everyone and this may act as a further incentive to succeed. An important friend with your personal interests at heart may see the situation quite differently. You must make up your own mind. There is opportunity right now to make a breakthrough. In a year of opportunity you must acccept a challenge. You cannot expect to have everything handed to you on a silver platter. Support comes in practical ways. You will be fully geared to put plans into action. Keep on your toes for any change in working conditions that will need consideration. Ability is there, as is opportunity. Do what you think is right for reputation.

18. SATURDAY. Sensitive. A bit of friendly gossip can do you good. Heavy love affairs will only weary you. More to the point, you are in for an expensive time if you get too heavily involved. Accept any breakdown in a relationship as a blessing in disguise. Keep away from pinball machines, gambling tables, and computer games when you are out in the evening. They have nothing to return. A fistfight could occur at a nightspot you visit. Either keep out of the action or use your diplomacy to quiet things down. Appreciate someone who can talk his way around any difficulty. Use your talents to entertain. You have a dramatic way about you that is pleasing. Make your partner aware of your feelings.

19. SUNDAY. Good. Enjoy an all-social weekend. Personal plans should be made for sharing with your friends. A new companion may come into your life for the first time. You can both look forward to further meetings. Feel at home with your friends. Relax and take it all as it comes. Any emotional ties should give you comfort and make you realize how lucky you are to have friends. Feel sure you are doing the right things. Be generous if asked to support any civic works project in which you have an interest. Artistic people will appeal to you. It is a day to keep up with what is going on around you in the local community. There may be some events you would want to participate in.

20. MONDAY. Quiet. Complete any outstanding financial transaction as soon as possible. Be prepared for a quiet day. Social engagements can be completed with good results. A contact made socially should be good for business and personal reputation. Get to know people of importance. You should be able to impress them and come to some agreement about a personal matter. Seniors will accept your views and be prepared to give you support. Settle down to a more private day once you have made initial agreements. Background details will need attention. Financial matters are becoming more important now that the social scene has been left to take care of itself.

21. TUESDAY. Mixed. Public officials can upset personal affairs perhaps inadvertently. In the business world, a more progressive mood is considered a risk by those who carry influence. You can be personally interested in the important reactions and discussions that may affect the reputations of many. It seems like a good opportunity to take a rest from the public eye. Note carefully all that is going on around you. Any attempt to make progress could be stopped or delayed for no apparent reason. Be wary before you attempt any new initiative. Use a private approach to anyone who is in your debt. Be sure of your ground.

22. WEDNESDAY. Slow. Look out for hidden flaws. If you are tinkering with an appliance take all necessary precautions to safeguard yourself. Electrical faults may come to your notice. Public officials are again thinking about you. They should be able to give you information in private that will help you progress. Consider your reputation if you are doing any company business that can lead to expansion. Do not put all your cards on the table. It will be greatly appreciated by those who cannot avoid publicity if you keep a low profile. Your turn for the limelight will come soon enough. Someone you know in the hospital may have an unexpected turn for the better. This may be just the time for a visit.

23. THURSDAY. Deceptive. You may want to unburden your feelings. The desire to let things go can be overpowering. Talking will give some relief, but you may bore listeners with your personal views. Be careful you are not misjudged. Everyone you talk to will not think as you do. There could be deceit and gossip after you are well out of earshot. Partners may find you hard to live with. They may agree just to get rid of you. Other people's problems can be a talking point. Do not decide you can have your way with whatever you want to promote. The opposition is crafty and will lead you on till you are out of your depth. Negotiations can be very tricky.

24. FRIDAY. Enjoyable. Show-biz folk can have a heyday. If you have an artistic talent put it to good use. You could be admired by many, so you should put on your best appearance and enjoy yourself. There is some danger that you could be vain. Get over this by sharing your charms and getting even more pleasure. If you have time and opportunity, look around for fashionable clothes. You are on the ball when it comes to choosing the appropriate outfits. Ladies will find that it is the right time to get boyfriends into a buying mood. Choose your company well. You will have no trouble getting a partner, so you should make the best possible choice to suit your mood.

25. SATURDAY. Productive. The morning can be hectic and may also be disorganized. You may be dashing around to a variety of places trying to make up for lost time. Mistakes are inevitable if you do not slow down. Public places, markets, and shops are a temptation, but for you there will be few bargains. So avoid doing anything out of the ordinary. A date may be broken unexpectedly. But there is no point in getting worked up about that. There should be an opportunity to start off from scratch on a new and much more promising arrangement. A financial deal can be completed. Make the initial contact today. This can be followed up during next week after the weekend interlude.

26. SUNDAY. Important. Attend to financial priorities. There is work to be done in preparation for tomorrow. Apply yourself energetically to getting accounts straight. Balance all records of working capital and see that you are fully conversant with transactions and payments. It is also a day to appreciate the good things of life. You should feel quite secure and satisfied with your lot. You are ready to do business with anyone who is prepared to meet you halfway. Take time to consider future steps. There may be a need to improvise at a later stage. But until then you must be confident that whatever you arrange is based on a firm foundation.

27. MONDAY. Good. Get off to a good start. There will be no hitches with cars to spoil it this morning. Get right into the consideration of business prospects for the future. There will have been a change over the weekend that puts a different light on the business world. Get down to working out ways and means for implementing this new situation. Opportunity is there to be exploited by the adventurous. This should be right up your alley. If you are looking for a different job, today could provide the answer. Be confident if you are to have an interview. You should be able to impress anyone. This is a day to let your hair down and spend money to good advantage, perhaps on new clothes.

28. TUESDAY. Rewarding. Stick to your own back yard. Yesterday's comings and goings could be enough for a little while. It is time to take it easy and find a soft shoulder to rest on. There could be some restrictions placed on your movement later in the day. You may just as well make earlier preparations to enjoy some local entertainment. Get in touch with the boy or girl next door if you feel romantic. You usually feel a need to be affectionate, so will probably attract a partner who is as sensitive as yourself. An evening class may appeal to you. Make good use of your artistic talents. Practice your crafts and share your pleasures with others or with someone special.

29. WEDNESDAY. Mixed. This is a day of ups and downs. Essentials are important, but very boring in many respects. You can be easily frustrated if you lose your sense of direction. Keep your nose to the grindstone. You know very well how much depends on your productivity. There may be delays at first, followed by a sudden burst of activity. Try to cope as best you can by good and sensible application of experience. Relatives may cause you some problems. You could help one of them out financially. This should ease some of the pressure and will make you feel somewhat better. Money spent today will not be wasted. Put more into a work project that will pay you back in the future.

30. THURSDAY. Sensitive. Home ties are strong. When you are in real need, the family seems to rally around. All age groups are in on a homecoming. This is the center of operations today and you appreciate the strength of its foundations. If your partner is under the weather you have plenty of other support around you.

Property deals can be financially productive. It may be somewhat too early to do business, but keep your eyes open for a bargain. Money can flow like water if you are not extremely careful. You will never stint the family. It is the hangers-on that give you problems. Do not encourage sharing with an unknown partner or close associate. There are limitations and you should make this known.

31. FRIDAY. Good. The property market is good. If you are looking around for a buyer, settle when a good opportunity comes along. Attend to any job that needs doing around the home. You could have a busy day tomorrow. Today there is more chance of your being able to take your time and do a thorough, reliable job. No one is likely to get the better of you in a bagain or an argument. You seem to know where you are going and are aware of your basic facts. Spend a bit of money on the home. See that the most important things are attended to first of all. You can do a lot of the work yourself, so your expenditure will be worthwhile.

AUGUST

1. SATURDAY. Productive. Resist the temptation to carry on as usual at business. This excessive attention to interests outside your home will cause tension there. Concentrate on domestic duties first of all. Then, if you have time, let your hair down and have fun away from home. Work around the house should be undertaken with care. Electrical installations can be replaced. If there have been problems involving time-wasting at work, think up new ideas that can improve performance. Please the family by getting more up-to-date equipment in the kitchen. You could be a bit rash with your money, so spend on practical things.

2. SUNDAY. Difficult. You feel very close to someone in a romantic way. A regular reunion may cause some conflict in the family. A parent may not see eye-to-eye with you and your lover. There is a temptation to go all-out and then take the consequences. Avoid this sort of unpleasantness. The present tension will not always be there. Make good use of the pleasures of today and the warm associations. Tempers frayed are nonproductive. Should you have entertainment on your schedule, be prepared for the expense it will entail. More guests than you invited may turn

up. Cope with this contingency by cutting down and sharing what
you had prepared, rather than by using all your reserves.

3. MONDAY. Enjoyable. Do your own thinking. Personal
plans are in the forefront of your thoughts. Some people will be
making wedding plans and getting down to detailed preparations
for the great day. Mothers should be preparing children for the
school days that lie not far ahead. This is the time of year when
children play such an important part in the daily round. Arrange
some entertainment for them. Join in their games and share their
interests while they are around you. Visit relatives you do not often see. Keeping in touch is important. You should let all the family know how you are getting along. Be happy to spend some
money on those you love. Flowers would be appreciated.

4. TUESDAY. Encouraging. Your efforts at work will be rewarded. Employers can be generous at times, so never refuse an
offer of a bonus for your hard work. Recognition gives a boost to
progress and productivity. You could be surprised at the ease of
making money today. Store owners will notice how the public
looks for practical and utility goods. Spending is no problem. As
much will come in as goes out. Business entertainment is useful
and enjoyable and it pays to be sociable. Meet influential people at
work and discuss everyday problems and progress in pleasant surroundings. Plans may be in the works for a social occasion.

5. WEDNESDAY. Productive. You may be restless and wish
to get on with your work. Exciting things can be happening. You
want to become involved in the action. With the adrenaline flow-
ing, your judgment may lack clarity due to your being hasty. Yet
your sense of adventure should win the day. Have no fears about
the final outcome. Nothing will be gained by holding back. Even if
things do not work out as you had expected, you will have gained
more experience. Despite early mixed feelings, you should know
your fate at the end of the day. You will be surprised to find you
did quite well after all the excitement. Reputations can be gained
by innovation and originality.

6. THURSDAY. Demanding. Take a rest. Avoid sharing your
work or letting anyone take over from you. It is a time when you
need to relax and reflect but without losing your control. Someone
may try to persuade you that he or she is competent to take over.
Resist such offers. You may have to consider helping a partner
who has fallen by the wayside. Do not get led astray yourself. A

romantic interlude could make you feel unusually happy. Enjoy this as a passing pleasure, but do not let it go to your head. An old flame can bring back happy memories. What is past is past, even though the memories are still pleasant. If you find it hard to concentrate, do not attempt to undertake any business of importance.

7. FRIDAY. Good. Try hard to be moderate. An employer or someone with financial muscle may make you a long-term offer. Your services must be good and this could be a worthwhile project. But high hopes of popularity or establishment of a name for yourself could discourage you from accepting. Come down off your high horse and consider practicalities and future stability. It's good to have a safe base from which to try your luck, but do not think a flash in the pan is the beginning and the end of everything. Your natural conservatism should come to your aid today. You could start to make steady progress that will be good for you.

8. SATURDAY. Disquieting. Try to be patient. This is your only hope today if you are to do anything constructive. Joint finances are the cause of argument and discontent. A partner will not see eye-to-eye with you on more than one count. Influential people are not easily persuaded. With this sort of opposition, you are better taking things easy and waiting until everyone has cooled down. Do not use family funds. Do everything you can to persuade a joint account holder to refrain also. If arrangements or negotiations break down, do not seek solace in the bottle. That will be a complete waste of time, money and pleasure. Keep a loved one at arm's length till you are in a more sociable frame of mind.

9. SUNDAY. Strenuous. This is day two of the financial argument. There is a need now to come to some practical decision about future action. The peace of the weekend can be shattered if you are bent on getting your own way, or a partner tries to shout you down. Work out a rational solution. There is always a working compromise to every problem. Those of you with a problem may get relaxation by doing something out of the ordinary. See someone who is a learned scholar or at least knowledgeable, and this will do you a power of good. You may feel less downtrodden and realize you did quite well at stating your case over the last two days. And with a little bit of luck, all will be well that ends well.

10. MONDAY. Sensitive. Trust those you know well. Established values mean more than anything. A close relationship can prove to be of great value. Settle a work contract without delay. The terms should be good and the other person cooperative. Look after your wallet first of all. You could have a soft-spot for someone who works with you. Consider various possibilities for the future. Traveling any distance is not deemed advisable. Apart from possible delays, there is the question of correct protocol in leaving work to fly off to some unknown future. Take legal advice on a problem, but do not expect an easy solution. A loved one can make traveling interesting, but not on a business trip.

11. TUESDAY. Changeable. Keep clear of publishers and the media. Publicity and overseas news are likely to be bad. Interests abroad can be shaky. Communications that are considered modern show signs of unreliability. You may be asked to make a hasty journey. Try to avoid it. You have better things to do nearer home. Apply your energies to increasing your bank balance. An invention could bring rewards immediately. Look for a change of jobs provided this will increase your earning power. You will feel adventurous. Do not be put off by stories in the newspapers or opinions of people in your profession who do not work for a living.

12. WEDNESDAY. Difficult. Make your mark wherever you can. You should try to remain dignified, since your reputation is important. Be careful where you place your trust. Someone quite close to you may let you down. Tears may be shed if you concentrate on business and neglect other personal ties. If there are good reasons for your actions, why worry? Be considerate of those who depend on you, but this is not the time to lose your sense of direction. Associates can be a source of worry if you allow them to sidetrack you or sweet-talk you. Some people do not seem to understand either the way you feel or your motives.

13. THURSDAY. Good. The pattern is taking shape. Effort and worry in the past should now be showing results. This is good for your ego as well as for your career prospects. Consolidate a working arrangement. Advice from older colleagues will give you the confidence to do the right thing. Financial activity is part and parcel of the day's functions. You should use your money to the best advantage. Substantiate your position with a sound bank balance. Profit will come if you are prepared to invest or put your resources to work. Entertain wisely those you respect and who have helped you get where you are today. You should be able to pull out all the stops without too much trouble and celebrate in style.

14. FRIDAY. Pleasant. The full effects of recent activities may be felt early today. After all your hard work it will be nice to know you recognized opportunity when you saw it. Business matters should be given a rest for a day or so. A working arrangement can be agreed upon early. This will tidy up a problem for some time to come. From now on solid progress should be made. Seek out friends, but do not become too closely identified with anyone. The comfortable freedom of a club is less demanding than the attentions of an intimate friend. You do not consider your partner in this light. Later you should have a social evening together.

15. SATURDAY. Demanding. You seem to have a chip on your shoulder. Don't take anything for granted and don't push too hard for what you want. Pleasure should come from being sociable. You will find this difficult. Perhaps the expense of doing the things you feel to be correct may be too heavy. Come down to earth and get your plans into perspective. Try to please, so take your loved one into your confidence if you are to solve a problem. If you find it too difficult to get on with people you may face a lonely evening. Consider your best course. It seems to be a matter of your pride. If others make you feel unwanted, that is one thing.

16. SUNDAY. Mixed. Last-minute efforts to promote a social service project may fail. Expenses can be too high. You may be looking forward to a more peaceful spell, so are not quite as enthusiastic about your humanitarian interests as usual. Expenses will not be so heavy if you keep up a relationship with someone you met recently through work. A change is as good as a rest. Influential people can have nice things to say about you this weekend. Do what you consider is the right thing. You will wish to please and are bound to look your best, whatever function you attend. You may have difficulty in keeping peace among your friends. Try allowing opposing sides to state their cases.

17. MONDAY. Sensitive. Put your foot down quietly but firmly if an employee has been neglecting duty. It is time to take minor but stern action in order to keep things moving. Your involvement may not be fully appreciated. Find other ways in which you can get your message across. Get away from routine or old-fashioned methods and try something new. Take private lessons if you think this will improve your earning power. Pay a visit to a health specialist who is likely to have good news for you. The pressures of the last few days may have worried you. Any way out of your difficulties can give relief, so be adventurous and daring.

18. TUESDAY. Productive. Go all-out for the main chance! Resources can be increased in more ways than one if you have faith and confidence. Concentrate all your energies on getting ahead. This will depend to a large extent on the funds you have available to sustain any future plans. Employees or contractors you hire on the outside may be a thorn in the flesh. Do not allow such people to retard your progress. You can get up-tight if hitches occur at a crucial moment. Move quietly ahead with your plans. Senior bank officials will be pleased to support you. Artistic ideas should be promoted. There are numerous ways in which you can increase your earnings, despite problems.

19. WEDNESDAY. Difficult. Be quietly confident early in the day. You could have a stroke of luck that you may want to keep to yourself. As the day progresses you may feel attracted to someone. It seems like a good day for romance, provided you do not push your luck too far. Avoid total commitment to any one partner. What you think or feel now may not be the real thing. Take pleasure from any relationship and show your love to someone you recognize as a truly sensitive person. Business deals are subject to misinterpretation. It may be difficult to know what your opposite number is thinking. Rather than risk making a blooper, you should avoid bargaining today. You could give away too much.

20. THURSDAY. Uneventful. You could be out of the front-line action. Much can be going on around you, nevertheless. Business prospects are good, depending on financial negotiations that can be under way on your behalf. Accountants should be able to get your finances in good working order and be able to report progress and personal profits. Look after personal matters. Just because you are not particularly needed, there is no reason to slack off. Get prepared for future action that is almost at hand. Make time to be friendly with a number of people who may have good news to impart. Take this opportunity to spread it.

21. FRIDAY. Variable. You should switch on the charm when you think it's necessary. Conditions will vary over the day and according to the company you keep. At one time you may need to take initiative and talk your way through an agreement. At another, be prepared to show pleasure and agreement in order to get your own way. Financial interests are all important. Career matters need action and you should have your wits about you if your are to make the progress you deserve. You may be operating on the fringe right now. But there is no reason why your talent and know-how should not be exploited on your behalf.

22. SATURDAY. Important. Be aware of your responsibilities. After a short period of waiting you will feel ready to take up the cudgels. Be positive and forthright in your dealings. A direct approach will get you a long way. You may hear that a local celebrity is making a personal appearance. This could be a good time to cash in on a deal. Get yourself properly organized so that all details are taken care of. Be prepared to work hard and long to make a profit on the day. A lot may depend on public reaction or the opportunity afforded the public to enjoy themselves. You should be keyed up to take full advantage of social conditions. A long-term health problem may show signs of improvement.

23. SUNDAY. Busy.   You have a full day ahead. There is no need to travel far for excitement. It will all be here in your own neighborhood. Be sociable. There is ample opportunity for entertaining or being entertained. All manner of people come your way, from the most influential to the next-door neighbor. Treat everyone alike, because you are in no mood to offend anyone. Though you have no ulterior motive, this should be a good day to make profits. Finances may not bother you, so there could be other gains coming your way. It seems to be the day for initiating some action for the future in the local community. News affecting relatives must be good on a day like this.

24. MONDAY. Harmonious.   Concentrate your resources. All activities may be taking place at a single location. Friends and acquaintances gather together in order to make an impact. Local interests are all-important, so you should get the local press and other elements of the media to help further your plans. With so much facing you, you will have little time to dawdle or consider one subject for very long. Try to avoid being impatient or brusque with others who may be trying to keep up with you. Cooperation will help rather than hinder. You are obliged to consider all aspects if the best result is to emerge from today's activities.

25. TUESDAY. Mixed.   Take care when you travel. If you have neglected to service your car, a breakdown could slow your progress. Expect problems at work. You could be feeling depressed and this will not help matters. It will be best to dig your toes in and get on with the job. Perhaps things will improve later. Avoid arguments that could get you fired. Jobs could be hard to come by. Undertake more responsibility, even if you have doubts as to your ability. You should give it a try, but be careful and go slowly at the start. Impatience is going to achieve very little. News you receive today may be hard to take. While you feel like ignoring your mail, it will be wise to look at it in case something important is missed.

26. WEDNESDAY. Easygoing. Take care of your mail now. It could be less frustrating than usual. There is a chance that you can tidy up a lot of loose ends and get down to making whatever preparations you feel necessary. Relatives come into the picture more frequently now that you have more time away from the pressures of work. A health problem that has been worrying a member of the family should be gradually fading away. This will allow someone else to relax. Get around in your neighborhood and renew contacts you have dropped over the last few days. There is still a need to be closely involved with neighborhood affairs, so you are not going to get out of any previous obligation.

27. THURSDAY. Exciting. A neighborhood love affair may be developing. Thoughts of marriage make it a day for dismissing all logical reactions. More practical action can be taken by those young folk who are looking for a home of their own. A firm offer can be accepted. There is time now to do something about repairs or replacements in the home. Partnership interests can be developed more fully. Though plans may be a bit vague or overly optimistic, someone will be prepared to help without a guarantee. Love abounds in one form or another. It would be impolite to upset anyone, but look after the practical side as well and consider all angles even though you're up in the clouds.

28. FRIDAY. Mixed. Mind your manners when out with neighbors and colleagues. It is all too easy to be familiar with people you meet and chat with almost every day. Today some may be a little touchy, or perhaps you are a little careless. You could be rebuked for going too far. This could cause a family upset if you risk its reputation for no good reason. Make amends somehow. A change in your attitude is called for and you should be quite honest about it. New developments at work should increase your opportunities. Consider the advantages that can arise from installing modern appliances in the home. A property arrangement may be made in record time. Welcome new ideas from the family.

29. SATURDAY. Important. Be quite clear in your intentions. A romantic encounter will mean a great deal to you. It is not something you will lightly dismiss. As the months go by, you could find that you are building up to a decision. A parent could be more cooperative than in the past. Romance is inclined to impress everyone at some time and you could have touched on a soft spot. Do not push too hard. But former attitudes have altered and you should be able to relax and enjoy the company you keep without interruption. It could be time to make yourself available if relatives are feeling friendly and want to see you. Think about the future and perhaps consider a date for the great day.

30. SUNDAY. Exciting. Positive action is possible so you can geta lot straightened out today. Prospects are good for the weekend and you should be able to relax. You know that you have put something in motion which will be followed up and dealt with by the appropriate people. All partnership matters can be dealt with directly and successfully. Joys can be shared. Relatives are actively cooperative and show their love in lots of practical ways. A mystery trip can prove most enjoyable. There may be news of a wedding in the family. A senior member may be able to give useful advice to the young people who are in love. All systems are go and future happiness is there for the taking.

31. MONDAY. Disconcerting. You may feel everyone is ganging up on you. It will be difficult to do anything right, though you could be intent on going ahead with your work. Employers are difficult to satisfy. Local problems can be a cause of much upset, but this is not your fault. Accidents can cause delays. Be careful with tools or hot metal. Workmates are likely to be overly enthusiastic and this can create more work rather than less. There could be some slight distraction that takes the anger out of any ticklish situation. A gentle word may help things along. It is difficult to believe all you hear. There is always more than one version of everything. You usually believe what you want to believe.

SEPTEMBER

1. TUESDAY. Disturbing. Hang on to what is rightfully yours. Before the day is over you could be in trouble with neighbors who could drain your resources. Keep on your toes for changing conditions. The unexpected attitudes of work colleagues can throw you. There may be disturbing news in your mail. Be decisive in the way you react and try to turn this to your advantage. Avoid signing agreements or negotiating better work conditions. Someone can be high-handed and this could depress you. The health of a relative can cause you grave concern. Do what you can to be of practical help. This will make you feel better. Apply yourself to whatever needs doing, whether household repairs or correspondence.

2. WEDNESDAY. Challenging. Develop your business interests. While there is a good opportunity, put into motion any work project that can bring expansion. A surprise you received yesterday can evoke some helpful reactions from the bigwigs. You are eager to do well, so you should be ready to grasp opportunity. Later on, you may be a little too dreamy. Provided you havestarted out on the right foot, this will be no loss. Sharing can be adubious matter. A partner can make you forget your worries or can distract you from your main purpose. Play this by ear. You are zeroed in on a good thing today if you keep your head.

3. THURSDAY. Good. Make hay while the sun shines. Support and advice you received yesterday from senior relatives should not be ignored today. Build on a sound structure. If you are thinking of marriage, this is a good time to settle the details. Some will actually tie the knot, while others must still make the final arrangements. Maintain peace with your fellow beings. If anyone wishes to cast doubt on your proposals, take note but do not be dissuaded. There is more going for you than you may think. Try not to take life too seriously or you will miss out on good times. Make every effort to enjoy local entertainment with your loved one. This is a day to make the most of a partnership.

4. FRIDAY. Disturbing. Cooperation may be difficult to come by. A partner may be reckless and wasteful, expecting too much of you. Do not risk your reputation by being too generous or giving way against your better judgment. Details can be a bit of a bore and this is the sort of pressure you could do without. However, the small things have to be mastered and you should not risk your health through carelessness. Watch out for your diet, which may be getting out of balance. You could be tempted to have a night out with your partner in order to get away from worry and drudgery. Do not put too much store by this outing. You could overdo it, only to have it backfire.

5. SATURDAY. Pleasant. Have a day outdoors with your partner. You should get a lot of pleasure putting your hard-earned cash to good use on behalf of the family. Bargains can be had through serious haggling. Consider practical ways of investing in the future. Look at the prospects available to the next generation as they relate to work. An apprenticeship can be arranged for some professions. A new pet will be a welcome addition to the family circle. Be prepared to consider a different approach to a family pension matter. Some of you will begin to take an interest in the occult for the first time.

6. SUNDAY. Enjoyable. Take the day as it comes for a change of pace. You may feel free and easy, and in no way inclined to plan too far ahead. This is fine and gives you plenty scope for improvisation. Interests can vary between work and travel. Anything too sedate will bore you, but you have a great curiosity about things that function. So it is highly unlikely you will settle for a quiet day. Let the family share your interests with you. This is a joint venture. Lovers will find the later part of the day a time for relaxation and peace. Take your loved one far away from the crowds and enjoy the weekend. Many of you will think of the future.

7. MONDAY. Unsettling. It will be most difficult to get any cooperation today. Your interests will differ from those of your loved ones. This could be through force of circumstances. Work and travel may take you away from those you love when they most need to have you around. Get your priorities right and explain them if it becomes necessary. The health of a relative may cause you some worry. Undertake whatever traveling is necessary. Though this may be troublesome, there is good reason to apply yourself. Delays may be encountered. Schedules may have to be altered at the last moment.

8. TUESDAY. Disquieting. Outside interests will take priority. Family will have to take a backseat if you want to make the most of your chances. A journey could be completed at the expense of home comforts. But you feel you must get something tidied up if anything of value is to be achieved. Negotiations could be tough. You will have to go to extremes to seek a compromise. Keep an open mind if you are to see both sides of the problem. Early rearrangements can start you off on the wrong foot. Accept such aggravation and settle down to the main considerations concerning reputation. Consider carefully before you commit yourself in writing or to oral agreements.

9. WEDNESDAY. Important. Past efforts are sure to be recognized. Your reputation should be strengthened and you will be one step nearer that goal you had set for yourself this year. Performance is all-important. You should be keen to display your talents. There is no call for false modesty. If you have difficulty with other forms of publicity, you should have none when it comes to the visual display of competence. Business should prosper. Consolidate gains and keep an eye open for more adventurous techniques that can keep you a step ahead of competitors. If you are employed, now is the time to make your position more secure.

10. THURSDAY. Changeable. Take advantage of diverse business opportunities. You may be inclined to put all your eggs in one basket. Make your own judgment. Reputations could be at stake, especially in the early part of the day. There could be some cause for concern in the family. Property deals should be treated with caution. Sign or agree to nothing connected with land or property. You could be in for a letdown. All is not what it seems. A working relationship can blow up in your face. Try to be diplomatic, but do not expect your actions to be reciprocated. There may be news of a relative in poor health. Be gentle with your partner, who may be upset. Love is never wasted.

11. FRIDAY. Productive. Enlarge your business prospects by attracting new clients. Concentrate your energies positively on material and practical aims. Friendship is an important factor if you are to make full use of the day. Cement local relationships. Attend to all those run-of-the-mill activities that keep business a viable concern. Neighbors will be actively cooperative in any social project you wish to promote. You should have no difficulty in getting your point of view across. Try to avoid personal involvement that will distract you from your main social endeavors. Someone may feel neglected if you appear to be more interested in friends.

12. SATURDAY. Enjoyable. Weekend prospects appear to be good. With two days of freedom ahead, you should have well-laid plans to enjoy the social scene. Entertainment and good company are essential ingredients and should be easy to come by. You are not likely to get too deeply involved. There may be a local attraction that intrigues without any underlying ties. Enjoy varied company. This is no time to tie yourself down to one companion. For those married folks, consider this a good chance to have a family get-together socially. Friends and neighbors will be welcome and will share your enthusiasm. You have many friends to see.

13. SUNDAY. Special. Why not take it easy? You may appreciate a rest after the fun-filled activities last night. Family gossip will be enjoyable. It is a day to let your hair down in the privacy of the home and in the company of those who know you best. Carry on with the weekend festivities in a more restrained way. Relationships can develop and old ties be cemented in a peaceful atmosphere. Make the most of the family group. This is your bulwark. If you are looking for personal seclusion, you can probably find pleasure in your collections. You may receive private information of a property arrangement that is pending. If you can help someone in need, do so. Make arrangements for family gatherings.

14. MONDAY. Disturbing. One again, you go back to the problems of the week. This is no time to take things easy. Traveling problems can cause delays. Mail may be unwelcome or held up, causing further frustration. You will want to promote a private project, but may find it difficult to persuade fellow workers. You may have to give up for a time. The opposition of a superior or employer can give you a headache. Have a thought for resulting complications. Keep a low profile if things begin to heat up. Do not commit yourself too far at any time. Relatives you saw yesterday may have had problems getting home.

15. TUESDAY. Mixed. Have your arrangements well planned if you participate in a public engagement. You should make private gains from any social involvement. Show the flag where necessary. Your reputation will benefit from public or private contributions to a good cause. Personal needs are important. You may feel you have to share, but can find it difficult to accept the situation. Make up your mind. You will lose momentum and direction if you are unsure of your way. Avoid making firm agreements. You will be obliged to consider hard facts, so may have to be very practical. But there are temptations that can lead you astray.

16. WEDNESDAY. Difficult. Personal plans and hopes can be upset by the uncooperative actions of superiors. Do not expect employers to give away more than is necessary. Influential people in the neighborhood can make it difficult for you to earn a living. You will need to be careful if security is to be maintained. A family matter will be difficult to settle. Any arrangement affecting property may be to your personal disadvantage. Keep the family from making plans for the future at this point. There will be a better chance for success a little later. Your personal plans are likely to disrupt the domestic front. See if you can raise support from neighbors or relatives who understand and appreciate you.

17. THURSDAY. Fair. Think long-term rather than in the present. You are fully capable of constructive action and thought. But you are equally capable of blowing everything sky-high by seeking immediate recognition. A public appointment could be attractive. Consider this in terms of your long-term security prospects. Seek advice from influential people if you are in a quandary. Someone of importance in your locality should be able to help.

This could be the deciding factor. Financial reward and family security are becoming more important in the general scheme of things. Make firm arrangements to have repairs done to the house.

18. FRIDAY. Strenuous. A fool and his money are soon parted. Think twice before risking your hard-earned money in any gambling ventures. Family plans need financial support. This will give much more satisfaction in the long run. Intuition may not be reliable today. If you have a hunch about a surefire winner in a race, let it go. A lovers' tiff can make the day miserable for some. Do not try to buy happiness. Patching things up will prove to be too expensive. If you are feeling sorry for yourself look for company. Being on your own will only make you more depressed so that you will tend to blow things out of all proportion. There are lots of things to do locally or around the house.

19. SATURDAY. Good. If you are working today, there is much to be gained. Get cracking early and look for a good return on your labors. Shoppers looking for a bargain should be practical. You get nothing you do not pay for, but do expect value for your money. Self-employed people should think seriously of future prospects. This is a time when you should be consolidating and making profits. Check on your bank account. If it is not what you expect, do something about it. Innovation should pay off. A change can be to your advantage, though hastiness is not advisable. Routine can prove less boring with the introduction of a new outlook or new friends. Interesting people can brighten your day.

20. SUNDAY. Fair. A public appearance early in the day can bring rewards. You should get pleasure from participation in a project that will pay dividends later on. Be generous with your money. It will be well spent. A stroke of luck may add to the joys of living. Enjoy the company of relatives and colleagues who have similar interests. There is room for romance, so you can live it up with a close friend. Get around in a quiet way. You have friends to see and will be well received. There may be some sensitivity to spoil the day if you neglect the home. Your partner could feel hurt or unable to keep up with you. Be considerate of others.

21. MONDAY. Worrisome. Get on with whatever job you last had in hand. A backlog of work can greet you, so you may have little choice in the matter. Fortunately you can concentrate, so you will be able to cope with whatever comes your way. Make your own decisions. You will get more done through personal initiative than by consultation. Colleagues will have differing viewpoints.

They will frustrate you and make you very impatient. Drive a hard bargain. If you have to make a journey, be prepared for hitches. But do be prepared, so that you can carry on despite delays, detours, and inconvenience. This is not a day to be weak. You have entirely too much to do for rest and peace.

22. TUESDAY. Uncertain. Some people are going to be difficult today. Let them alone, if that is how they feel. You have other fish to fry so you need not be despondent. Think of the blessings of home and never mind the erratic behavior of colleagues or co-workers. Harmony can be jeopardized if you entertain a dissident. This may give you cause for second thoughts. You should be able to talk your way out of any problem. You probably have the support of influential people, so you have quite a lot going for you. Others may not appreciate this and could try to stir up trouble. You will survive and be another step ahead of the competition.

23. WEDNESDAY. Mixed. Consider your security before taking any initiative. Your judgment can be clouded. Some of you will be in love, while others can simply be deceiving themselves. Settle no agreement while in this sensitive state. Enjoy the benefits, but expect only what you are entitled to. A partner can be hard to please or may not show appropriate appreciation for your efforts. You should take no one for granted. This is hurtful and someone near you is very upset today. As you are feeling generous, why not try some home entertainment? This will keep you from making silly mistakes and give you the chance to be friendly. Think about home decoration. Get ideas from your friends.

24. THURSDAY. Lucky. Feel free to do your own thing. Ideas you had for home improvement can be investigated. Try something a bit unusual for a change. This should brighten up the scene. Dealings on the property market may get a boost. Look out for the unusual bargain or a property with an unusual difference. You should be full of bright ideas about the planning and decoration of your home. Those of you on the lookout for property can stumble on a bargain in a unexpected place. Settle any agreement at work. Contracts can be made in good faith. This is a good day to get your house in order. Security is always a main consideration.

25. FRIDAY. Fair. Something could be brewing that can upset the domestic scene. Wait and see. A regular get-together with someone you appreciate should prove rewarding. You will concentrate on one, rather than spreading your net wide. Romantic feelings can take over if you let down your defenses. Concentrate on developing an artistic outlet. You have talents that have remained hidden too long. This is a good day to bring them to the surface and give pleasure to others as well as yourself. Artistic types could be attracted to you. Accept this, but do not allow your imagination to run away with you. Be receptive to good ideas.

26. SATURDAY. Difficult.   A domestic problem needs to be straightened out. Any business involvement will be resented by the family. You will have to use all your diplomacy and wits to avoid a head-on collision of interests. Be honest with all those who are concerned or you will end up in the doghouse. Look after the minor details and the larger matters will tend to fall into place. You may be able to call on the support of relatives if there is need for arbitration. If things get out of control, enjoy yourself. You should be letting yourself go in some ways, so you can anticipate excesses and a few white lies in order to keep the peace.

27. SUNDAY. Mixed.   Nothing is likely to go according to plan. The gremlins seem to have invaded the system. It's a good thing, perhaps, that this is not a working day. You may have difficulty getting your thoughts organized. Local folk are likely to disrupt your routine. Do not be too dependent on relatives or nearby neighbors if you have a major task to complete. Thoughts of the working week ahead can spoil your enjoyment of the weekend. Relatives who call seem to talk shop all the time. Any attempt to get away from such aggravation will be frustrated by unexpected events and thoughtless people. Make the most of the day, however. Do something energetic to relieve the tension.

28. MONDAY. Demanding.   Domestic conditions can be very trying. If you are determined to carry on with work, be prepared for family squalls. You may be accused of neglect by your loved ones. Take all this with a pinch of salt. You are well aware that performance and production are all-important, so get on with your work. Hand out a bit of flattery. This will oil the works and give you a better chance for making progress. A workmate may become attractive. This could make you think quite seriously. As you may be in a very sensitive state of mind, you should be extra careful of your actions or intentions. An older person, or the boss, may turn on you. You may not know the reason, so try to find out.

29. TUESDAY. Variable.   Try to do things on your own. Should you be too deeply involved with others there is likely to be a flare-up. Personal ideas and initiative at work should lead to promotion or recognition. Colleagues may take a different view of your progress and this could cause arguments. Cooperaton is out of the question at the moment. You may be inclined to overdo strenuous work. A strain is possible if you try to lift heavy things. Pride and a sense of urgency may overrule good judgment. Despite the aggravation you can achieve a good deal. Curb your impatience and moderate your language to get what you want.

30. WEDNESDAY. Good. You will appreciate a rest after the storm. You could be whacked out. A soothing hand will be appreciated. Look for support and comfort from those you know most intimately. Enjoy life with a loved one and do not seek activity or involvement with the world in general. Seek peace in creative ways. Your artistic talents can now be utilized if you hope to find any kind of satisfaction. Be gentle and friendly with all you meet. Entertain if you feel like it, but do not put yourself out too much. A select company will be far better than a host of friends. You could disturb the equilibrium if you go too far with your plans.

OCTOBER

1. THURSDAY. Satisfactory. Active cooperation is what you need. Without this a great deal of your efforts can be wasted. Recognition will not come easily, but that is not your main focus at the moment. It would be much better to maintain good relationships with your everyday contacts. In this way you can build up your resources on a reliable basis. Partners in business may not see eye-to-eye with you. Let this ride for the moment. Do not trust such people. They may put appearances before essential cooperation and achieve nothing. Rely on your own judgment and on the friendship of those you meet every day. Relatives are friendly.

2. FRIDAY. Manageable. Seek the advice of a parent or senior member of the family. You do not like to take family business out of the nest, so listen to wisdom at home. If you are having a problem meeting family commitments, remember this is nothing new. Provided you keep your head there is no fear of wasting money. But you will need to discipline yourself. It is all too easy to give in to the demands of children. Arrive at a working agreement that will make your family income more secure. It may be a good idea to have insurance premiums paid in advance at their source. This can save you worry over missing a crucial date and expense. Look for a permanent arrangement to free you from such aggravation.

3. SATURDAY. Good.   Spend some money on brightening up the home. This will be a good investment and will add to the value of your property. Take note of family views on investment. Get an all-round opinion for future transactions. It seems an appropriate time to do some research with an open mind. Methods and rewards should be considered seriously before action is taken. Property matters can be settled without disagreement. You should find happiness in the company of someone well-known to the family. Entertain at home. A trip to see someone you admire may follow later in the day. Prepare the way with a bit of self-promotion. This will do no harm and could even help you.

4. SUNDAY. Harmonious.   Get moving early in the day. If local interests kept you at home yesterday, make an early start. The wide-open spaces beckon you and yours. Visits to family can be undertaken. Equally important, you are also in a position to entertain. The main thing is to meet friends and family you see infrequently. Look up travel schedules for future vacations. It may be wise to plan ahead in order to get the best treatment. Students should have a good and productive weekend. A break from regular studies will prove beneficial. Develop your interests and broaden your mind generally. There is nothing like travel to do this.

5. MONDAY. Sensitive.   Nothing fits into place today. You may be glad to avoid routine and long for the open road. But even that can provide its quota of problems. Traveling will not be the pleasant pastime you had expected it to be. Working conditions create problems. Imported material is not up to usual standards. A deal with an overseas firm is more trouble than it is worth. Try to keep emotions under control, although that will be difficult. A working relationship can save the day. You should be able to resolve a lot of problems in the quiet and peace of home. Security is strengthened by a rearrangement of your working routine.

6. TUESDAY. Strenuous.   You are full of ideas. Concentrate on those that seem to offer the most reward and have a sound basis. Creative urges are strong, so you could be a bit wayward. Opposition may be met from a parent or senior member of the family. If you seek to show off too much you are likely to be brought back to earth quickly. Family ties may prove to be overriding. A partner could let you down. You have your own ideas and this may rule out cooperative action. So do not expect help from others. It is usually best to go your own way. Consider your reputation in all aspects. There are some who would like to get you down off your pedestal. See to it that your position is secure.

7. WEDNESDAY. Productive. It should be a happy day to be away from home responsibilities. Business will be much more attractive and work more stimulating. You can make a lot of headway and be given the room to develop and expand your efforts. Concentrate on the job at hand. Do not waste any time on trivialities. It may be difficult to include some things, so ignore them and get on with something else that fits into place. This is a day of opportunity. You cannot please everyone, even those who depend on your labors. But despite this, you should be able to make a great deal of progress that is essential to your future prospects. If the family feels neglected, try to explain the pros and cons to them.

8. THURSDAY. Difficult. You can get carried away with idealistic plans. Seek the cooperation of willing partners in whatever you contemplate. Only genuine support will be offered, so you need not be suspicious. Opposition to your aims will have to be faced. A deep-seated resentment may be stirred up in some areas. Be firm in your reaction. Try to guide your personal talents for the benefit of people who can be steered toward a humanitarian goal. You may have to choose between using such talents for purely personal or social advantage. If a balance cannot be struck, something may have to go by the board. You might rationalize the choice. If you opt for social advantage, you will be apt to reap benefit.

9. FRIDAY. Disconcerting. This would appear to be an uneventful day. You could have difficulty in getting any idea or project accepted that you think is worthwhile. Dumb insolence or a blank stare might greet you. For those involved with children or education this can be frustrating. Try to forge ahead anyway and remember that you are trying to improve the lot of someone who needs help. No one is particularly reliable. You will be far better off on your own, keeping your distance in company and remaining friendly or somewhat aloof. Avoid intimate involvement. You may be misunderstood and that would not benefit you.

10. SATURDAY. Rewarding. Make the most of weekend privacy. Settle down to interests that have been neglected too long. You will be energetic and so can make adequate plans for work that will benefit the whole family. Take into consideration all matters connected with the home that you can handle yourself. Where you need advice, a member of the family with more experience will be ready to oblige. A parent can be extra helpful and set your mind at rest. Consider a long-term contract for house maintenance. This seems like a good time to make firm arrangements. Lay plans for a lengthy schedule that will attend to the basic needs of the family. Their hard work should be recognized.

11. SUNDAY. Pleasant.   Collect your thoughts. Planning is essential while you have peace and privacy. Opposition to some scheme may make you ponder the pros and cons of the present situation. Take note of any advice or support offered by someone of importance. It would be sensible to entertain such a person in order to cultivate a private source of strength for the future. Should you take life too seriously, this could be a worrisome day. You may try to do too much or think you are hardier than is the case. Avoid taking on too heavy a responsibility and thus endangering your health. A friend in need may be glad of your attention.

12. MONDAY. Uncertain.   It will be a day of changing emphasis. Workaday problems make life uncertain early on. Be prepared for changes and erratic behavior from your colleagues. An opportunity to make headway can come later. Someone may pass the word to you in private. You seem to be in favor with the fair sex and at war with men in general later in the day. This may mean a complicated evening for you, so play your cards with care. Romance seems promising and this will suit you. Your ego can be boosted. Look out for squalls at home if you disturb the family. A member of the family may take a dim view of some of your activities, and you must expect some criticism in the process.

13. TUESDAY. Exciting.   Something you started yesterday may build up today. Your lovelife can become more and more interesting. Emotions may run high, but you will find this exciting. If you are married there is a possibility that your partner may take a poor view of your manner. For those without ties, this could be a day to develop a new relationship. Be on your guard that you do not misjudge your opposite number. You could get carried away and perhaps lose out if you are not honest with yourself and your newfound friend. You might wind up behind the eight ball or may be led up the garden path. So be romantic, but avoid entanglements. Make good use of your artistic and creative talents.

14. WEDNESDAY. Strenuous.   Do not push your luck. The urge to go your own way can be strong. Given a bit of rope, you could hang yourself, figuratively speaking. You could be tempted

to seek public favor. What you have to propose to any backer or
business friend will not be received well. It is too risky at the moment. Your security can be threatened if you take on too much
and do not heed the advice of people with influence. This may be
frustrating. Stay away from any property deals for a week or so.
You can do a lot of homework in the interim. Look for moral support or just comfort from a partner who has helped you before
when you were in trouble. This will help you cope.

15. THURSDAY. Sensitive. You could feel like splashing your
money around. Your first priority should be the home. You may
not be looking for bargains, but you should have a clear idea of
what you are after before you hit the stores. Deal directly and you
should get your money's worth. The young and unattached may
have more problems. You are eager to please. What you wish to
do can be very expensive. Try to impress someone you admire
with your natural talents. Should you have to resort to buying your
favors, this will cost you a bundle. There is a possibility of going
too far, in some respects. But if you are making someone happy,
you will take it all in your stride.

16. FRIDAY. Satisfactory. You will be aware of your true
worth. Take a good hard look at yourself, your prospects, and
your abilities. This should give you heart and confidence. Apply
yourself to whatever has to be done and see that you get due reward for your labor. No one will sell you short today, possibly because you have made your mind up to get your rights. Your
finances should be sound. You will feel you are getting somewhere. You may be tempted to sign away some asset. Someone
could try to talk you out of hard-earned cash. Keep clear of such
temptation. Children may be expensive. If you have to pay a
school fee this could be unavoidable.

17. SATURDAY. Promising. Make the most of public popularity. You who are in the business of merchandising should have a
great day. Any way in which you can demonstrate your talent or
your potential should pay dividends. Show-biz folk will do well.
Though some influential people may consider this is not your true
future, they will give you support that will encourage you. As long
as they understand what it is that you are seeking and the financial
background, this is all you need expect. What you do in public is
your own affair. Security can be slack in some way. Look after
property if you have doubts about the safety of valuables. A partner may be a weak link in any property transaction.

18. SUNDAY. Useful. An obsession of yesterday may seem less important today. You could feel more relaxed or uplifted, and so able to think more clearly. Disbelief or confusion can be clarified if you apply your mind to some outstanding problem. Be patient in handling anyone who has got it wrong. Activity in your neighborhood should be good for you. A relative can be thoughtful or you, in your turn, can be extra considerate of a relative in need. Plans can be made for future family travel. These are early days, but you should be prepared. You may have two or three relationships going at the moment. Stop to think if this is wise. You can waste time and talent by spreading resources too far.

19. MONDAY. Demanding. Traffic problems can delay your start. Try to be patient, for this could be the pattern for the day ahead. As the day progresses you can become more and more frustrated. Being an emotional person you will soon get uptight. Think about those stomach ulcers in the future and let things take their course. If you can get things organized, all to the good. It may be difficult to stick to a schedule. Try to avoid wasted journeys. You could be distressed by news of a sick relative. This is one of the areas where you can use your sympathetic talents constructively. If others want to be contrary, let them go their way.

20. TUESDAY. Satisfactory. Make your holiday arrangements final. Come to an agreement with other friends who share your recreational interests. Take up a new hobby that will give you more contact with artistic and articulate people. Some may start another collection if one is nearly complete. Avoid dealings in property. You may think you are on to a good thing, but there will be flaws in your reasoning. At the moment you could be very sure of yourself. This can blind you to other issues, some of them quite serious. When you are quite satisfied, you can take the initiative. Sharing responsibility, however, is not recommended. A partner or opposite number is likely to let you down.

21. WEDNESDAY. Good. Complete arrangements for a family get-together. You should know how many you can accommodate, so can arrive at a firm estimate for food and beverages. Stock up, if necessary, and put enough aside for the unexpected guest who will be made welcome. Consider the impact of your efforts on society. You could go overboard and make a splash, or you can restrict your operations to manageable proportions. Be conservative and you will not lose your good reputation. House reconstruction can go ahead. This could be part of a long-term project. It will add to the size of the structure and provide needed security to weak spots. Get modern safety equipment installed.

22. THURSDAY. Challenging. Some of you may be starting another chapter of life. This can be a most important step. For some it can mean a new home and fresh responsibilities. Your maternal instincts can be stimulated, as home means so much to you. Think of your background, the past, the stock you came from. As this is a year of opportunity, consider what you want to make of the future. But remember how much depends on your understanding of the past. It is a day, therefore, on which to be optimistic. If your nearest and dearest finds you a little distant, be loving and kind. You have all to gain and nothing to lose by sharing with those you love.

23. FRIDAY. Uneventful. Concentration on a personal interest can keep you from general activity. Some may be obsessed with their children who could need special attention. Others can be intrigued by the power and ability of a child they meet. Young lovers may be deeply moved by the thought of becoming parents. Try to be constructive when in such a mood. Make plans if that is all you can do. Pay some attention to little ones if it is within your power. Use your intuition to advantage and get what you are after. You can be a step ahead of those who have to reason logically. Later on you may appreciate how much you can enjoy yourself by being interested in a great variety of subjects.

24. SATURDAY. Enjoyable. Once more, Saturday gives you a chance to show off your skills. Business and shopkeeping should be good for those who live by their own efforts. The public will be enthusiastic and should appreciate a novel approach if you have the good sense to experiment. Your lovelife should be active. You can have more than one iron in the fire. This can keep you very busy as well as lending variety to the weekend. See that you get your fair share of publicity. You might be given a pleasant social outing to keep you in a good mood. If you feel adventurous, you should be glad to show off your talents. A meeting with someone in the law profession or government service is possible.

25. SUNDAY. Rewarding. You will not have any time to waste today. The remainder of the weekend should be gainfully occupied in doing those outstanding chores in and around the home and the premises. Ladies will straighten out the home while menfolk get on with heavy-duty jobs of repair that have been left untended for too long. There could be some hitches. Do not take things too seriously or you will make yourself miserable. By the end of the day you should be well satisfied with your progress. Consider seriously a proposal regarding a property transaction. Look into the mechanics of buying and selling. Get yourself acquainted with all practical aspects. Consolidate any gain you have made.

26. MONDAY. Productive.   There will be a lively start to the working week. Your services may be in great demand. Rise to the occasion and you will gain in prestige. Reputations can be made today if you care to apply yourself. No doubt you may feel a little adventurous again, so can experiment in order to broaden your horizons. If you have prepared your ground carefully there will be no fear of failing today. So go ahead and have faith in yourself. You should be able to enlist some support before the day is over. The cooperation of important people in show-biz or of those who understand the market will help, once you have broken new ground. Your enthusiasm and know-how will inspire confidence.

27. TUESDAY. Tricky.   Reach an understanding with someone who is willing to cooperate. This is a good time to talk and arrange joint affairs. Plans must be laid prior to any action. You could be very sensitive to whatever is going on around you. Use this in a positive manner and sound out any situation before you commit yourself to action. Should you be fearful and act in a negative way, someone could quite easily play you for a sucker. You would then lose out altogether. All people do not think as you do, although you may think someone in particular is perfect. If your kind feelings are reciprocated, this will be fine. Avoid arguments in the home.

28. WEDNESDAY. Sensitive.   Patch up any disagreement you have had recently. There is no need to have family quarrels. A recent hitch in a relationship can be put to rights. Some of you will be considering marriage and getting organized for the great day. Others may be even further advanced toward the altar. By now you should have been able to reach an understanding on important details. Business partnerships which have been through a trying period lately may receive a boost. This is something you should treat with some reserve. Someone at the top could be setting a trap. Risk at the moment is unlikely to pay off.

29. THURSDAY. Worrisome.   An influential person in fashion or show-biz may apparently be of help and wish to cooperate. There are two sides to this coin. You may gain a friend who carries weight, but you could easily lose money or risk family funds. Try to judge which is more important. Consider the timing of any such proposal. There could be a substantial loss of revenue if you are too immersed in one aspect of a joint venture and so miss its deeper implications. Someone may be looking for an opportunity to cooperate, or may be more inclined to gain control. Be on your guard. Look after a long-term asset. Consider reinvestment if you have money to play with.

30. FRIDAY. Manageable.   You are determinedly poised ready to promote the family funds. This is the time to come to a fair decision about joint resources, based on sound working practices and public reputation. Look ahead with confidence. Be happy to improvise after due consideration of all important facts. Take advantage of a progressive offer from someone who knows the legal position in business. A public official could be of assistance and should be welcomed. A great deal of joint monies may have been spent recently on entertaining, hobbies, and other pleasure projects. This is the time to put your foot down.

31. SATURDAY. Exciting.   Hit the road with close friends and family. This is a day to get clear away from everyday chores. You should be feeling great and at peace with everyone. Some will travel far to join the one person in their lives. Love blossoms in all corners of the globe. Partnership interests are promoted by the friendly attitude of all sorts of people. Good publicity comes for those in the theater. A top-rank promoter can do some of you a power of good. Do not be too shy to advertise your talent. Be happy to travel if you are given the opportunity. Students with hopes for the future should be able to put across their truly creative ideas. Children and young people should have a good day.

NOVEMBER

1. SUNDAY. Upsetting. You could be feeling under the weather a bit. A journey planned earlier may have to be postponed until you are able to cope. It is just one of those things, so do not get in too much of an uproar. Practicalities may weigh heavy on you. While you have great ideas for the future, you are obliged to think of the everyday responsibilities and chores that seem to restrict your progress. There could be news of a near relative, possibly an in-law, that arouses your compassion. Do something practical rather than just worry. Students could find this a frustrating weekend. Preparations for future examinations can be more than usually burdensome. Stick to it.

2. MONDAY. Demanding. Stand on your own two feet. Public appearances count for a lot. You should seek recognition in your own right while being aware that someone else may be giving you a push. Influential people can be forceful or persuasive. If you are looking for progress, you may be wide open to exploitation. Your judgment is all-important, so do not put too much trust in any partner or intimate friend who offers advice or assistance. A partner may be rather confused. Your aspirations may not be fully appreciated or shared, so a loved one may be upset. There is little hope of changing your attitude. The bit is between your teeth now and there's no stopping you. Make good use of your talent.

3. TUESDAY. Useful. Taking chances may pay off. Even so, all will not be plain sailing. You could get an opportunity to make good. Prestige can rise if you time things well. Opposition from home may upset your schedule. Try to avoid friction, even if you have to bite your tongue to keep quiet. Should you have to make a major decision, take time to consider the pros and cons. Patience and consideration are on your side though you may be impatient for results. If engaged in any bargaining, have your groundwork done previously. A well-prepared case will win the day. Positive action will overcome any argument. Be careful in the home. See that all is secure.

4. WEDNESDAY. Variable. It is hard to satisfy everyone. Though you may be feeling it is time to relax, there may be many details to tidy up. Arrangements can be upset. Your point of view will not be acceptable to someone who is concerned with the way you handle your public affairs. Take on no transaction connected with property if you want a quiet day. Such business is likely to be complicated. Previous property deals may have complications you did not see earlier. Be on your guard for someone who will try to talk you into something you can do without. Your partner may have ideas that help you out of a difficulty. When the business of the day is through, this is a good time to enjoy social activities.

5. THURSDAY. Difficult. Watch your step or you can overdo things. There is a temptation to go all out in order to make a point. This attitude will arouse opposition from people in authority. Show-biz people should avoid confrontation with producers and other influential top brass. Be content to please the public without thinking too much of your own self-satisfaction. Social life can be upset by the interference of people who could control your destiny or have the power to block your plans. Humanitarian interests may turn you on at the moment. You will not get far with your plans until you can enlist the help of the big boys with the money.

6. FRIDAY. Ordinary. Make a list of things that need to be done. Get on quietly with your work. The upsets of yesterday may have left you a little shattered, so do not push yourself. Life is rather like a jigsaw puzzle at the moment. Before you break for the weekend see that you are prepared for the jobs you have in mind. Be sociable without getting out of your depth. Business finances will need to be put straight today. Do not attempt to start any new venture. You should be buttoning things up rather than looking for new business. Though you may have a busy day, you should not become too involved with people. Try to get some privacy, especially later in the day. Above all, keep cool and calm.

7. SATURDAY. Good. Now you will have the time to get on with your own private jobs. An early start will help if you have weekend shopping to do. You will not want to be involved in hustle and bustle today. Quiet efficiency should be your goal. With a fair bit of work to do around the house, you will appreciate the opportunity to be left to your own devices. Feelings may be touched if you are separated from a loved one. Others may have to leave you on your own, which is what you want. But you will become somewhat nostalgic if you are not fully occupied. You can't have it both ways, so buckle down and get on with your good deed for the day. Don't lose sight of those private jobs you had lined up.

8. SUNDAY. Mixed. Look for a change if you are getting bored. A little bit of public excitement should break up any feelings of isolation you may have. Should you be behind schedule with your efforts of yesterday do not take it too seriously. Somewhere along the line there is likely to be a stoppage. So make the day one you can enjoy. There will be another day tomorrow or next weekend. Think of a friend who may be in need. Your sympathy could be aroused for an older person who has fallen on hard times. You should be able to cheer someone up if you use your initiative and act informally. Don't be a stuffed shirt.

9. MONDAY. Misleading. You may feel uncertain about a relationship. Be cautious rather than adventurous. A close associate may not be everything he claims to be. Look after your own interests as a main priority without being selfish. Cooperation may be hard to come by, so you are better off making your own decisions. If you have a legal matter to contest, be well prepared. The opposition is likely to produce something out of the blue. You could be involved with a slippery client or customer if you are engaged in a business deal. Consider the needs of your true partner. If there is a genuine need to comfort and support someone you love, make a good job of it. Make your feelings clear.

10. TUESDAY. Challenging. Personal desires can be fully expressed. Look for genuine support from influential people if you have something creative to offer. The business side of the coin may be more heavily involved. You might have to choose between security at home and possible personal development in public. Encouragement from those who know your inner potential can lift you high enough to handle any problem. But guard against taking too many risks or becoming too sure of yourself. Pride can go before a fall. The family may have their own interests and be involved in making progress in a way different to yours.

11. WEDNESDAY. Worrisome. Involvement in family affairs can lead to complications. The small print on any agreement can be more important than you think, so take care of details. A certain amount of haggling can throw you off your guard and waste a lot of valuable time. You have personal matters to complete. Do not get rattled by the chatter of people who have little appreciation of your needs. Business expansion has been threatened recently and will still remain uncertain today. You need to think clearly before making any decision. Be as tactful as you can. Remember you are in the driver's seat and should be able to control negotiations.

12. THURSDAY. Productive. Use your charm and you will get all you deserve. Work should be a pleasure. Some will meet a new friend at work and from this beginning a romantic experience can start. Given the right approach, you should be able to make money. Be prepared to spend wisely if you are looking for a bargain. Your taste should be especially good today, so get something nice for the home if you see it. Provided you use judgment, you are on a winning roll. Be cooperative and obliging to get the best out of the staff at work. Should you try to push your luck or exercise too much pressure, you will fall apart. Your cash flow will suffer if you gamble immoderately.

13. FRIDAY. Encouraging. An influential person who should know better may wish to receive financial backing. You should have things going for you today. This could attract a lot of attention and someone may look to you for the go-ahead or financial support. Do not allow yourself to be forced into doing a service in order to gain a favor. You are being taken for a sucker by someone who is lazy or not a true friend. If they want to get ahead, let them take the risks along with you. But do not ever accept the burden on someone else's behalf. You will get a long way on your own because family will cooperate actively. Business friends and fellow workers, who have a sense of originality, will also pitch in.

14. SATURDAY. Good. The weekend will get off to a good start. With free time you can make the rounds among relatives and neighbors. Get up-to-date with all you have missed in the past week. Enjoy your natural pleasure in the company of children. Their activities in local affairs should give you a feeling of warmth. Any activity that brings you in contact with articulate people should be encouraged. The local paper may report something to your advantage. Intimate ties are especially meaningful. You will want to do things together with your partner. Be gentle and relaxed. Use your imagination. Seek to develop relationships within the family by keeping in touch with a wider circle.

15. SUNDAY. Disturbing. You may be surprised at the attitude of a relative. Perhaps a shoulder is needed to cry on. There may be some unhappiness in others that you can help clear up. Health problems can come to the fore. Use your versatility to cope with any problem that arises during the day. It may be necessary to change your diet, which may currently be out of balance. Someone you are fond of may have to work today. This will throw your anticipated schedule right out of whack. Don't worry too much. It could be worse. You may be inclined to get upset and do too much running around. This will be fruitless and could give you ulcers.

16. MONDAY. Mixed. Early travelers can have problems. Overnight delays will take some time to clear up. Be prepared to improvise. Try to keep your cool if you hear upsetting news. First impressions are not always right. Though you may appear to start out on the wrong foot, you will get organized eventually and all will be well. There could be some trouble with employees right at the start of the working week. No one is very happy on a Monday morning. Avoid early negotiations with discontented staff. They will be more cooperative when you can produce a workable proposition. That should give them more scope and basic security.

17. TUESDAY. Good. There should be a much better start to the working day. After the pressure of yesterday it can be a pleasure to be with your colleagues. They will also be in a much better frame of mind today. Domestic conditions should be considered. It may be a good time to select material for decorating your home in the future. Prepare quietly for entertainment. You may wish to invite a colleague home for a meal. As you are feeling friendly, you should share your goodwill. Think ahead to the holiday period at the end of the year. Try to be prepared in advance by getting the basics organized. Use your charm to get the family on your side, so that you are not left with too much to do.

18. WEDNESDAY. Demanding. You are in the mood to get your house in order. An early start will give you the headway you need for coping with a busy day. Positive thinking is required and you are ready for action. Organize your day. Be prepared to stick to your schedule. Despite some interruptions later in the day, you will get straight to the point in whatever you do. Business interests may be distracting. Remember you are dealing primarily with basic matters on which your security depends. You therefore cannot expand too much at the moment. Once you have made your position secure, you will be more free to develop at will.

19. THURSDAY. Productive. A regular engagement comes round again. You will concentrate on one interest for a part of the day. If you decide to focus your attention on one subject, some people may feel they are being ignored. Use your good judgment as to your priorities. A child or children may take up much of your time. There could be a need to concentrate on some creative venture that you feel should be interpreted or publicized. Loving support can come from a partner who is on your wavelength. Because you are particularly sensitive, you could be either vulnerable or totally impervious to outside intervention. Be cooperative if you want best results. Your creative talents could be in heavy demand.

20. FRIDAY. Strenuous. Though work still goes on you will want to enjoy the day. It will offer a good time for shopping. You can be well employed in selecting presents and other goods for the Christmas period ahead. Get out of the house and travel a bit more than usual in search of whatever may have special appeal. You may be inclined to spend a little more than usual. Try to be practical without losing that taste for which you are noted. Children may have to be excluded from today's operation. They are likely to make their presence known, so you should be firm if you hope to get anything done. Reach an early and firm understanding with them before you set out. They will repay you in kind.

21. SATURDAY. Pleasant. Put your best foot forward today. If you are obliged to work today, do so with high hopes. You have a need to put all of it to good use. Many outlets will interest you. The boredom of work will be lessened by the variety of occupations you handle in just a few hours. Artistic interests come naturally. You can apply yourself with purpose, so you are not likely to lose an opportunity to do yourself some good in the bargain. Use your judgment. Your reputation depends, to a good deal, on the reliability of your work and your sense of service. Honesty will be rewarded. For those dealing with the public, this is particularly appropriate. If you have a free day, enjoy a public outing.

22. SUNDAY. Productive. Carry on with the good work. This looks like a weekend in which you will get a mountain of work done. You can also lay the foundations for the holidays at the end of the year. Cooperation comes easily. Every one of the family should pitch in with whatever has to be done. If you are in charge of operations, allocate the jobs. Otherwise you will have more helpers than there is work to do and something will get missed. Leave no stone unturned, as they say, and no task untended. This could be the last chance many have of getting things shipshape this year. Make good use of the opportunity.

23. MONDAY. Deceptive. This will be a day of surprises. You will find little is likely to go according to schedule. Follow your hunches in some cases. A relationship can take on unexpected importance. You may find that working conditions are unpredictable. Look on the bright side and with a bit of polish or diplomacy you can have everyone eating out of your hand. Personal ties can be strengthened if you use your good sense and tread carefully. A partner may be very loving or hypersensitive. You will have to gauge the situation for yourself. It would pay you to be considerate and loving with intimates. A business partner may be trying to pull the wool over your eyes.

24. TUESDAY. Satisfactory. Someone may encourage you to be extravagant. Take no notice of business acquaintances who have little idea about family commitments. Cooperate with those who matter to you. Pay attention to the young members of the family. It may be a youngster's birthday and you should show your love. Arrange a family outing. You may hear of a forthcoming engagement in the family. Take the family out for the day if you get the chance. If not, take your loved one to a show later on. There are lots of things you can discuss with partners. See that everyday matters are attended to down to the smallest detail.

25. WEDNESDAY. Mixed. Conserve the family funds. Discuss with your employer any matter that can increase the family income. Pension rights may need to be considered. Your bank manager can give sound advice if you have additional income to handle. Self-employed folk should be able to button up important contracts with the person they report to. Do not waste time with an assistant if you can get hold of the big chief. Having made ground, do not lose everything by being careless or stupid. You may be tempted to let yourself go. This will be selfish. Think of those who depend on your goodwill for their sustenance.

26. THURSDAY. Useful. Business prospects look good. Make the most of your chances and this will fatten up the family coffers. Work with a purpose and to a pattern. There is little time to spare for pleasure or recreation. Any time taken off will undermine your main ambitions. While you have the active cooperation of partners and colleagues, it would be unwise to divert your activities. Someone may try to talk you into a deal that will have no future. Keep away from any investment dealing in sporting goods or pleasure outlets. Talk about future holiday arrangements is untimely. Deal with matters of the moment which need your direct attention.

27. FRIDAY. Successful. You are now in a better position to talk over holiday plans with the family. See that passports are up to date and other necessary matters are taken into consideration. You should be able to make the complete arrangements tomorrow if all goes well. Before committing yourself to any family expense, get your partner to agree and involve the family in your deliberations. A family powwow can resolve a lot of questions. Your friends at work will be interested in your plans, even if they are not also involved. On the other hand, your employer may take a dim view of your ideas if it will upset schedules. Your first consideration should be for the family, however.

28. SATURDAY. Disquieting. Stick to your original plans. This will not be easy and you may think everything is stacked against you. But it is better to try than be frustrated through inactivity. Students could be faced with last-minute hitches as they seek a free weekend. Many of you will find you have to work after you had expected to be enjoying a free day. Traveling can bring problems. There could be delays at airports. Customs people can be uncooperative. Stick it out if you want to see some result for your labors. Do not expect good publicity if you have plans for self-promotion. Health problems may interfere with your early plans. An in-law may be feeling down in the dumps.

29. SUNDAY. Disconcerting. You may have had a restless night. Do not expect sympathy. Perhaps everyone else has had a bad night also. If you are tense there may be little you can do about it. For some there may be a continuing need to work. This is probably because of some emergency that throws everything out of schedule. Try to keep your cool insofar as possible. There may be little reward at the moment for your efforts. Family or loved ones may be missing when you return home. There will be good reason, no doubt. An engagement may have to be overlooked and this could disappoint your partner. You could wind up in the doghouse until you can come up with a way to make amends.

30. MONDAY. Quiet. You will start they day off under mixed influences. Feel optimistic. This is a day to straighten out your business life. So take time to reflect and look around you for those indications of the prosperity you expected last January. Take stock while everyone is getting back into the swing. Frustrations of the weekend may have given you food for thought. Possible emergencies which may have arisen can sharpen your mind to future prevention methods. At times you may wonder if you should have taken a certain course of action. Fate will sort things out as they should be. You may be thinking of future business combined with social matters. Make provision for everything as best you can.

DECEMBER

1. TUESDAY. Encouraging.   Your stock should be high. If you play your cards right today you have much to gain. You will learn that you're popular with all. Relationships should prosper. A lively interest in someone of the opposite sex will do wonders for both persons. Look after a friend who may become a partner. Your better half will be feeling warm and loving. Start the day on an unconventional note. The early bird catches the worm at business as well as in the park. Work will go with a swing if you are allowed enough freedom to do your own thing. It is a day to improvise or try something different. This will prove attractive to more than your friends at work.

2. WEDNESDAY. Fair.   You can be bursting with love and goodwill. Nothing is likely to stop you if you feel you are on the right track. Emotion can be your strength, given a happy response. You seem to be in tune with the one you hold dearest. You also have time for most other people you call friends. If there is a division of interests or someone thinks he or she is being neglected, make them feel at ease. There is no reason to doubt your sincerity. Passions can run high. You may have a new friendship that is developing rapidly into a much closer tie. You will know in a little while whether or not you are infatuated or really in love.

3. THURSDAY. Worrisome.   Someone may think you are an easy touch. If you are handling business finances hold to the traditional values and try nothing that could be open to doubt. You may think you are on to a good thing and can be misled. Partners may be very loving. They will probably have ulterior motives. Among friends you will not mind, but beware of those who flatter in business. A legal wrangle can work against your interests if you have been deceived. It may be possible to mislead some folk, but not all. The attention of friends may leave children at a loss to understand you. Think of those who cannot reason too clearly and explain what you are about. Club activities should be enjoyable.

4. FRIDAY. Mixed.   Look for a quiet spot. You may find it difficult to get away from people who talk too much. Working conditions can be made miserable by the gossip and interference of inquisitive and malicious people. Do not have your resolution undermined by a careless word. Keep your own counsel. Traveling may be disrupted by a detour due to repair work on the road. Trying to keep aware of all that is in progress can be very tiring. Use modern methods to keep up with the times. If you do not have modern tools available, don't start complaining. You will get nowhere by trying to persuade employers of their shortcomings.

5. SATURDAY. Demanding. You may very well have a headache. Irritation due to the recent past events could cause you a sleepless night. If you took any pill to combat this, you could have a sort of a hangover. A friend may offer to do what you had intended to, out-of-doors or at business. This will give you a break. Rest may do you good. On the other hand, you may feel it only right that you attend to the needs of others who have problems. Do not take life too seriously. Any frustration will bring a challenge you should meet. All your resources may be tested before the day is out and you will then know where you stand.

6. SUNDAY. Challenging. You could feel much relieved, but not quite up to par. Have a lazy day if that is possible. Otherwise, you may attempt something and fail. This will make you feel inadequate and deflate your ego somewhat. As the day progresses you will gain confidence and soon be back in fighting trim. Enjoy some energetic pastime which should liven you up and make you much more compatible. It is essential that you get on your feet as soon as possible. This is a day for personal interests. No one else is going to care very much about them. You cannot survive on sympathy, but will soon put that right. A bit of emotional inspiration is basically all you need now. That will serve as a challenge to you.

7. MONDAY. Changeable. Others do not understand the way you feel. A major disagreement could be brewing. You should try to keep out of their way and follow your own interests. No good can come from disagreeing with those you would expect to show compassion. If you have to meet someone halfway, be as dignified as possible. You have to keep up appearances no matter what the differences. Some respite can be had through sport or active interests. Make full use of your talents. At some later date you will be in favor and must not let yourself get rusty. To avoid sharing is no sin, especially when you feel you should go it alone.

8. TUESDAY. Uneventful. Get on with your own life in whatever way you choose. Make the most of any opportunity that comes your way without expecting too much. Personal affairs need to be considered in some detail. You have your own plans to set in motion for the remainder of the year and will not have another opportunity like this again before the Christmas break. Get yourself organized. After all, this has been an eventful year and you want to end it with all flags flying. Look ahead, considering your financial state first after you have fully collected your thoughts. Working conditions are complicated at the moment. You have a lot going for you, however, if you handle yourself properly.

9. WEDNESDAY. Changeable. Put your wits to good use. A working condition can be turned to your advantage if you are on the ball. Just spot the opportunity and say the right word at the right time. If you are thinking ahead about a wage increase, prepare your plans now. Do any talking or writing you feel is necessary. You will be better organized for a direct approach tomorrow. But today you must prepare the ground and sow the seeds. You can be a bit heavy-handed if you have had a night out enjoying yourself. Look after your cash till you are sure there is more where it came from. Getting near the holiday season puts pressure on the checkbook, especially if you are spending on children.

10. THURSDAY. Encouraging. This is the day to make a hit with the boss. Bonus day is here. Some will be told they are being promoted. It will also be a good day for business. Hard work eventually pays off despite the gloomy predictions of some people. Influential people know what is going on and will look to the future with optimism. You should feel this also. Some people believe in luck. It often strikes where least expected. If you feel you have earned your keep this year, it is partly the result of good judgment, but more perhaps, of application to your work. Your bank manager will be glad to help with any plans you have for your savings. Consolidate whatever you have gained up to now.

11. FRIDAY. Satisfactory. It will be a day of mixed blessings. Progress should be made at work with the active support of your employer. Business can prosper, given the full cooperation of people who rank high in industry. Personal problems can occur through children who may be a bit of a handful or unwilling to listen to parental reason. You should be able to cope with any problem if you use your good sense and allow for the vagaries of humanity. An active mind should keep you ahead of the field. You may hear romantic news about a neighbor or near relative. This could make you think of the past and your own relationships.

12. SATURDAY. Pleasant. Play it by ear for a change. Whatever the day brings, you can count your blessings with respect to the less helpful possibilities. Superiors or people with influence are still feeling helpful toward you. Take advantage of their aid if you have something to promote. Others in the working situation may be less cooperative. Bad feelings can be caused through gossip or idle talk. Try to avoid unnecessary travel. If you have to get around, take a friendly companion. Your lovelife should be good and this will brighten the day. Your partner should be extra cooperative and any recreation should be shared.

13. SUNDAY. Challenging. Don't take life too seriously. If you feel you have a rough day ahead, spend an extra hour or two in bed. There is probably no need to bother yourself too much. Workaday worries can bother you if you have time on your hands. When you are emotionally upset, you can become despondent quite easily. Perhaps you can turn this to advantage by doing a bit of careful and constructive preparation for the coming week. Some of you will be expecting to take on added responsibility in the next day or two. Look forward with conviction and be prepared to welcome this essential recognition of your worth.

14. MONDAY. Misleading. Domestic chaos may get you off to a poor start. Do not take this to heart. If there are problems at home you will be able to master them in due course. Try to keep yourself organized, as it is possible that others who depend on you could be in a bit of a flap. Look after basics. Despite the unreliability of those who are supposed to cooperate with you, it is essential to keep your feet on the ground. Have no dealings in real estate, despite whatever the temptation. Avoid legal encounters in this respect. Nothing will be clear and you could end up making absolutely no progress. A romantic episode in the family may cause some domestic bad feeling.

15. TUESDAY. Important. Prepare for a day of decision. You are likely to take on added responsibility. This may be due to pressure from an employer or because you are taking over from a senior who cannot handle it. Accept such responsibility in a positive way. This could be an important day in your life as it affects your career or business prospects. Keep in touch with the outside world. There are opportunities which give you a chance to put a word in the right ear at the top. Your activities may not find favor with a loved one. Perhaps you cause others to worry if you press yourself too hard. Do not let this deter you.

16. WEDNESDAY. Successful. You are more relaxed after the pressure of yesterday. Expect cooperation and love from those who share your intimate life. Children can attract a great deal of attention which you will welcome. The going is much more inactive. You will think you are through the rough spots, and are probably quite right. A regular appointment with someone you feel for should be kept. As you are a sensitive person, you may be interested in developing a psychic ability that gives pleasure to those you meet as well as to you. Your mind is very active, even though you may be able to relax physically. Keep your wits about you for an opportunity to make progress.

17. THURSDAY. Tricky.   Someone may really turn you on. If your emotions are fully aroused you could find it difficult to control yourself or events. This could lead to all sorts of problems or to a fuller appreciation of someone who shares your creative interests. You could be tempted to go it alone. This may get you into hot water. On the other hand, there is no reason why you should not demonstrate your initiative and ability. Hasty actions can get you into trouble by accident. Impetuosity can get you into financial trouble if you indulge yourself in unwise speculations. So, avoid that pitfall which would more than likely get out of hand. Using your intuition may not be the wisest policy today.

18. FRIDAY. Mixed.   Settle agreements with partners. End the working week on a cooperative note with your associates. If you have had a trying time make amends by showing goodwill to all you meet. The working day may be frustrating. Perhaps you feel impending pressure from a superior who is not quite sure of prevailing conditons. Do not prejudge an issue. Wait for its outcome before deciding on its merits or drawbacks. A close friend may be particularly obliging. Spend some time and money on children. Thoughts of the approaching festive season may prompt you to go shopping after work has ended. If you are buying presents for the young, think of the future. Try to make them feel more grown up.

19. SATURDAY. Challenging.   This will be a busy day for all workers. Shopkeepers and others who depend on the public trade should work with a will. You will be in demand. Employees may be obliged to put themselves out because of the unexpected volume of work. Or they find that extra effort is called for by employers. If your plans are upset, try to make the most of the situation; use your intelligence. Avoid being difficult. You can gain more by showing initiative and versatility. Take advantage of the weekend to do your own shopping. Busy markets should offer bargains, so look out for the merchant who is prepared to discuss prices. Someone could be in a generous frame of mind.

20. SUNDAY. Useful. You can concentrate your thoughts on an important issue. Some may be thinking of future work prospects. If you are looking for a change, this is a good day to crystallize your ideas. An initiative could follow. A health matter could come to a head. Make up your mind if you have to decide on the sort of future treatment you wish to have. Spend some time reflecting on events of the past year. It may be time to consider changes that will set you off on a new start in the year ahead. You are not likely to be diverted from any task you undertake. See that you are well prepared for any undertaking that lies ahead.

21. MONDAY. Rewarding. You may have a strong desire to please. Make your intentions and feelings clear and you will be accepted with eagerness by all. Make peace early with anyone you have crossed swords with in the past few days. It is best to start as you mean to continue. In the main, you will find that others will respond to your peaceful approach. A romantic encounter can give you a boost. It takes two to make a bargain and your initiative should pay dividends. Should you be strongly attracted to someone of the opposite sex, use your charm to make the most of it. There could be a certain amount of risk. But there would be no pleasure in loving if you were afraid to take a chance occasionally.

22. TUESDAY. Buoyant. Count on this as a day for agreements. Marriages can take place; arrangements finalized; engagements sealed. All sorts of people will feel they are on the same wavelength at last. Financial contracts can be agreed on and family can unite with family in a truly remarkable display of good faith. End-of-the-year celebrations are popular while everyone is in the mood to be friendly and considerate of others. Last-minute office parties will take many away from the drudgery of work. Many will share a confidence with a friend in a way not previously done. The spirit of goodwill can bring new friends and stir the emotions to a new pitch of common understanding.

23. WEDNESDAY. Demanding. End-of-year expenses could be high. Be reasonably philosophical about this. It frequently happens at Christmas, even in the best regulated of families. Provision should be made for the entertainment and pleasure of the children in the family. Costs could be high. You may need to consider different possibilities in order to do the best with your resources. Try to avoid putting the family into debt. It would be best to do your homework thoroughly. Lovers may be in a quandary about pleasing their dear ones. As a rule, you will be inclined to overspend. Do not let anything come between you and your beloved.

24. THURSDAY. Good. Get all loose ends tied up today. Finalize as much as possible if you are obliged to be at work. The family funds may look better than you had expected after all the hustle and bustle. Make your feelings known to employers who may be feeling generous at this time of year. Future prospects and security can be discussed. Some will receive well-earned bonuses that put the funds ahead for the post-holiday period. Relax and cooperate freely with family and friends. Even the most hard-pressed of you should feel more relaxed as the great day approaches. Family unity is the most important feature of Christmas.

25. FRIDAY. Merry Christmas! New horizons will have opened up. Those who entertain at home will have family and friends from far away to bring joy into this day. Some of you will be far from your own fireside. But you will be in the company of dear ones you seldom see otherwise. Wherever you happen to be, this is a great day. Nothing should stop you from enjoying yourself to the fullest. As ever, the children attract the most attention. But the message of the day is not wasted on adults, either. Philosophical thoughts will move you to a full appreciation of the importance of family ties and the effect that you, as a person, have on those near and dear to you. Be joyful and count yourself fortunate.

26. SATURDAY. Difficult. After the prolonged excitement comes the letdown. This is the accepted norm of the so-called morning after the night before. Those who entertained guests will have a full day getting things back to normal. Take this in your stride. A number of problems may have to be straightened out. This is frequently the case when no one is very interested in keeping order. Traveling back to base may prove a bit of a hazard. Regular services are not likely to be available. If you feel in need of peace and quiet you are likely to be disappointed. The adventurous who wish to get out-of-doors to let off steam may be careless. They must be prepared to take things as they come.

27. SUNDAY. Mixed. Ambitious people will be thinking of the year ahead. Those with love on their minds will feel the moment is right to impress the one who matters. You should feel confident that you are able to carry family responsibilities. Look to the future with confidence and make plans to start the year ahead at full speed. Family folk will be running through the accounts and getting themselves organized for the January sales. You are always on the alert for a bargain. A person you respect in the family circle may not share your optimism. You will have to see who is right. Do not put too much trust in partners. They may be envious.

28. MONDAY. Good. It will be back to the daily routine for many. This could be a relief. You can get stymied by all sorts of jobs that are outstanding. But you might also make considerable progress. Promotion prospects are good. You should be popular and feeling confident you can cope with anything that comes your way. The relaxation of the past few days should have given you a new lease on life which you can put to good use. You act like a new broom that sweeps clean at your place of work. Go along with ideas that will modernize and improve all working conditions. A new year should mean a new approach. Do not be old-fashioned. Use your judgment, which is particularly good today.

29. TUESDAY. Sensitive. You could be called upon to arbitrate a nasty dispute. People you respect will give you support in what could be a ticklish situation. Fortunately you have a sense of proportion that allows you to understand the feelings of others. Be a friend to anyone in need. A partnership could be under pressure, but will prevail if true feeling and understanding are allowed to influence the issue. A parent could give a blessing on a union. Extra expense may be incurred as a result of social activities. If you are having a night out, look into your funds beforehand. You might get a surprise when you see the bill. Be sure to treat your partner to the best, whatever the expense.

30. WEDNESDAY. Mixed. A lovers' tiff may develop. Should you feel cast aside, there will be an opportunity to renew ties with your club friends. They are still making the most of the post-Christmas spirit. Friends may provide more consolation than lovers. Some matter affecting your involvement at a social level may have to be argued out before the New Year. Make your opinion well-known. You are bound to stir up some opposition, so should be quite clear about where you stand. If you are to be a public figure there is no point in hiding your light. But do not expect an easy route. You could lose some support, but probably gain more friends who share your aims.

31. THURSDAY. Important. Welcome the New Year in with selected friends. You are a person who naturally thinks of family and close friends first, so do not reach beyond this limit. On a special day such as this, you can be philosophical. It is an ideal time to reflect on the past with an eye to the future. The old year will have had many problems, but also a great deal of reward. For this, you can and will be thankful. All those you love may not be with you. This cannot be helped. Make a fuss of those around you in your own quiet way. Look forward with confidence to 1988 and all of the challenges of the unknown. You will be prepared.

October—December 1986

OCTOBER

1. WEDNESDAY. Satisfactory. Do not take life too seriously. Provided you set out to enjoy yourself and share a lighthearted day with those you encounter, today will pass fairly easily. If you have inescapable ties or are obliged to seek working cooperation, you may have problems. You could say this is not a good day for work. Associates and colleagues are inconsiderate and will make life miserable if you allow it. Separations may be unavoidable, whether for benefit or necessity. You could have to choose between a stand-up argument or a withdrawal. Superficial interests can take you away from this heaviness. Do not take your love life too seriously. Be happy to flirt with someone who is nice company.

2. THURSDAY. Encouraging. Make use of helpful partners. You may find you could do with some short-term assistance, perhaps with a heavy shopping load, for instance. Accept an offer and enjoy the relationship you make for its true worth. A friend in need is a friend indeed, they say. Shopping can be rewarding today. You are open to choice offers and should take advantage of this momentary bargain period. Your partners in business or at work are full of energy. This is good because you can take it a little less energetically yourself. You will find these same colleagues have ideas that can save work although you have to give the matter some thought. A family gathering is agreeable. Promote such get-togethers.

3. FRIDAY. Rewarding. It will be a day for starting a domestic project. For some, this could mean a new home or moving from one home to another. Such an event is always important to home-loving Cancer natives. No doubt you have gone into the preparation thoroughly and are confident the right move is being undertaken. Any connection with property, whether buying or selling, should be to your advantage. For newlyweds, it will be pleasant to find neighbors and friends who wish to help. For others, this is the day to start some basic operations that will lead to later success. You will have prepared the ground and are now on the way up. When a good opportunity like this presents itself, go all out.

4. SATURDAY. Disquieting. It is difficult to get your own way. Since it is the weekend, you have quite a lot to organize and accomplish. People around you are not cooperative. Even the family seems to have ideas that are different from yours. This may mean a change of schedule, a reassessment of priorities or a straightforward difference of opinion and the consequent upheaval. You will use your common sense, a real Cancer virtue, and handle any problem as you think best. Make no move that can be avoided, especially of a domestic or property nature. It will not be an enjoyable start to the weekend. But you can make the most of it and try to forget whatever you cannot change.

5. SUNDAY. Uncertain. Continue to keep your interests light. At some point you can be under pressure from someone who wishes to monopolize your attention. You do not feel responsive to this sort of restriction, so you should shy away from acquaintances or romantic admirers who persist. When you feel good and ready you can consider love and the ultimate consequence of intimate relationships. At the moment you are not in the mood. There are other ways in which you can find light relief. Children are always attractive and in return share their pleasure in your company. They have no strings attached to their affections. For some this is a nice quiet day to enjoy your hobbies.

6. MONDAY. Happy. It feels good to be alive. You want to express yourself freely. For those who are self-employed, it is a day to work with a will. For the artistically employed, this is a day to feel free and creative. Many Cancer natives will be occupied in the acting profession. Their sense of the dramatic makes them natural actors and actresses. For them, it will be a particularly rewarding day. Romance is in the air and you want to enjoy life with someone on your wavelength. You will find there are many who feel as you do. This should result in a happy day. People you meet will respond to your goodwill. This is a good day to have a break from work. An extended weekend or the beginning of a vacation will be well chosen.

7. TUESDAY. Difficult. You may need someone to cheer you up. When things go wrong you can be easily depressed. Other people's feelings are so easy to pick up and this frequently adds to your own doubts if you are under the weather. It may be difficult to put on a brave face. Seek the company of someone who is outgoing. This will stir you into positive action, because you really are not one to vegetate and grow miserable. It is always much better to share a problem or get your feelings out of your system. There may be a good deal of aggravation where you work. If you are given responsibility, take it without considering it as a burden. Even if there is no immediate return for your efforts, there is a future to look forward to. It may take time, but it will be worth waiting for.

8. WEDNESDAY. Unsettled. Try to avoid acting on impulse. You may be more than usually emotionally motivated. This will tend to make you overdramatize and your judgment could therefore be faulty. A lot is going on around you that will add to this state of unrest so you are likely to react in a way that makes a sensitive situation volatile. If you feel discontented, try to do something constructive to ease the situation. It is pointless to grumble. Conditions can be uncertain, though not to your disadvantage. Changes can work to your benefit, though you may not think so at the time. Be prepared for unexpected changes or quick promotion to another job or responsibility. It seems like a day when anything can happen.

9. THURSDAY. Fair. The day should improve as it goes on. There seems some lack of clarity or decision. This may be most obvious by the attitude and behavior of those around you at work or at home. A number of people seem to have little idea of priorities or where they are going. If you are involved with them, it places you in a quandary. You will need to be patient and tolerate quite a bit of delay if you have things to get on with. Personal projects can be promoted, if they are things which you developed and on which you can concentrate without interference or involvement. Partners or closely related allies will assist you in this sort of endeavor. It will be a good day to seek entertainment.

10. FRIDAY. Pleasant. You should do your own thing. Family will not agree with your sense of priorities, but that cannot be helped. You have the urge to enjoy romantic company and there is no time like the present. It is the end of the working week and Friday evening is generally a good time for relaxation. An appointment you keep will be enjoyable. With yesterday's indecision you were not sure if it would materialize. In the main, it is a day to enjoy yourself and do the things that turn you on, rather than be too restricted by sense of duty or control of parents and family. If you are inclined this way, it is not wise to expect support if something falls through. You are on a tightrope in some ways.

11. SATURDAY. Mixed. You have money problems. You must decide whether to restrict the family outlay this weekend or to buy something you consider a bargain. Your partner's opinion will differ from your own and this is something you have resolve jointly. There is no point in arguing too much. Face facts and deal with the situation practically. With a weekend here again you may have to do domestic tasks that have been waiting since last week. You may have a lot else to do and the change from routine is not always a welcome diversion. Heavy work around the house can tire you, but you will be pleased with a job well done. If you persist in finishing what you set out to do, there may be little time for recreation.

12. SUNDAY. Fair. Be considerate with those you love. You are under some pressure to assert yourself and may not be easy to get along with. No doubt you have worries or have made plans and cannot rely on others to carry them out. Restrain yourself and avoid being either selfish or aggressive. This suggests your judgment is a bit awry and you are not likely to get far by antagonizing people who have your best interests at heart. It could be an opportune time to entertain people who can further your interests. For this there must be domestic peace and order. Discussions can lead to new developments you have hoped for.

13. MONDAY. Productive. Traveling can be to your advantage today. The attraction of distant places can be strong from different standpoints. Business travel will be advantageous and there is the possibility of mixing business with pleasure. You may travel with your partner or close associate, or fly to make an appointment with someone you are linked closely with. There can be a measure of necessity in your journeying. The tenor of the day is helpful and not superficial. Relationships will need to be purposeful, not flirtatious. There is much lasting pleasure to be gained from your activities today. Health may be worrisome. This may apply to you or to someone you know who may need your sympathy.

14. TUESDAY. Rewarding. It will be a day to use your intuition to good advantage. Routine does not interest you at all. The daily work grind or the need to stick to a schedule is tiresome. You feel like extending yourself, taking a chance. To some extent this is fine. You are a good business person, so you will not be careless. Speculation may be beneficial, provided you are well versed in the prevailing situation. It may be that you are lucky today and something of value falls in your lap, without your having to take a chance. When you feel like this it is natural to look for someone to share your joy. In consequence, your love life will be good and you can further enjoy yourself. Go places with someone you love.

15. WEDNESDAY. Deceptive. You are very sensitive to what goes on around you. This is a day when you should listen, take note of what is going on, but withdraw from activity or decision-making. Partnership and family, of course, take priority in your affairs. You will understand quite early in the day that there can be some confusion which will negate any positive ideas you may have. You may also find it difficult to concentrate. This may mean you are in dreamland, or are bemused and not particularly practical. In business this may show especially in attempts to publicize. At the moment you will not get good publicity or may go off in the wrong direction. Do not waste money on such speculative outlets.

16. THURSDAY. Satisfactory. You can accept routine more readily. Though you feel no strong urge to get up and go, there seems to be more possibility of sorting things out to your satisfaction. You are able to collect your thoughts and can consider plans or projects. Those around you, too, seem to be more evenly balanced than they were yesterday. Perhaps it was the vibrations you felt yesterday that caused the confusion. You could be tempted to jump from one extreme to another if you are worried about schedules. Try to avoid this change of attitude. It would be far better to reflect on events and progress up to date in order to prepare yourself constructively for the future.

17. FRIDAY. Demanding. This is a day of decisions. There may be no end product to emerge from any of these decisions, but you will be faced at some stage with a view counter to your own. You may be tempted to rely on your emotional nature to cope. This will not necessarily be the right course. Influential people, or those to whom you would naturally show respect, will not see eye-to-eye with you. This can easily have domestic repercussions. Any property deal is likely to be hard work or not easy to settle. You may be fully extended and need to take complete stock of your emotional and psychological resources. A good deal can be learned if you keep your cool and are considerate. You may have to seek professional help for a health problem. This may not necessarily be yours.

18. SATURDAY. Disconcerting. You may be feeling fragile or fragmented. Because of the pressure of the past few days you are a bit uncertain about a lot of things. You should not, therefore, be inclined to take any risks or expect too much reliability from any quarter. You can find some light relief among social friends you meet with about once a week to discuss the world and its ways. Keep the involvement easy and detached. This is no time to heed anyone's advice or take serious matters into consideration. You want to be friendly and are sensitive to those of your acquaintances who appreciate that the weekend is for relaxation rather than business worries. Divorce business worries from weekend pursuits.

19. SUNDAY. Restful. Be happy with those you love and let them know it. Sunday is a family day and the day when you can relax with your loved ones. For you who are single and in love, it is a good time to make the most of your blessings. Equally, for the family it is a natural time to enjoy the close harmony of the circle you all appreciate so deeply. Outside relationships may be considered interference. Though you are not normally inhospitable, you will have your priorities clear. Casual friends are more likely to upset you than make life pleasant. You do not want to travel far. You know you could be happier right here at home with your dearest friend than dashing about with a group of acquaintances.

20. MONDAY. Disquieting.   Be conservative and tread carefully. There seems to be no letup yet. You are well aware of the financial priorities you have decided this year, so you will be keeping a careful eye on family expenditure and business economics. Neither appears to be very healthy at the moment and there is no good indication that you can do a lot about it, except by hard work and avoidance of waste. This is right up your alley. If your partner does not appreciate the point as well as you, you may be able to do a bit of educating. This will certainly be better than arguing or disagreeing about money. Be as patient and tolerant as you can. Some people find it very difficult to understand budgets.

21. TUESDAY. Variable.   You have difficulty putting your point across. There are views other than yours which may carry weight today. This opinion is not necessarily from someone close by, so you have a potential problem of communications. Business from overseas can be difficult to agree on. You may not be able to satisfy your foreign market. Though you would like to fly out and settle distant problems, you cannot do this at the moment. Earlier agreements you have made now need to be honored. You will do this, of course, even though your resources are likely to be strained. Whatever you feel, it is a good day to keep to essential routine. The peaks and valleys come and go. Reliability counts.

22. WEDNESDAY. Fortunate.   You have unexpected good news. Your material well-being has been a source of concern recently, but it seems this was unnecessary. You are helped in a way you had not previously considered or expected. Developments are likely to follow. There will be no fuss. You will be able to do more things constructively by retaining a low profile and getting on with essential preparations in the background. You may be surprised by the help and support you get from an unexpected quarter. Be diplomatic and consolidate any gain you are making. There is a possibility of a legacy. Go about your business with confidence, keeping your own counsel where appropriate. Try not to do too much advance planning until you learn what is involved. Things will go smoothly if you avoid haste.

23. THURSDAY. Deceptive. Trust your own judgment. You will find your partner is either not constructive or likely to fly off on a tangent. In business, it is better to rely on your own assessment, or your own ideas, than to become too heavily involved in joint proposals. The domestic situation is erratic. Cooperation is not reliable and you do not know what to expect. Be prepared to do your own cooking or to go your own way at some point in the day when you would usually expect joint involvement. You may find this is to your advantage as you can boost your ego a bit by doing something that allows self-expression. Avoid taking a chance. Be careful about possible opportunity. It may be genuine or it may not.

24. FRIDAY. Good. This is a time of year when you can enjoy living. For the next three or four weeks, you may at some time feel the urge to develop your talents. It can be an enjoyable period for those in love and those young people who are looking forward to raising a family. Today is generally smooth and helpful. You should find it easy to express yourself, so be at peace with all and you will be able to relate easily. You will be appreciated and sought after. Make headway with creative projects. There is plenty of cooperation to make your way more easy. You can enjoy sharing your pleasure with loved ones. Perhaps a birthday party is organized. Or everyone might want to find foliage to photograph.

25. SATURDAY. Difficult. You need to make your way with care. The weekend duties will not be easily accomplished. Too much needs to be done with too little help or means. You know how much depends on your ability to keep going and persevering, so you can discipline yourself. There are few bargains to be had and you feel in no mood to throw your money away. As you may not see any light at the end of the tunnel, you should not expect favors from anyone at this moment. Other people appear to have their own problems. This reflects directly on those with whom they have contact. Be positive, accepting the restrictions, and exercise personal discipline willingly. Resources are most important.

26. SUNDAY. Frustrating. It will be a day to stretch your tolerance. It is just as well that there is less opportunity to spend today. The review of family accounts is not heartening, but at least you can come to a realization of the position and get a grip on the problem.

Decide to cut costs or plan for reduced spending in the immediate future. With this sort of atmosphere, it is hard to please. It's not a good day for romance or letting your hair down. Pay attention to your partner. You are not the only one with problems and may be able to share your joint worries. This depends on the pressure you exert on each other. Try to keep demands moderate, though this will be difficult. You are responsible for the family budget.

27. MONDAY. Variable. Enjoy your relationships. You are still aware of financial limitations or pressures, but today you feel that the best things in life are free. Your loved one will be appreciative of your attention and this will take you out of the mundane struggle. Some of you will decide on marriage. This is a time of year to think of home and a future family. You are never a wild speculator, so you should be able to make a wise assessment of your opportunities. Some aspects of the day are not satisfying. There may be aggravation about agreements concerning business or money. Keep clear of such involvement if you can. Delay any transaction about which you have reservations. Give yourself more time to study the proposal and get others' opinions of its worth.

28. TUESDAY. Mixed. Routine can be a bore. You feel like enjoying more freedom to do your own thing, but are only too aware of the need to persevere with essentials. It will be nice if you get through the day's schedule and then do something that allows this use of your creative potential. A break from work routine would help. Make employers aware of your ideas. Since your mind will be on other things, be sure you concentraate enough to avoid mishaps. Health is important. This is no time to take risks or be careless. You may wish to visit some friends nearby. Even here, avoid being distracted while traveling. Your brain is working at full speed, but you may find it out of coordination with your pen. Be careful what you write.

29. WEDNESDAY. Disquieting. Avoid being dependent on others. This will be no hardship if you are looking for personal progress. You will find many people to be unsteady or erratic, so your personal judgment will outweigh advice tendered or help offered from associates or even some members of the family. Neighbors appear to be at sixes and sevens. All working arrangements are suspect. This may be a reflection of conditions. If you feel unsettled, try to avoid hasty action. There will be enough around you to give warning of possible detrimental consequences. Do not force the issue if agreement seems difficult in any personal liaison. Bide your time; more promising opportunities will follow.

30. THURSDAY. Deceptive. Play everything by ear. All that happens today will not be apparent. There is considerable tension in areas where you would least expect it. The family is not in harmony. You could have news of a split among your relatives. This undermines your security since the family has such significance in your life. You need to be constructive, so if there is anything you can do to help, be sympathetic and positive. Your own romantic life is potentially eventful. There is no knowing which way it may develop. It could be out of this world or you may be misunderstood. Your intuition usually sees you through. Be optimistic and generous.

31. FRIDAY. Good. It will be a good day on which to end the month. You have the weekend to look forward to and everyone around you seems to be in a good mood. Salary or bonus payments can be higher than usual. You merit both reward and respect after the pressure of the last few weeks. This is a time to develop your inventive theories for practical application. For the self-employed, it is a time to make the most of new ideas and more progressive methods. Innovation can be time-saving. You are well aware of traditional values, and have for some time been conscious of the need to harmonize the old and reliable with the new and the progressive. This is a day when you can blend the two with great effectiveness.

NOVEMBER

1. SATURDAY. Fair. You can start something new and exciting. For some this could mean marriage, for others the recognition of a lasting relationship. The day can be romantic and appeal to your emotional aspirations. You feel forces that may be difficult to control, but are at your disposal. You have to be true to yourself and keep your targets well within view. You know you have to be constructive and not overly emotional. You will have a desire to put all your eggs in one basket. This is fine if the basket is the right one. Your security has been much on your mind this year and you have updated ideas about expressing your true inner feelings. You are not one to keep a low profile and retreat into yourself.

2. SUNDAY. Variable. You will want to enjoy yourself. Material consequences may not interest you and instead you can enjoy the day to the full with friendly people of your own choosing. But in the excitement of the moment, you may take on more than you had bargained for. Family entertainment could stretch finances to the breaking point. It will not be easy to neglect your friends, but you can cause some upsets if you are too free with your money or too free with your affections in the wrong place. You are in a good mood, so keep things smooth and try to avoid distractions that may result in problems. It would be a pity to spoil the weekend, especially when both days have been so successful.

3. MONDAY. Uncertain. You are not really in tune with the work scene. It would be nice if you could follow up yesterday's activities with a long weekend. If you are forced to get back into the weekday routine, make the most of it. Some may have a severe headache, which will not improve matters. For others there may be repercussions from the weekend that will cause acute depression, perhaps over money matters. For the majority, though, there is a chance to follow up your gains, and you spend the day in anticipation, if not actual receipt, of your good luck. A new relationship is likely to turn out well and lead to a more mature liaison. Take the day as it comes and do your best.

4. TUESDAY. Variable. Keep your eye on the ball and avoid distraction. You will need to look after detail. The small print is important, and it will have a useful purpose, provided you are aware of its significance. Read whatever you must sign beforehand. Concentration on the practicalities will pay dividends. Look after all matters connected with work or the employment of others in your service. There should be openings. Routine is important, but it is likely to be upset. There may be a need for diversification. You have to keep on your toes in order to know which way to jump for the best result. A great deal depends on your mental agility and ordinary common sense.

5. WEDNESDAY. Deceptive. It is not a day for being too practical. Before tomorrow you may wish you had been more down-to-earth. So much of the pleasure of today will depend on your state of mind and your ability to keep your feet on the ground. It can be a most romantic day. You will feel more sensitive than usual, so you will be able to respond easily to the feelings expressed by others. Close contact may be disturbing or overpowering and it may be better to enjoy romance from a distance. You may receive a letter from someone dear to your heart. For those engaged in study or taking examinations this could be a fortunate period. The loner is more likely to benefit than the married Cancer native.

6. THURSDAY. Excellent. Everything in your life runs smoothly. Things go with a swing. Your partner and all the family seem to have matters in true perspective. There has been better news about the family finances which caused so much worry a few weeks ago. For the young in love, it's a day to make happy progress. For the newly married, there may be hopes of an addition to the family. There is creative growth all around which will affect you in your own personal way and give you joy. While you are feeling like this it is always easy to get support. Business projects will gain backing, and family projects will not lack for cooperation and moral support. Make the most of these upbeat conditions and lay the groundwork for future projects.

7. FRIDAY. Exciting. Take the opportunity to settle a deal. While everyone appears to be in a cooperative mood, you should take immediate advantage. Make any necessary agreements that are likely to be of help in the near future. Problems you have had concerning children will now be largely alleviated. You will find the young members of the family are a pleasure and a constant source of inspiration. You may hear news that gives encouragement. Some idea of yours is finding favor out of town. It will do you no harm to make a visit to the local library. You should find that the information you collect will be worthwhile. You may be romantically moved to announce your engagement. It has been an eventful day.

8. SATURDAY. Difficult. The weekend starts off on the wrong foot. Instead of peace and harmony, there are problems. Your partner does not agree with your priorities where money is concerned. The family finances could be under pressure again if you do not come to some arrangement about joint limitations. This is always a sensitive area of human relationships, especially in a year when you have to discipline yourself to work or do without. There has been a temptation to overspend. Any excess is likely to cause an emotional flare-up. If you value cooperation, you will need all your patience. For those in love, be content with small rewards.

9. SUNDAY. Variable. You will feel like letting your hair down. In due course this may be possible, but duty in one form or another will demand your attention. Try to avoid arguments on this sensitive Sunday morning. Retain your composure and be on your best behavior. A change of scenery in the afternoon will be good for everyone, perhaps through a visit to distant friends or relatives you have not seen for some time. This is a good opportunity to exchange family news and views. Having talked everyone into a better frame of mind, you can now clear up any problems that have been bothering you over the weekend. Your partner is likely to be more cooperative and settled.

10. MONDAY. Productive. You will soon get into your stride. There are problems to deal with, but their solution will bring satisfaction and probably a good return for your efforts. There is room for expansion. Foreign markets are good so you may find it pays to deal with business colleagues in overseas agencies. The response to your individual efforts is heartening. Being allowed to develop your creative or original talents is always a sure way to arouse your enthusiasm. You may meet a new friend while on your travels today. Your energy and enthusiasm are infectious and you will not be short of admirers. Mix business with pleasure. This will lighten the day and keep you from overdoing it.

11. TUESDAY. Rewarding. Put your point of view across with confidence. You may have a busy time making long-distance calls. It would be wise to get as much business done with overseas customers as you can manage. The foreign market remains good. You should express your individuality as well as you can. This will attract attention which you need to help you promote your aims. Be prepared to make deals with large concerns, as well as the family business. In your own way you should find you have a better chance to express your creative talents. This is, of course, enjoyable as well as rewarding. Research will stand you in good stead. Having done your homework, you can answer all queries with confidence.

12. WEDNESDAY. Variable. Be direct and get your priorities straight. If you persevere with whatever you have to do, you will find things drop into place. Be guided by older people if you are in any doubt. You have respect for age, which will help, but need to go your own way to establish your individual identity. Be business-like and practical. In this way you will avoid mistakes and distractions. Those who have dealings with the public can expect a good day. You are on the right wavelength for putting across your point. Your sympathy will be appreciated. Listen to good advice on technicalities from those who have more years of experience. Try to keep your spending under control. This is not a favorable day to chance your luck or be extravagant.

13. THURSDAY. Fair. It will be a day for public involvement. You will find it difficult to keep out of the limelight and this will suit your purpose. You must make your presence felt if you are to gain ground this year, so you are prepared to seek publicity when the moment is right. Business or work should benefit from this activity. Romance does not really seek publicity at the moment. You are prepared to do all that is needed in order to make your mark while you have the material and expertise at hand. Your inventiveness should be rewarded. It is not the time to expect support from others if you are not prepared to go out on a limb and show what you can do. You have to demonstrate your faith in whatever area you expect to get help by putting your cards on the table.

14. FRIDAY. Sensitive. Use your Cancer talent to discriminate. You are blessed with common sense, which will be needed today. You may feel a compulsive urge to do something that is deeply felt. There are pitfalls. Cooperation may come from some quarter, but be sadly lacking in another. You may find friends and you will feel the urge to be friendly. At the same time there can be trouble with those you love if you put new friends before family responsibility. This can be a most delicate situation that can blow up all too easily. Keep everything on a moderate level and you will avoid major problems. Avoid confrontations and use all the tact you can.

15. SATURDAY. Mixed. Make the most of travel. This is a good day to widen your horizons in whatever way suits your purpose. For many it will mean the chance to get on the highway and head out of town. Foreign travel or contacts from overseas will be to your advantage. If you are leaving your native land for a distant place, perhaps to reside there, appreciate the feelings of those you may leave behind. A certain amount of family sensitivity pervades today. You are very attuned to disturbing vibrations and will find good use for your natural sympathy and understanding. If you are preparing yourself for later responsibility in society, make the most of your chance to study.

16. SUNDAY. Important. It's a day for straightforward decisions. This is not a day to beat around the bush, take chances, or look for trouble. You will be obliged to use good old common sense, since you may have a lot of important decisions to make. There will be a choice between enjoying yourself or looking after the business. Finances are all-important and can be strained if you are careless or speculative. For those with strong relationship ties in the making, it will be a day of possible consideration that can end in agreement or separation. The outcome will probably lie with you. If you remember that there are two sides to every question, you will be all right. Just take time for careful evaluation.

17. MONDAY. Difficult. It will not be an exciting start to the week. There is some unhappiness or aggravation at work. Your colleagues appear to be suspicious. There is a lack of trust which you will sense at once. Your energies will be fully extended and you will need to apply yourself with little apparent possibility of extra reward to compensate for the additional effort. The whole atmosphere is likely to depress you if you allow the feelings of others to impinge on your own. Keep busy and concentrate on what you have to do. This should keep you occupied enough to disregard the undermining effect of dissension around you. Think of the needs of the day. Let tomorrow take care of itself.

18. TUESDAY. Variable. Keep your own counsel calmly. The atmosphere has not changed much among your everyday colleagues or acquaintances. It will pay you to keep quietly to yourself, without offending anyone. Some people around you are very sensitive and likely to go off on a tangent without warning. Be prepared for erratic behavior or disjointed actions. There is some secrecy of attitude and some very direct action. It's not a situation you can easily equate. Be careful if you are handling unfamiliar tools or machinery. If any equipment is known to be unreliable, have it fixed. You may need to do some private arranging. Make sure it precedes a pleasant surprise.

19. WEDNESDAY. Deceptive. You are not in the mood to trust many others. Conditions remain uncertain and you are much too sensitive to ignore the warning signs. The family appears to be infected by this prevailing lack of determination. You find it difficult to get a positive assessment from even your dearest partner. It will be unwise to let uncontrolled emotion substitute for common sense. Your sympathy will be extended to whomever really needs it. If you find some people you meet in the course of the day are holding up your progress through their indecision, avoid being with them. Someone in this situation will try to hoodwink you.

20. THURSDAY. Good. It looks like a successful day. You have great plans and they seem to be coming true. Earlier in the year you made arrangements to travel. Today is the great day when the world is before you. Individual talents have been well used and you are in line for recognition. The creative Cancer native is no mean performer so you will have pleased many with your endeavors. People may attribute your success to good luck when you are enjoying acclaim. In truth, it is an ability to use good judgment, but you are not in the mood to quibble when your ability is recognized. Be happy with someone close to your heart. Enjoy a trip away from the crowd. For business types, it can be a rewarding day.

21. FRIDAY. Harmonious. You are at peace with the world. To be in love means everything today. You are confident and thoroughly in tune with all the friendly vibrations around you. For lovers, it is a time to make plans for the future. For more mature partners, it will be a happy day to enjoy the mutual satisfaction of shared experience. The end of the working week gives an opportunity to celebrate your joy. You can forget about schedules and routine tomorrow. Tonight is for pleasure and a day of rest to follow. You will find you are appreciated. Someone with influence will speak well of you. For the artistic, it will be a day to reveal your latest creation.

22. SATURDAY. Variable. Take the chance to stay in bed. There is not a lot to turn you on this morning, so you are just as well out of circulation. Someone with a good memory can stir up trouble. It is odd that people always recall the bad moments. Be prepared for alterations affecting your plans or engagements for the day. You will not be happy about someone letting you down. Local interests do not intrigue you. You have ideas about wider involvement. Life is restricted today. Look to your finances if you have ideas that may lead to spreading your interests. Perhaps a move out of town to a new job would relieve the pressure you feel. Consult other family members and get their reactions to such an idea.

23. SUNDAY. Good. It's a day for positive thought and planning. You have the day free from the pressure of mundane routine, so you are able to think out loud about your ideas for the future. Yesterday started you off and you can sense how to go about making beneficial changes. The longer you think the clearer it becomes. Your friends do not provide any ideas. You are the catalyst who turns the ordinary into the extraordinary. An appreciation of your functional needs can be made in a flash. You may have worried about work or its value at this stage. Future attitudes and needs are no longer in doubt. As a result you feel a great deal better. And that allows you to plan for enjoyment and relaxation.

24. MONDAY. Unsettled. It is difficult to avoid the Monday morning feeling. You need a little distraction, or better still, the chance to do work that is wholly dependent on your ability. If you are obliged to do a routine job, it will be more than usually boring. People around you are not very sociable. It is difficult to make headway with people who expect you to produce. They seem to forget their end of the bargain, which is to encourage and make conditions amenable. Everyone has a problem. There is good news in the mail. Forget work and think of your loved one. It will be easy to express your feelings in writing. You feel the need to be sympathetic. That emotion will be appreciated and will go a long way to cementing a relationship.

25. TUESDAY. Sensitive. Keep on the right side of everyone. This is no time to try anyone's patience or push your luck too far. Most particularly, there is a danger of saying the wrong thing or writing in bad taste. Be very careful when conversing on the telephone. A slip could be most difficult to correct when you are not visible to the eye. You may be a little too hopeful or optimistic, and may not have a true picture before you. This can lead to a disappointment for you or for someone who expects more than you can give. Be very sure you know your capabilities. If you can safely handle a personal responsibility, do so. If you are not prepared, be footloose and fancy-free.

26. WEDNESDAY. Deceptive. You may be let down unexpectedly. This may seem to be a normal run-of-the-mill day. For some perhaps it will be, but for many there can be an undercurrent of uncertainty or confusion. You should avoid accepting too much at face value. While you need not be distrustful, it will be wise to maintain vigilance. Dealings or direct transactions may not be what they seem. At home your partner may have a troubled day and need support. Relationships of any meaning could be under pressure because of uncertainty. One partner may suspect deceit or treachery. Avoid clinching any deal. Take time to read the small print; you don't want to get yourself locked into some bad deal.

27. THURSDAY. Good. Try to get your body into good working order. This is something you can readily undertake, because you cannot be efficient if you are under the weather in any way. This could be a good time to arrange the annual checkup for all the family. Parents and grandparents will offer advice. You are always appreciative of family strength which is maintained by respecting the old and encouraging the young. Take the advice offered. At work, too, you will benefit from sound words of wisdom from a senior colleague. Having arranged to have the details looked after, and cleared the decks, it is a good time to look ahead. You know your ability, so you can fix a date for accomplishing your goals.

28. FRIDAY. Successful. You know where you are going. Do not be deterred. Some will try to make you change your mind. This is a bit late since you had sorted out your position earlier. You are noted for your tenacity and resilience, and will bounce back before you break. Stand your ground in your own manner without giving offense. Others will see your point of view and concede. At this point, you should be feeling more secure financially. You will need some backing if you are to get what you want. Your partner will be cooperative, and by working in unison you should do well for yourselves. Take advantage of a profitable day for property and re-sources. This may involve real estate deals and/or the sale of stock.

29. SATURDAY. Fair. Relax for the weekend. Forget old quarrels and enjoy today. You are not usually a resentful person, but you may have heard news that stirred up past unhappiness. Put it out of your mind and get out and about to make the weekend light and carefree. Traveling can take you into pleasant company or may bring you a pleasant surprise. You are quite a romantic, especially when separated from the cares of daily routine. Someone is likely to say nice words to you, which will warm your heart. There is the promise of a future rendezvous. You may feel you need to do some preparation before you get too deeply involved. One or two facts have to be assured. Inquiries must be made.

30. SUNDAY. Quiet. It will be a pleasant day to do your own thing quietly. Any fact-finding you need to do will be accomplished in pleasant conditions. You appreciate the opportunity. For some a visit to church will be more than usually peaceful. There may be time to tour a Sunday market or other public center that has its own particular flavor of the lazy weekend. Children give pleasure be-cause they are so open in their enthusiasm when out with the family for the weekend. In a relaxed atmosphere they seem to respond more easily to persuasion by their elders. Cancers who are school teachers are aware of this. Romance, too, has its quiet moments. It is never beyond you to get the best out of romance.

DECEMBER

1. MONDAY. Disquieting. You may not feel at your best. This will probably be an emotional thing, for conditions are not against you. You may feel it is essential to close a chapter and start some-thing new. Any working conditions that are not just right for you will keep you from making up your mind. This lack of decision will unsettle you and perhaps make you moody, if not ill-tempered and at cross-purposes with yourself. It will not help if you have to attend to minor tasks and cannot get out to spread your wings. You are probably better off looking after the essential details. If you keep order at your fingertips there is less likelihood of trouble from out-side affecting your progress.

2. TUESDAY. Variable. You are itching to get on the move. With Mars well into your house of travel, you will feel the urge to widen your horizons. Look for business expansion and be prepared to fly at a moment's notice. You will not have an easy time, but at least you will know you are taking positive action. If you have to accept routine conditions you may get impatient. Bear with it. Work is potentially rewarding in the last month of the year. You are not likely to find that work is a snap, but it should be well worthwhile. This is a good time to be single-minded if you are studying for examinations. Family travel with a purpose is probable.

3. WEDNESDAY. Successful. You will be unusually sensitive to the feelings of others. This will, of course, apply first with your partner, your loved ones and those who share your everyday life. There is understanding and cooperation from this quarter. Business associates may be a bit more adventurous than of late and agree with your ideas. You are not one to take unnecessary risks and they know this. The urge to travel can be fulfilled. This may well be a business excursion. The possibility of expanding areas of trade will be dependent on your enthusiasm and drive. You are prepared to work hard and cultivate more interest in your concern.

4. THURSDAY. Important. Be prepared for added responsibility. There may be some doubt as to whether you are rewarded immediately. However, it seems you are the best one to handle a situation that has escalated to problem proportions. You are well able to stand your ground, but this will not be an easy task. Buckle down to work and you will cope well. There are other things you would wish to do as pressure mounts. Get your priorities straight. Handle one thing at a time. For those who may have a health problem, it is a day to accept your lot. You have the strength to endure a great deal and should win out. Life has its consolations and you realize there are dear friends and a family who love and support you.

5. FRIDAY. Satisfactory. A day on which you should blow your own trumpet. Make sure your unstinting efforts of the recent past are noted in the right quarter. You should have a good publicity project some time this month. Support and understanding will come from different directions, giving you a balanced approach. You are looking for recognizable reward, so you can expect to make solid progress if you are prepared to get on with the job. Events of the day can make you feel romantic and generous. You need to relax and find an outlet for your feelings. It may be difficult to adjust to normalcy after the pressure you have experienced.

6. SATURDAY. Unsettled. Attend first to whatever has to be done at home. There will be little pleasure this weekend if you do not get the weekend tasks attended to before starting with recreational ones. It may be fortunate that a visit you had proposed is not now on. This may have upset your schedule to some extent. You have been wondering whether all the recent pressure at work was worthwhile. Be careful if you are considering a move. It is not a good time of year to be making changes and you should do so when you feel enthusiastic, not as a reaction to upsetting conditions. Look after the family finances. This is a good time to take stock. The year is coming to a close and you must get your house in order.

7. SUNDAY. Mixed. Try to take things easy for a little while. This is not the best of days, mainly because other people seem to be impatient. You look forward to this day in the week when you can work at relaxing hobbies and do so at your own speed. Try being diplomatic if your proposed schedule is to be disturbed by interruptions over the telephone or through the failure of people you normally depend on to deliver on time. If you are denied consideration or cooperation and can do little or nothing about it, it is best to accept the situation. You will meet up with someone who is cooperative and you will find your day is brightened for it.

8. MONDAY. Changeable. It will be a day of ups and downs. You feel quite happy about some of the events and situations, yet there is a basic lack of harmony somewhere. You have hopes of travel or getting away to different surroundings, but are too idle to give it second thoughts. You slip into routine, then find this is broken for no good reason. You feel great and then feel upset because of distractions. This gives you an upset stomach. The fact that you cannot concentrate on essentials will muddle your day. It is difficult enough having to keep your eye on the job at hand on any Monday. You can be more relaxed when the daily chores are over.

9. TUESDAY. Deceptive. Your judgment can be unreliable. It may be your own lack of perception or the vague meanderings of others around you that makes today so uncertain. Home conditions are not all they should be. Your partner may behave oddly or have something going that is not the usual routine. You will feel this unpredictability in everything. It follows that you should be on your toes to avoid the unexpected. While it may be difficult to stick to routine, you should not commit yourself to any deal that is not watertight. People may be deceitful or the conditions in which you operate can be unreliable. All that glitters is not gold.

10. WEDNESDAY. Fair. Look after the little things in life. Detail is important and you will be constantly reminded of this during the month. It will mean keeping your nose to the grindstone, but that is better than making a serious mistake through carelessness. You have been recognized already as a responsible person and to-day you can receive some recognition. If your employer is in the right mood your requests or advice will be noted. The self-employed Cancer native will find that others wish to cooperate. Business is looking up. Your security or defenses are important. While you are fit, make plans for a rainy day. Enjoy your love life.

11. THURSDAY. Happy. You are confident of success. With everything fitting into place you work with a will, knowing that you can reach the goal you aspire to. As in every case of success, you have support from those who love you. Your partner makes it quite clear that your mutual aims coincide. Business prospers as you con-centrate on the essentials and look to the future for expansion. A new connection is made, with promise of closer cooperation. The evening is to be enjoyed while you feel happy and sociable. You should go out to your local entertainment spot and celebrate in good spirits. At this time of year there are a number of parties.

12. FRIDAY. Pleasant. It can be an expensive day. The holiday period is nearly upon you and there is much to buy. Prices are high at this time of year, but there is a deadline, so you have to get these things that suit only the Christmas occasion. It is nice to think ahead and picture the joy that prevails at this festive season. This will help you face the prices. Remember it is only once a year. There is good news of a holiday booking overseas. For some, the actual journey can start. The exchange rate is turning in your favor and that helps the day along. You feel happy and can make new friends easily. Avoid taking risks or being impulsive. It can be an enjoyable day.

13. SATURDAY. Quiet. You fit into the weekend routine easi-ly. The change of momentum is appreciated, though you have quite a lot to do, as usual. At your own speed this is a pleasure. You should take the opportunity at some point during the day to get out with your friends. There is a lot to discuss and many experiences to relate, but this is nothing out of the ordinary. The weekly routine can be dramatized in retrospect, and you enjoy exaggerating in fun. There are new members of your circle who will grow to be good friends in the near future. A little business left over from the week can be tidied up nicely in the quiet of home.

14. SUNDAY. Unsettled. You may want to visit a friend in the hospital. Patients look forward to the weekend when visiting hours are longer and friends have time to spend with them. You are the natural visitor, full of sympathy and understanding and you don't pry. A word in the right place can do good, for you or for someone else. During the week you may have little opportunity to do important business in some quarter. Now you can attend to this omission with some success. Avoid involvement with anyone in secret if you are talking business. But much will be gained by this. You can be misled if you try to outwit someone, so be open and aboveboard.

15. MONDAY. Frustrating. Take everything as it comes today. One cannot ever be prepared for the unexpected, so the best attitude to adopt is one of relaxation. This will be very difficult. A lot of tension pervades everything and every place. Avoid taking risks. Try to be as precise as you can so that you are not caught unawares. You may have a brainstorm. Avoid acting on it right away. Be cautious and sleep on it. Tension may cause your fellow workers or associates to lose their sense of timing. This can cause problems. In these circumstances an aggressive person may try to take over. Try to keep things in proportion and avoid overdramatization.

16. TUESDAY. Restful. You will welcome a calmer day. Yesterday provided the ideal atmosphere for giving you ulcers. Today you should relax and make the most of a lull in the action. For those having a routine, this is a good time to renew or recapitulate. In your own quiet way you should find time to do a favor for someone you care for. Your sympathies are appreciated in many public and social services where a gentle word of encouragement and understanding can work wonders. While you do not feel like being very energetic, this should not deter you from using your creative talents in a natural way. It will be a good day to absorb knowledge.

17. WEDNESDAY. Exciting. You feel sure your intuition cannot be wrong. When you feel this way you are not inclined to seek advice. Rather, you will go your own way and test your resources against one and all. Personal plans are important. You are not being selfish, just realizing that personal identity must be established before progress is made later in the week. You are magnetic. Your positive actions are attractive to someone near you. Obviously your initiative is not based on selfish desire and your friends know this. Seek out a foreign connection and work on it. There should be some potential for development here. Enjoy romantic company later in the day and gradually unwind if the day has been exciting.

18. THURSDAY. Demanding. Establish good relations with overseas visitors. This is an opportunity you have waited for and it should not be wasted. A good deal depends on overseas business and influence. The opportunity to make contact will be appreciated and you should use all your diplomatic skills to make any meeting worthwhile. Go out of your way to please. There will be impediments, problems of communication and possible misunderstandings. Your patience will be put to the test, but you can remain a reliable link, provided you keep yourself under control. Results of your endeavors may not be apparent for some time and it may appear to have been an expensive outing.

19. FRIDAY. Disquieting. You will be pleased when the work week is over. This seems like a day of little achievement and a good deal of missed opportunity or wasted effort. There is nothing you can really put your finger on, just a general vagueness that can dishearten or confuse. Someone gets upset later on in the evening. It may be a love tangle or perhaps a shadow of the past emerges that should never have been brought to light. Avoid being implicated in any intimate dispute as tempers can be easily sparked. There seems little hope of a quiet, romantic evening. Most of the excitement seems to center around love relationships and the shortage of ready cash. That alone could spell an uneasy tension.

20. SATURDAY. Variable. If you work on weekends, develop your local outlets. This is no time to be wasting energy away from the customer on your doorstep. Some of you may be looking for a change of job to start the new year. Consider the possibilities carefully before committing yourself and avoid looking too far afield if you are definitely going to change. Travelers may find there are problems at airports and other terminals. Prices are still high. Shopping is increasingly expensive as Christmas comes nearer. You cannot get truly organized, and you're having difficulty in finding entertainment. Distractions keep you from concentrating.

21. SUNDAY. Mixed. Make this a family day. The natural day of rest is traditionally one of peace with the family. You have respect for tradition and find it hard to get out of good old habits. Near the end of the year, you need no excuse to call the generations together. Advice and news will be exchanged. You learn something to your advantage. Given a spare hour or so, you will catch up on your letter writing. It is getting late in the year and you must write to friends before vacation. This is not a day to consider traveling if it can be avoided. The weekend is short, but there is no end to the good you can accomplish in limited time.

22. MONDAY. Difficult. Problems have been created over the weekend. Something has been left unattended and there are serious repercussions. Your colleagues are not at all happy, which means there is less attention to work and you have to keep things going under your own steam. You realize how short your money supply is. The Christmas spending spree is not yet over and there is no sign of bargains. Money worries can sour relationships. Try to avoid upsets because of excessive spending. Worry also leads to unnecessary health problems which you do not wish to add to your problems. Preparation is always full of frustrations and problems.

23. TUESDAY. Disquieting. Be careful what you say and do. You are likely to be a bit careless or thoughtless today. It will be only too easy to upset someone with a careless word. You are very sensitive to this sort of hurt yourself, so you should naturally be careful. But occasionally something slips out and you regret it. Maybe your mind is ahead of your performance. This will make you impatient, if not intolerant. Be careful not to upset those who can be of future service to you. If your job is in any way dangerous, look to basic safety rules. Do not risk losing your job due to an injury at this time of the year when most people are beginning to relax. If you have your own business, look out for careless mishaps.

24. WEDNESDAY. Deceptive. You are busy with last-minute preparations. You can make them either happy or industrious. There are a number of attractions and involvements all going at once. Consider your priorities and act upon them. For those of you who are working for the common good it will be particularly comforting to know your efforts are appreciated by many who depend on your love. Whatever your role, be prepared for misunderstandings and hitches. Christmas preparations always have last-minute setbacks. Do what you can yourself and leave nothing to chance. The inevitable problems with transport can put family plans at risk.

25. THURSDAY. Merry Christmas. Nothing should go wrong today. The annual day of thanksgiving and family reunion has too much to offer for anyone to be miserable. Your sympathies are always stirred on Christmas Day as you think of those who are not as fortunate as you and you try to do something about it. It is not a time for negative concern, but one for doing a good turn wherever you can. There will be the usual round of local visits to exchange greetings. The telephone will work overtime and can bring distant relatives into your home. Everything has, as usual, turned out all right in the end. With the worries past, you feel better.

26. FRIDAY. Fair. You will be in the mood for a change of air or scenery. Nothing extreme, just the chance to be with someone you love in a relaxed environment. For young lovers it is a day to carry on with plans for the future. There is no pressure and romance can flourish. At home the family atmosphere remains gentle and there is more movement and signs of personal initiative in the way the day is spent. This is a smooth Christmas period for you, the sensitive Cancer person. Many of you will fall in love and some will be married before the working routine commences. Neptune the romantic is doing its work well. Parents will find the day relaxing after the preparations and excitement of yesterday.

27. SATURDAY. Enjoyable. This will be an emotional day with possible farewells. You have found the last few days to be most exciting. A peak may be reached today. For some it will mean a loving departure, for others the realization of deep affection not previously known. There is an air of unreality in some respects. This does not easily fit into your pattern of living. If your idealism is stirred, do something about it. Think kindly of the old you see off on their journey home. They may not have the energy and expectation of the youngsters. Emotion is a bulwark of your nature. Give your love and support wherever you think it is needed.

28. SUNDAY. Quiet. It has been a long vacation and a busy one. Now you should rest and gradually get back to normal. There may be new pets to look after as Christmas seems to have brought you presents that you can mother or fuss over. You can regain some contact with your local friends at the club and share some time exchanging news on everything you have missed over the last few days. Catching up with the news is almost a full-time occupation for a little while. For some it will have been a busy time looking after the pleasures of others. You are well aware of this role, being a natural host or hostess. Now it is the proprietor's day off.

29. MONDAY. Disturbing. You take a while to get back into your stride. There is a certain amount of chaos or disorder to disrupt the beginning of the working week for those who have to return. Traveling has its complications. Provided you do not rely on public transportation too heavily you should accomplish all that is necessary. It will take a little while to get things working smoothly, so avoid making sudden decisions that may catch others unaware. Equally, do not react too abruptly to whatever comes as a surprise. You may find it best to go your own way, expecting little from others. This will keep you occupied and relieve depressing feelings.

30. TUESDAY. Disconcerting. It will be a day of mixed blessings. You may feel inspired and full of original ideas, or be obstinate and reluctant to change your viewpoint. This may be reflected in the company you are obliged to keep. Do not take anything or anyone for granted. You will not know what is really on anyone's mind, so do not prejudge. Relationships of a long-lasting nature can be precarious if the partners are not honest with each other. Young romance, on the other hand, should flourish. Stick to those things which allow you room to maneuver and superficial freedom. Avoid deep involvement. Do not travel far in search of amusement.

31. WEDNESDAY. Good. Memories are always stirred at the end of the year. This is always a moving and emotional day for all you sensitive and home-loving Cancer natives. Naturally it is a day when nostalgia is rampant, old ties remembered and happy memories cherished. This has been a good year for many, a year when you worked hard and made progress. You look forward with hope and will make this day and night one to remember. Partnerships are particularly sensitive. Many couples will rededicate themselves to future affection as in the past. For many young couples, this will be the beginning of an adventure of a lifetime. Wherever you are going, the going is fair and the new year beckons brightly.

HOROSCOPES

Arrow publish an individual Super Horoscope book for each sign of the Zodiac, the definitive *Handbook of Chinese Horoscopes* by Theodora Lau, and the *Book of Chinese Beliefs* by Frena Bloomfield. There is also a series on *Chinese Zodiac Signs*, with a book on each of the 12 years. These books can be bought in your local bookshop or you can order by using the form below.

SUPER HOROSCOPES 1987
Each at £1.95

_____ ARIES
_____ TAURUS
_____ GEMINI
_____ CANCER
_____ LEO
_____ VIRGO
_____ LIBRA
_____ SCORPIO
_____ SAGITTARIUS
_____ CAPRICORN
_____ AQUARIUS
_____ PISCES

Also available

_____ HANDBOOK OF
        CHINESE
        HOROSCOPES £2.50

_____ BOOK OF CHINESE
        BELIEFS £2.50

CHINESE ZODIAC SIGNS
Each at 1.25

_____ RAT (1900, '12, '24, '36, '48, '60, '72, '84)
_____ OX (1901, '13, '25, '37, '49, '61, '73, '85)
_____ TIGER (1902, '14, '26, '38, '50, '62, '74, '86)
_____ RABBIT (1903, '15, '27, '39, '51, '63, '75, '87)
_____ DRAGON (1904, '16, '28, '40, '52, '64, '76, '88)
_____ SNAKE (1905, '17, '29, '41, '53, '65, '77)
_____ HORSE (1906, '18, '30, '42, '54, '66, '78)
_____ GOAT (1907), '19, '31, '43, '55, '67, '79)
_____ MONKEY (1908, '20, '32, '44, '56, '68, '80)
_____ ROOSTER (1909, '21, '33, '45, '57, '69, '81)
_____ DOG (1910, '22, '34, '46, '58, '70, '82)
_____ PIG (1911, '23, '35, '47, '59, '71, '83)

Postage _____
TOTAL _____

ARROW BOOKS, BOOKSERVICE BY POST, PO BOX 29, DOUGLAS, ISLE OF MAN, BRITISH ISLES

Please enclose a cheque or postal order made out to Arrow Books Limited for the amount due including 15p per book for postage and packing for orders both within the UK and overseas.
Please print clearly
NAME ....
ADDRESS..
....
Whilst every effort is made to keep prices down and to keep popular books in print, Arrow Books cannot guarantee that prices will be the same as those advertised here or that books will be available.